PLACE *of* PRIVILEGE

YOUNG, BLACK AND IN AN UNEXPECTED PLACE OF PRIVILEGE

MARK ROBINSON & RAYMOND SMALTZ, III

Place Of Privilege

© 2021 by **Mark Robinson & Raymond Smaltz III**

Place of Privilege, LLC
For additional information regarding bulk purchases, or author booking engagements, go to www.placeofprivilege.com

ISBN:
Hardcover: 978-1-7366215-2-3
Paperback: 978-1-7366215-1-6
EPUB/Ebook: 978-1-7366215-0-9

Cover Design by 100Covers.com
Interior Design by FormattedBooks.com

"You don't have to have been a classmate of Mark and Ray's, as I was—or be a proud alum of Dalton, as I am—to be horrified, ashamed, and infuriated by so much of what they recall from their high school days in the early 1970s. Their candid, fair-minded approach vividly depicts the perils of life as a Black student at Dalton—and shows how their inner strength in the face of racism, their willingness to confront authority, and their determination to overcome obstacles saw them emerge with confidence and self-assurance.

Forthright and heartfelt, rich with erudition along with historical context and perspective, *Place of Privilege* makes a vital contribution to understanding our troubled present and our challenging past. For today's students and their parents, it's an invaluable guide."

Chris Connelly
ESPN & ABC News

CONTENTS

DEDICATION

To Laura and Teri.

AUTHORS' NOTE

The stories we share in this book are based primarily on our own personal recollections and therefore the details of these stories are "as we remembered them" or in some cases "as we failed to remember them." We have interviewed more than 100 people, including teachers, administrators and other Dalton alums in the preparation and writing of this book. At the end of the day, however, memory is truly all we have. In the likelihood that we have gotten some details wrong, we say, "You're probably right, and we apologize."

In a number of instances, we have omitted the names of individuals from the stories we share. This is an attempt to preserve and protect their privacy. If we mention a name in a story, it is meant to pay that person a sincere compliment and no insult, slander or libel is intended. In many cases, it would be simply impossible to tell the story without naming names.

This book is not intended to be gossip or a tell-all. It is simply a memoir of our lives as two young Black men in an unexpected place of privilege.

PREFACE

This book is a different kind of memoir. It has two authors. It is a narrative of two lives, two journeys braided together by a shared experience in a most uncommon setting, the Dalton School in New York City. There are shared truths and shared insights into the impact that Dalton had on us, and in the effect we had on Dalton. You will hear, hopefully, two different voices. That is how we told our story.

Remembering and retelling our stories (as best as we could) has been fun and occasionally illuminating. Many things are seen and understood differently in hindsight. A few of the stories are a touch gossipy. Frankly, that would be hard to avoid. But mostly they are heartfelt and deeply personal. More important, however, the title of this book comes from the shared recognition that Dalton did not simply affect us in the moments that we were there. Dalton affected us—and in meaningful ways changed us—across the full span and trajectory of our lives.

It does not surprise us, therefore, that even now Dalton continues to have an influence on our lives, and that we continue to have an influence on Dalton.

In the summer of 2020, the summer of Dalton's 101st anniversary, traumatic national events touched everyone, including inside the bubble of the Dalton community. People in communities all across America rose up in protest against the murders of George Floyd, Breonna Taylor, Ahmaud Arbery, Rayshard Brooks and so many others. Protests decrying police violence against Black men and women. Protests against the unrelenting oppression of systemic racism. The summer of 2020 became a moment in time when change seemed inevitable, even inside the insulated and removed world of the Dalton walled garden.

In a lengthy and at times emotional and overwrought letter to the entire Dalton community, Jim Best, the Head of School, announced that Dalton needed to own up to its shortcomings and had chosen this moment to declare its commitment to creating and preserving an anti-racist community at Dalton. The school administration began conducting "meaningful conversations" with its communities of color, including students, parents and alumni, and asked for insight, perspective and guidance as the school endeavored to become better.

We don't know if Dalton will succeed in its pursuit of this lofty mission, but for now we take them at their word that their intentions and actions are sincere. Consequently, the two of us did not hesitate to step forward and become involved when Dalton asked for help. The two of us are now part of a six-person Dalton Black Alumni Task Force (DBATF) that will work to establish a permanent infrastructure and process between the school (both the administration and the school's minority students) and the Black alumni.

August 14, 2010

The French Culinary Institute (now the International Culinary Center) on the corner of Broadway and Grand Street in New York's SoHo neighborhood is one of the finest cooking schools in the country, a training ground for some of the nation's best chefs. The ground floor of the building is a restaurant where the school's best students put their skills through real-world rigors against the discerning palettes of finicky New York patrons. The restaurant is small. It does not need to attract crowds. The meals cost a small fortune, and are worth every penny.

On this day in mid-August, the "intimate" restaurant was invaded by a party of 10, who had arrived for Sunday brunch and a gathering that might be considered "historic." Although this was conceived as simply a coming together of old friends who had not seen each other in a long, long time, it was something more. This was—as far as we know—the very first Dalton Black Alumni Reunion. Even in its very small scale (six of the 10 of us were Dalton Black Alums), nothing like this had ever happened before. Yes, the very first time that more than two or three of us were assembled together for this stated purpose. This was definitely the start of something. And what better way to start something, than with champagne, good cheer, and some of the finest food in New York.

Brought together for this event were Chris Rose '75, Desiree Pilgrim-Hunter '75, Bob Hunter '76, Toni Lynn Dickinson '77, Ray Smaltz '74, and Mark Robinson '74, along with our respective spouses. The choice of venue for the brunch was automatic, since Toni is a master chef and was an instructor at the French Culinary Institute. It was her students preparing our feast. And what a feast it was! We arrived to the restaurant in late morning and did not rise from the table until mid-afternoon. Some of us barely able to stand up.

Although we all knew we were in a place of elegant sophistication and refinement, all attempts at dignified decorum immediately flew out the window as the unrestrained joy of seeing each other after so many years took over. Toni Lynn was just a freshman when Mark and Ray were graduating seniors, but everyone remembered each other. Everyone had stories to tell.

Desiree had everyone bent over with laughter at retelling the story of her Dalton prom night.

THE BRUT EXPERIENCE

The boys had gone to Stan's house to get ready for the prom before picking us up at my apartment. When they arrived at the apartment, I opened the door and ushered them in. OMG! This oh-so-strong odor took over the whole apartment and took our breath away.

The girls had come to my apartment to get ready for the prom. We could hardly breathe. Here were these three guys in powder blue tuxes with ruffles, cummerbunds and matching shoes! They told us they had taken showers with Brut soap, then used Brut deodorant and body powder, then topped that off with generous doses of Brut cologne. Just imagine!

Then they told us the hilarious story of their taxi ride. Apparently, they almost choked the poor driver to death with the fumes. He had to open all his windows just so he could breathe. The boys gave him a generous tip to prevent him from throwing them out of the cab. They even managed to bring my doorman to tears with their combined aromas. Needless to say, the one thing we didn't have to worry about this night was body odor from the boys. We just needed plenty of fresh air!

August 14, 2010 was the start of something. There would be many more gatherings after that, including an ill-fated backyard barbecue where Chris Rose somehow never showed up to bring the barbecued spare ribs and the rest of us teased him mercilessly.

A few years later, another group of Dalton Black alumni, this group mostly from the 1990s, began to coalesce, at first through email and social media. In 2015, organized by Bunmi Samuel '95, a group of a dozen or more Black alums met for dinner and drinks at a Harlem restaurant. The gathering of this group would be the genesis of a Black alumni group now known as the Dalton Crew, which number close to 80.

In all these years, and it has been 67 years since the first two Black students graduated from Dalton in 1953, Dalton has never (until now) communicated specifically with its Black alumni, or even recognized its Black alumni as an actual group or constituency of the school. Not once. In fact, we were somewhat surprised to discover that Dalton (even still) does not have any idea just how many Dalton Black alumni there are. They cannot even make an "educated" guess. That is because the school has never maintained any internal census of students to record ethnic self-identification (i.e., "How do you identify yourself?"). The fact that the school never considered it important to know this kind of information may give us some insight into the school's attitude toward engaging with and supporting its students of color. The school does, after all, spend a tremendous amount of time and resources thinking deeply about the lives of its students in so many other ways.

This is, regrettably, a recurring theme within this book. Time and again, Dalton seems either unable or unwilling to see us. In fact, allow me to take a moment to underscore this point. Recently, a friend who also happens to be a Dalton classmate and an esteemed professor of English, asked me to articulate the thru-line of this book. Most definitely, this is it, that for Dalton we have always been invisible.

In the beginning (and for quite a long time), when we had no presence at Dalton, no one noticed our absence. And no one missed us. When we were there, they did not see us. (My oldest brother, a baby in the Dalton nursery, was literally invisible.) Dalton's first Black students entered the school in 1949, and yet for more than fifty years afterward, there was not one single official action, symbolic gesture, public statement or formal policy that acknowledged the presence of minority students. Not one. And as alumni of color, Dalton has made no effort to learn anything about us or to communicate with us.

We. Are. Invisible.

Today, Dalton's Black alumni groups are just beginning to make their presence known, and heard. With any luck, Dalton will be paying attention and perhaps they will see us. With any luck, they will also read this book.

CHAPTER 1

The Paradox and the Sphinx

THERE ARE PRIVATE SCHOOLS ALL across the country, places with better resources, better teachers, better budgets. By definition, these schools are not for the public. They are private. They are exclusive. They are for those who can afford better. Rarely does that include Black students. In the 1960's, it almost never did.

And then there are the ultra-elite private schools, the super schools; places where the resources, the curriculum and the tuition are comparable to the best liberal arts colleges. These are schools that taught computer programming to high school students using the same state of the art machines that NASA used, and offered classes in Russian taught by a Russian countess. These are schools that served London Broil in the cafeteria, along with eclairs that rivaled the French patisserie around the corner. These are schools where lineage is a factor in the admission process. These are not schools for those who can afford better, they are schools only for those who can afford the very best.

These are places of privilege.

Think that's an exaggeration? Let's put that in terms of simple dollars and cents. In New York, the average tuition (2018/2019) for a year of private high school is $24,011. That's $2,000 per month. And that is an average that includes many subsidized parochial schools. New York's ultra-elite private schools are in a different league entirely. At New York's top 100 private schools, tuition begins at $50,000 and continues to climb like a Saturn rocket. The Dalton School, our alma mater, boasts one of the lowest tuition rates in its peer group, with $51,350. One year of tuition at THINK Global, a progressive "alternative" school on the Upper West Side of Manhattan costs $85,500. What if you have more than one child?

What kind of income do you need in order to climb this walled garden?

Sure, most of these schools offer financial aid and scholarships for students who cannot afford the prohibitively high tuition. But unlike colleges and universities that also have huge endowments, the admission process at these private schools is not "need-blind." That means that the applicant's need for financial assistance becomes a significant factor in the school's decision whether to admit. It means that financial disadvantage becomes admission disadvantage. Unless the school is trying to fulfill a diversity objective, this means that minority students with excellent grades and test scores are not competing equally with their affluent white counterparts.

What happens then is that the school's own diversity objectives become a Catch-22. Minority students are admitted, but then automatically assumed to be less worthy of a place at the table, because "diversity consideration" was given. So is it worse to be stigmatized by your teachers and fellow students, or to be excluded altogether? You might insist that there has to be a third option. Most of the time there is not.

Furthermore, when they are the beneficiaries of financial aid or scholarships, students and their parents relinquish a degree of agency in their relationship with the school. The school knows that you did not pay "full sticker price." The school knows that you are the recipient of their generosity. That takes a lot of the punch out of your role as the "customer" and the school knows it. They want you to know it too. You can complain. You can advocate for your child—up to a point. Beyond that, however, they politely suggest that you consider other school options for your child.

The next time you are seated in first class on a flight somewhere, ask the flight attendant—as I did once—if they know which passengers got their first class seat through a mileage upgrade and which passengers paid full price. The answer came with a knowing glance and a smile, "Oh yes, we know."

This is the difference between *having* privilege and being *given* privilege.

They don't call them "private schools" anymore. The term was abandoned, no longer politically correct. It implied exclusivity. It implied elitism. Of course, even without the old obsolete label, these traits were still entirely true. That was never going to change. But the old label was simply bad for image management in the new millennium, and so it was retired.

Today, "independent schools" are fully committed to the values of diversity and inclusion. Today, it is explicit to their mission to "level the playing field."

Yes, but we have a different perspective; a point of view borne of our own experiences as young Black men attending one of the most prestigious, most exclusive, most "private" schools in the nation.

The playing field is never going to be level.

In this book, Ray and I are going to try to explain that. We're going to attempt to explain the paradox of how the most prestigious "independent" schools in the country can be so zealously fully committed—simultaneously and concurrently—to both exclusion and inclusion. It's not hypocrisy and it's not deceit. It's paradox; two conflicting realities that are both true. And where else would you expect that to be possible, after all, than in an extraordinary place of privilege?

In the mid-1960's, for a variety of complex reasons, The Dalton School, and many others like it, chose to be inclusive, chose to admit Black boys for the first time. Ray Smaltz and I would not be here, we would not have a story to tell, if not for the fact that Dalton, one of the most elite, expensive private schools in the country invited us in. And once we were in, we were most definitely part of their closed community, a walled garden. It quickly became clear to us that whatever culture we might have brought with us to our new, wealthy white environment, it would be ignored, dismissed or rejected in favor of their own social customs and mores. Our experiences in our own communities, our history, our family upbringings were overwhelmed and overrun (both intentionally and unintentionally) by the Daltonian outlook on life, no matter how unrealistic those options may have been for us. It was up to each and every Black and brown student at Dalton and elsewhere at other independent schools to figure out how much we were willing to adapt, assimilate, or transform in order to achieve. Every day that we went to school we found ourselves navigating an elaborate matrix of choices and decisions; when to be like them, when to be like their expectations of us, and when to just be ourselves. Even so, as boys who were just beginning their teenage years, "being ourselves" was a question we were only beginning to work out.

This push and pull of assimilation versus self-actualization had one other critical variable; our families. We were in private school because of our families. Because of our parents. They sent us there. They wanted us there. They invested in us (quite literally) their hopes and dreams that we might have a better life, a better future. Their dream was that the magic of these places of privilege would rub off on us and imbue our lives with great possibilities. They wanted us to succeed in *that* world, but that meant pushing us away from *their* world. Although they too were probably conflicted about this impulse, they wanted us to turn our backs on the world we came from.

It was like a struggling mother putting her baby up for adoption so that it could have a better life. In the end, even good intentions and good outcomes leave everyone wounded and damaged.

Bring us in, but keep the essence of us out.

The private school paradox of exclusion and inclusion became like the riddle of the Sphinx. The Sphinx, of course, was the legendary mammoth creature that guarded entrance to the great temples of Egypt (and the city of Thebes, in Greece). All those who failed to answer the riddle correctly were devoured and destroyed. Those who could answer correctly were granted admission. And ironically, the answer to the riddle was a metaphor for how our individual nature changes over time. Some of us understood this. Some of us recognized what was being asked of us. Sadly, Ray and I both bore witness to the crushing defeat of more than a few of our Black fellow students who failed to solve the riddle of the Sphinx and did not survive their private school experience.

Does that mean that to survive, and to thrive inside the temple, we must acknowledge and accept the changes imposed upon our individual nature? We'll see.

We have chosen to use our own experiences and our own stories as a window into a different world, a place that gave us an "education" in the broadest, most transformational meaning of the word. Without diminishing or making less of the abilities that Ray and I already possessed, Dalton gave us tools and perspective that changed the way that we engaged with the world. Sure, we both retained a very strong connection to who and what we were before Dalton. But whether we intended to be or not, Dalton bestowed on us privileges we never imagined and enabled us to plant at least one foot permanently in the world of the ultra-elite.

In New York, the crown jewel place of privilege is The Dalton School; one of the most prestigious, elite prep schools in the nation, recognized globally for its visionary progressive educational philosophy. Whenever popular culture needs a readily recognizable reference for the alma mater of the extraordinarily rich and famous, they simply say "Dalton." Time Magazine called Dalton "the most progressive of the city's chic schools and the most chic of the city's progressive schools." Dalton, and the extraordinary places of privilege like it, are where the purebred 1% are taught and groomed to become the next generation of America's power elite.

Ray and I came to Dalton in the second half of the 1960s. For nearly 50 years, Dalton's high school had been a very proper—and quite prestigious—school for girls. But now Dalton decided to make the biggest change in its history by embracing—in one sweeping decision—both coeducation and integration. Change seemed to be the only viable choice for the moment. This was, after all, a period of unprecedented, involuntary, wrenching change in America, and few, if any, were optimistic about the outcome of that change. It was a time of omnipresent conflict: young vs. old, Black vs. white, north vs. south, haves vs. have-nots. The Civil Rights movement. The Black Power Movement. The Anti-War movement. Everything moving. The assassinations of MLK and RFK led to riots, despair and fear.

It was in this historic, revolutionary time and place that the board of trustees of Dalton felt compelled to reach out to the previously unfamiliar communities of New York and actively recruit minority students. Black boys.

The Dalton trustees committed themselves and their school to a radical course of actions that would not merely embrace change, but would attempt to shape that change into a better, more progressive, more inclusive and more diverse future.

Why did they do it? What was their strategy and what was the benefit they saw? What did the presence of this small group of Black boys do to change Dalton forever? ...Assuming, of course, that they changed Dalton at all. And what happens to Black boys who are placed in this strange new world, without any support system, without any precedent and without any rules of engagement?

It is a long way to look back to the second half of the 1960's and the first half of the 1970's. Do any of those memories still matter to anyone?

Are the truths that those memories reveal still relevant to anyone? After all, for the young men and women who are in school today, even their parents were probably not yet born when Ray and I were in school. Perhaps our experiences are now nothing more than ancient history.

Or perhaps not.

As part of our research for writing this book, Ray and I interviewed more than 50 other minority students from our era and just as many post-millennial minority students. We spoke with teachers, administrators, parents and a handful of subject matter experts. What we learned was that certain statistical, quantifiable metrics have made enormous progress since our time in school, while certain other metrics appear to be frozen in time from 50 years ago. Why some numbers have changed dramatically, while others haven't, is not so much a mystery, but more a part of the private school paradox we have only begun to describe.

Has the drive for diversity and inclusion over the past 20 years or so made things any better, or are the ultra-wealthy still gaming the system for their own advantage and privilege? Despite the recent headline-grabbing scandal involving college admissions and the rich and famous, the answer isn't quite so simple or obvious.

By reaching back into our own experiences and sharing stories, we'll answer some of these questions. We will offer our own perspective on how attending school in a place of privilege changed our lives, as well as how our presence there changed Dalton and other places like it.

THE BOYCOTT & THE STRIKE

Before we can talk about our own personal experiences—and why they matter—it is worthwhile to take a moment for a quick review of what was happening in New York City schools in the 1960's and the inter-relationship (or conflict) between public and private and the dynamic forces that drove them.

In 1954, when the United States Supreme Court ruled unanimously to strike down the Jim Crow system of "separate but equal", it was in a court case about public school education. More than buses or bathrooms or lunch counters, the classroom was the heart of our nation's segregation. And the classroom was its most toxic factory. In Brown v. Board of Education, the

Supreme Court declared an end to school segregation with the banging of a gavel, but the rest of America soon found out that reality fell far short of the legal ruling. The aftermath of the court decision launched several decades of urban flight; white families avoiding integration and abandoning the crowded cities for suburban sprawl, creating "bedroom communities" and rapidly expanding small towns.

The families that escaped the cities and moved to the suburbs were able to send their children to local public schools where the students were pretty much demographically homogenous, exactly as these parents wanted. All across the country, school district funding in suburban communities is determined by local property taxes. That means that affluent communities— the tony suburbs that surround big cities—are able to endow their local schools with generous budgets so that no legitimate school need goes unmet. Furthermore, these affluent communities benefit from the generosity of well-funded, highly active PTA's with helicopter stay-at-home moms (or dads) and employers that are happy to match local charitable contributions dollar-for-dollar.

Fairfield County, Connecticut, the home of Greenwich and Westport and my own town of Ridgefield, is also the home of the widest income gap between rich and poor of any county in the nation. Affluent communities stay that way by aggressive political and grass roots lobbying against the threat of "affordable housing" invading their neighborhoods or their school districts. These families don't worry whether the playing field is ever going to be level. They own the field.

The families that remained in the cities, the affluent urbanites that eschew country and suburban living except on jaunts to their weekend houses upstate, have their own school solution.

Private school.

Northern urban centers like New York City did not have forced segregation backed by Jim Crow laws. The North was supposed to be much more enlightened. Northern cities like New York had "neighborhoods." They had "ethnic enclaves." They had ghettos. And in these cities, Blacks and whites casually crossed paths on public transportation, at work or even in the department store. There was no "colored section" at the movie theater. In these cities there was the patina of liberal harmony. But in these cities Blacks and whites did not live together, they did not worship together, and they did not go to school together.

This last issue—the school issue—was a problem for urban politicians and policy makers. Housing and religion were much tougher to tackle, but with schools, at least they would try. Motivated partly by the legal precedent set by the Supreme Court ruling in Brown v. Board of Education, and partly by a progressive political platform, city politicians worked to integrate local school districts. And yet, for a decade after Brown v. Board of Education, their efforts continued to fall very far short of their intended objectives. New York City schools that enrolled mostly Black and Latino students tended to have inferior facilities, less experienced teachers and severe overcrowding. Schools in many Black and Latino neighborhoods were so overcrowded that they operated on split shifts, with the school day lasting only four hours for students. There could not be any evidence more dramatic of the extent to which minority students were being short-changed and left behind.

What's it like to study biology from a textbook that never even mentions DNA?

What's it like to attend a school that has too few school psychologists and counselors—but plenty of in-school police officers?

Once again, education became an effective tool for separating and controlling the destinies of segments of society. This time, instead of separation based upon socio-economic class, the educational divide was along racial lines.

One way or the other, the playing field was never going to be level.

All across America, this was the height of the civil rights movement. In August of 1963, a quarter of a million people marched on the nation's capital to advocate for civil and economic rights for African Americans. Martin Luther King Jr. delivered his iconic "I have a dream" speech on the steps of the Lincoln Memorial. A year later, President Johnson would whip Congress into passing the Civil Rights Act of 1964. This was supposed to be our time.

Bayard Rustin, one of the key organizers of the March on Washington, came to New York just a few weeks after the march to meet with Rev. Milton Galamison, a local pastor and civil rights activist. Together they would organize the New York City school boycott of 1964, a protest they felt was necessary to call public attention to years of inaction and no progress by New York school officials. The event is almost entirely forgotten today, with hardly anyone alive who remembers it, and it is unlikely to be found in any history books about that period. And yet, the New York City school boycott of 1964 was at the time the largest civil rights protest in American history, with more than 460,000 students refusing to go to school.

460,000 students. Only 250,000 people attended the March on Washington.

This did not happen in Alabama or Mississippi or Georgia. It happened in New York City, where local politicians and school board administrators said they believed passionately in integration. And yet, according to a study completed by UCLA and The Civil Rights Project, New York City has some of the most segregated schools in the country. Popular public opinion, however, was in stark contrast to the grim reality in the classroom. Popular public opinion was that this could not be true in New York. New York was a progressive, cosmopolitan city of the world. New York could not possibly be segregated. In fact, New York School Superintendent William Jansen instructed school and Board of Education staff that they could not use the word "segregation" when discussing the topic, and instead should refer to "racial imbalance." The New York media were active collaborators in the culture of denial and largely refused to provide any press coverage to the boycott. That is why most history books make no mention of it. Like an ostrich with its head planted firmly in the sand, the New York Times insisted that there was "no official segregation in the city." In their eyes this was not a legitimate protest. The boycott was a "violent, illegal approach of adult-encouraged truancy." They dismissed the civil rights demands as "unreasonable and unjustified."

One month after the boycott, a counter protest was organized by Parents and Taxpayers (PAT), a coalition of white neighborhood groups who brought 15,000 mothers to the steps of City Hall with signs and banners that read "Bussing Creates Fussing" and "Don't Let the Courts Dictate Our Children." In New York, the 15,000 PAT protesters were more powerful and more successful than the 460,000 protesters from the month before. In a poll conducted by the New York Times in September 1964, 54% of white New Yorkers thought "civil rights was moving too fast." According to the front page, above-the-fold story in The Times, most white New Yorkers felt that Negroes "were receiving everything on a silver platter." These were New Yorkers.

The New York Board of Education did nothing more for the remainder of Mayor Wagner's term in office. In 1966, John Lindsey was elected mayor and efforts to address New York's "school problem" were renewed. Black community leaders throughout New York had been calling for local control of school districts, arguing that the central board was unresponsive to their neighborhood needs. The Lindsey administration launched a test program called the Ocean Hill—Brownsville Experiment, in which this minority community in Brooklyn was given autonomy from the central Board of Education and permitted to manage its own school district.

In September of 1968, local administrators from the predominantly Black and Hispanic school district of Ocean Hill—Brownsville dismissed 19 teachers from their schools and told them to report to the Board of Ed's central office. They weren't fired. They were just told they needed to work someplace else. This was an attempt to assert "local control" and manage what was best for the local schools. The teacher's union, the United Federation of Teachers, was not having any of it, and pushed back hard. The teacher's union led its members on a 36 day strike that crippled the school year and broke the back of the local control movement that Black and Hispanic communities had been fighting for. Minority parents and community leaders had lost.

Just as in 1964, the coverage and reporting of the strike by the New York media was heavily biased along racial lines. The New York Times described the Ocean Hill—Brownsville community leaders as "crazy, anti-Semitic Black nationalists." And just as occurred in 1964, public opinion turned against the city's minority community. New York City's liberalism, apparently, had its limits.

Of the 1.1 million students enrolled in New York City Public Schools, only 14.7% are Caucasian. That seems like an almost unbelievable statistic. Where did all the white kids go? They went, of course, to private school. In the late 1960's, a great many went to parochial schools throughout the city, mostly either Catholic or Jewish. Although parochial school enrollment has declined significantly in the past decade, in 1970, parochial schools represented roughly 85% of NYC private school enrollment. At the time, these schools were quite affordable, even within the means of working class families, with annual tuition of only a few hundred dollars. As a result, the opportunity to escape the integrated classroom was an option available across the socio-economic spectrum. You didn't have to be rich to go to private school.

But what if you were rich? What would your options be then?

If you are rich, you attend the ultra-elite private schools, the super schools; places where the resources, the curriculum and the tuition are comparable to the best liberal arts colleges. If you are rich, you are not escaping the integrated classroom. That world never touched you anyway. If you are rich, you don't have to escape anything because the world is built around you. If you are rich, you exist in your own solar system, where the planets are Collegiate and Trinity and Horace Mann and Nightingale and Brearley. And Dalton.

Places of privilege.

This is how we got here, the speed-reading version of how we arrived at the world of public and private schools at the time and place when our lives, Ray's and mine, intersected with Dalton.

CHAPTER 2

"THAT LITTLE GIRL WAS ME"

"T*HAT LITTLE GIRL WAS ME."*
These words were spoken by United States Senator Kamala Harris during a 2019 primary debate for the Democratic nomination for president. With those five simple words, Harris wove together the separate strands of debate over federal education policy, our nation's civil rights and racial segregation history and the personal struggles of a little Black girl just trying to go to school and be a six year old. It's all there. It was personal and it was shared history. Harris was part of just the second class of Black children to be bused by the Berkeley, California school district to an integrated school, more than two decades after the Supreme Court ruling in Brown v. Board of Education.

It was 1971 and the parents of Kamala Harris were doing what every good parent tries to do. They were doing the single most aspirational, most transformative thing that any parent can do for their child, send them to a good school. The fact that those five words were spoken by a United States Senator, a former Attorney General and a candidate for the White House, makes it crystal clear that Kamala's parents knew exactly what they were doing.

These were values and experiences that Ray and I understood deeply and personally. Our stories could be laid alongside the story of Kamala Harris and the elegant symmetry would be immediately apparent, a bond greater than anything found in Ancestry.com. For each of us, while our stories are personal, they are about more than just ourselves. They are about themes and truths and journeys that are shared by some and are mile markers for many others. Where we have been helps all of us understand where the road goes next.

Our names are Ray Smaltz and Mark Robinson. It says so right on the cover of this book. "Place of Privilege" tells our stories of being sent by our parents to attend a good school and make that the springboard to better opportunities and to a better life. In our case, the local school district did not bus us to an integrated school. No, our story is just a bit more one-in-a-million than that. To make our story possible, amazing things had to fall into place just right. And they did.

The Dalton School on the upper east side of Manhattan in New York is one of the most prestigious, most exclusive and most expensive private schools in the country. Dalton is written about and talked about as an extraordinary place. A place of privilege. To be of that world automatically means that the rest of the world sees you differently. Treats you differently. But for nearly half a century, the Dalton School did not admit boys into the high school. Never. Not even for its wealthiest parents. Until it did, just at the moment when we needed it to. And because there had never before been boys in the high school at Dalton, there most certainly had never been Black boys in the high school. Never. Until it did, just at the moment that we needed it to.

And in that heretofore unprecedented moment, when Dalton decided that now was the time to admit Black boys to the high school, the last piece of the infinite jigsaw puzzle was picked up and placed onto the board. Dalton looked around and chose to admit Ray and me. Luck? Preparation? Destiny? Ability? My best guess is all of the above. There are stories of how we got there. My story is different from Ray's. And once we got to Dalton, our stories traveled some very interesting parallel paths, although—ironically—our paths rarely ever crossed.

From Ray

Mark and I have been asked several times about when our friendship first began at Dalton. Honestly, our friendship didn't really begin until thirty-five years after graduating from Dalton, when Chris Rose, Mark and I had dinner together at a P.F. Chang's in the Westchester County Mall in the winter of 2009. I'm embarrassed to admit that we weren't the least bit close during our five years together at Dalton.

From Mark

Ray and I never explained how the two of us met and became friends at Dalton. We wrote the whole book and somehow never touched upon this subject. The reason, oddly enough, was quite simple. Ray and I were never friends at Dalton.

Ray came to Dalton in seventh grade, a year before me. By the time that I arrived in eighth grade the following year, Ray had a head start in making friends and settling into the Dalton ecosystem. By eighth grade, Ray was returning to familiar faces that were all new to me. As I arrived in eighth grade, I was the new kid trying to find my way, trying to figure out how to be accepted, how to survive.

This lack of synchronicity, combined with the differences in our backgrounds and the differences in our personalities, were the likely causes that Ray and I did not connect at Dalton. And when I say that we did not connect, I don't simply mean my eighth grade first year. I mean that for the five years that Ray and I were classmates at Dalton, we did not connect.

From Ray

In fact, out of a graduating class of ninety-two, I can say that I knew all of the other minority boys in the school; Jay Strong, Paul Driver, Luis Pacheco, Kenny Collins, Raymond Rivera, Ricardo Ramirez and Benson Fong, but I never had the opportunity to take a class with Mark, share a homeroom group, or even join the same school committees. We were two ships who kept passing each other during the day, weighing our anchors at various different social ports along the way, but never seeming to find a common pier to engage each other.

From Mark

Ray said to me recently, as we searched our memories for shared moments at Dalton, that he honestly doubted that there was ever a time in those five years that the two of us sat and had a one-on-one conversation of any substance. I'm pretty sure he's right. In a school as small as Dalton—when you can count the number of Black kids on one hand—that's pretty damn amazing.

There was no *un*-friendliness between us, no conflict or tension. There were no negative feelings. We simply traveled in different circles during our time at Dalton and it never occurred to either of us that we should do anything to change that.

From Ray

There were times during school when I would see Mark with a camera around his neck, as he documented the comings and goings of the students and teachers at the school. He even managed to capture several different pictures of me during our time together, where I was completely oblivious to his presence, which was probably why I only learned of his work from the school yearbook. Hell, Mark recently showed me photos of our basketball team that were in his collection from our Dalton years together and I wracked my brain trying to remember if I ever noticed him behind the camera.

Mark captured candid images of me that stood out from year-to-year. When I was young, struggling to find my place at the school, Mark's photographic work documented to everyone that Black, Hispanic and other minority students at Dalton were just as much a part of the social fabric of the institution as the white students and that our presence mattered.

From Mark

Ironically, Ray has often remarked that he considered me his unofficial photographer. I was a yearbook photographer and Ray was a star athlete. Ray's favorite photos of himself are pictures that I took.

From Ray

There is an age-old phrase used by sports coaches for many years; *"It's not how you start—it's how you finish."* Well, in the case of the friendship between Mark and myself, it's not how our friendship began, it's how it's going to end. That will be as "brothers-in-arms" who experienced a unique social experiment in the 1960s, of bringing young Black and Hispanic males to private schools of privilege and seeing how they could either adjust or fall to the pressures of a challenging liberal arts education in a racially charged time in our country's history.

From Mark

So it's funny—and quite a bit unexpected—that 35 years later, Ray and I would become not just friends, but good friends. And so have our wives. With the passage of time, age and maturity, we are now able to see and appreciate the common bonds between us that we overlooked as high school kids at Dalton. We didn't comprehend it at the time, but Ray and I shared this important, transformative experience as the earliest young Black men at Dalton. That shared experience changed our lives forever. And that shared experience has now forged a powerful bond between us.

But it took time and distance and perspective to see that. So here we are. In fact, it took Facebook to bring Ray and me together. So kudos to Mark Zuckerberg. Facebook accomplished something worthwhile.

From Mark

Ray joined Facebook in January of 2009 and he and I began communicating on Facebook through a Dalton School alumni group almost immediately. It didn't take long for us to begin making plans to meet up in person and move beyond just the social media communications. On February 17, 2009, Ray, Chris Rose (another Dalton classmate) and I met for dinner at P.F. Chang's in the Westchester Mall in White Plains, a carefully chosen geographic midpoint, since we all lived in different places. Although the passage of time has altered each of our physical appearances substantially since our old yearbook photos, we had no trouble spotting each other and recognizing old, familiar faces. It had literally been 35 years since we had laid eyes on each other, but the decades did nothing to diminish our re-connection.

From Ray

After warm hugs and backslaps, we sat down and ordered a handful of appetizers, since no one was in any rush to study the menu or order dinner. We talked and laughed and recounted stories from our old high school days, combined with autobiographical narratives of what each of us has been doing since graduation. After roughly three hours, we noticed that somehow we never bothered to order dinner. We had eaten the appetizers (long ago) and just kept talking and talking. After 35 years of disconnection, new friendships were born.

From Mark

By the end of our conversation that evening, we began to recognize that there were many stories from our high school memories that still carried emotional punch. We also recognized that those high school memories—and that very specific place and time—had a great deal to do with shaping and creating the people we had become. At pretty much the same time, all three of us came to the conclusion that these stories and memories mattered to more than just ourselves, that there was value and purpose in sharing these stories with others.

We each recognized that our memories—our stories—represented an intersection of time, place and protagonist that was both unique and fairly historic. It was something special. We could tell others about what we saw and did, and what was done to us. We could describe that world. Paint a picture.

We could testify. As in court. As in church. As in a rally on a corner.

From Ray

"We should do a book. We should put these stories in a book." I can't attribute the quote to any one of us, because all three of us probably said it. And in that moment, this book was born. We made a pact to write it together.

"Place of Privilege" would be a book about the ways that attending Dalton shaped and changed our lives, and the ways in which our unique presence there also re-shaped and changed Dalton.

From Mark

As we have described, Ray and I hardly spent any time together at Dalton. The recollections in our stories rarely overlap, if at all. Ray has his stories and I have mine. And yet, despite those differences, there is much commonality in our experiences. There are shared truths and shared insights in the impact that Dalton had on us, and in the effect we had on Dalton.

A BRIEF HISTORY OF DALTON

The Dalton School began 100 years ago in 1919 under the original name The Children's University. The school was founded by Helen Parkhurst (a disciple of Mme. Montessori), a brilliant but highly eccentric educator who was a major antagonist of the educational status quo at that time. The original name, The Children's University, is highly suggestive of both the child-centric focus of the school's teaching philosophy as well as the high-minded and expansive breadth of the curriculum. Child-centric learning definitely ran counter to the American tradition of ritualized learning and rote memorization administered by a teacher who had no time for individual student needs. And an expansive curriculum challenged the popular acceptance of the sacredness of the 3-R's. The school immediately began attracting the attention and admiration of educational intellectuals. What Parkhurst originally dubbed "The Laboratory Plan" was now being cited in academic journals as "The Dalton Plan." First Lady Eleanor Roosevelt became an outspoken booster of the school. Some of the finest schools around the world, from England to Japan to Chile, were copying The Dalton Plan. Dalton was a global role model.

Although Helen Parkhurst was an outstanding educator, she was not a particularly good administrator or financial steward for the school. Even though Dalton's student body were among New York's most well-heeled, the decade of the Great Depression nevertheless took its toll on Dalton's endowment. In the post-war late 1940's, the country was still struggling to rebound economically. Expensive, elite private schools still had their reliable enrollment, but alumni and parent donations and school endowments were seriously anemic. Dalton had fallen on hard times financially.

By 1942, Helen Parkhurst's inattention to her fiduciary duties apparently led Dalton's board of trustees to appoint Charlotte Durham as the school's new headmistress. Dalton's future—and therefore also its legacy—were in jeopardy. Dalton's trustees turned to the federal government for educational grant funds and desperately needed financial relief. As the story goes, the government said "Sure. On one condition." Dalton would need to shed its lily white exclusivity and begin admitting Negro students. Facing an existential choice, Dalton's trustees relented and admitted two Negro girls into the Class of 1953. Dalton may have been one of the very first elite New York private schools to admit Negroes. (*Just girls, for now.*)

In the 1950's and early 1960's, Dalton kept its head down, laid low and faded a bit into the background of the elite New York private school solar system. Schools like Spence, Chapin, Collegiate and Horace Mann were also attracting New York's finest families. Rather than being a star, Dalton had become just one of the planets; still a heavenly body, but now one of several. Dalton never stopped being a good school, but it had stopped being a "great" school. This demotion did not sit well with the school's board of trustees, nor with the school's parents. They were paying top dollar for Dalton tuition and getting less in return.

In exchange for its pricey tuition, Dalton (and to some degree, all of the elite private schools) promised three things; 1) an education based on the most rigorous and most expansive academic standards, 2) the satisfaction (i.e., bragging rights) and status of attending a school of enviable prestige and stature, 3) an almost assured admission to an ivy league or other top college for its graduates. During this period, Dalton continued to deliver on promise #1 and promise #3, but it was buckling a bit on promise #2. And that was intolerable. It was not acceptable to Dalton's core clientele. Perhaps that is why, in just the very short period from 1960—1964, Dalton had four different headmasters. Dalton's board of trustees were—quite probably—in panic mode. The school was in need of a major course correction.

And that is precisely what Donald Barr brought.

Many of the plans for Dalton's transformation were drafted by Barr's predecessor, Jack Kittell. However, Kittell was a bookish educator from Kansas, with a stiff, awkward demeanor that lacked the personal dynamism or political savvy of Donald Barr. Kittell may have drafted the plans, but he simply couldn't get them done. Donald Barr, on the other hand, was an express train that was leaving the station with or without you. Or if necessary, steaming right over you. Kittell wanted to grow the school, but it was Barr's vision to make Dalton a "hot" school, the kind of school that wealthy parents fought over to get their children admitted. Donald Barr was all about *Make Dalton Great Again.* Make it the school that got talked about, that got bragged about.

Immediately, Barr dramatically increased the size of the student enrollment simply because the admission of boys was incremental to the existing female student population. He increased the size of the faculty and brought in an entirely new cohort that was—on average—half the age of the existing genteel faculty (many of whom had already spent an entire generation teaching at Dalton). Many of the new faculty were just out of college. And with the newly enlarged faculty, he was able to expand the size and breadth of the curriculum to include Russian and Statistics and lots of very cool electives.

The most transformational change, however, was to make Dalton coeducational by admitting boys to the high school. That changed Dalton's identity overnight. Dalton was no longer prim and proper and refined. It was raucous, rambunctious and highly energetic; all of the adjectives that you might apply to teenage boys. And in a maneuver that was a master stroke of strategic timing and political savvy, Barr simultaneously recruited and admitted Black boys in that very first class of boys, so that the Dalton community swallowed all of the medicine at once, rather than fight each battle separately.

It would be impossible to overstate how much coeducation changed Dalton. For example, high school boys have Phys. Ed. requirements and expectations of a whole other order of magnitude. A brand new gymnasium was built because of the arrival of boys. An entire department of Phys. Ed. faculty needed to be hired. And of course, most important of all, varsity teams—in football, baseball, basketball and wrestling—were created from scratch.

Varsity teams might seem like nothing more than "just one more" element in the coeducation build-out, but nothing could be further from the truth. Varsity teams meant competition and rivalry against the other schools in the elite New York private school solar system. What better way to announce that you are ready to reclaim your status as King of the Hill than showing up on the field of battle. Varsity competition meant team support and boosterism from students, parents and alumni. And boosterism, with all its inherent loyalty and chauvinism, was also a major new revenue stream for the school. People gave money to support their teams. Lots of money.

However, (and this is pretty damn important), varsity teams are only as good as their last victory. And you don't have many victories without talented athletes. Suddenly, Donald Barr's strategy of admitting Black boys to the high school simultaneous with coeducation becomes clearer. Alan Boyers, Dalton's Director of Athletics, went on a city-wide scouting mission. This meant reaching beyond the preppy Upper East Side boys who were now coming up from Dalton's middle school. This meant scouring the city to find boys who were natural athletes, boys who played on winning junior high school teams. And—most fortunately for Mr. Boyers—Dalton was now interested in recruiting Black boys to the high school. Alan Boyers' Black student athletes would be the backbone of his new varsity teams.

We can't say what high-minded values and principles may have been part of the motivation for Dalton to decide to admit Black boys in 1966. Dalton did not make any public pronouncements about the importance of diversity, or even civil rights back in 1966. Nor did any of the media coverage at the time address this topic directly, although we are sure that it was a frequent topic of conversation. We can only speculate. But one thing is certain. Black boys were extremely useful in Dalton's new ambitions for athletic dominance. And as our stories will tell, Dalton definitely expected us Black kids to step up and do our part.

But we each had a life before Dalton. Ray and I had a dozen or so years of life experiences with family and neighborhood friends and public schools before Dalton. Those first dozen years shaped who we were. Who we are. And those first dozen years determined what we brought with us when we arrived at Dalton. So our next chapter describes what we were coming from before we got to Dalton.

CHAPTER 3

What We Were Coming From

Mark Robinson

I N THE WORLD OF MY childhood, my definitions and perceptions of "home" and "school" were fluid and generally spilled into each other. It was sometimes hard to tell which was which. Home and school shared many common attributes and experiences. And they shared a common cast of players.

While most kids celebrated the unambiguous separation of these two domains, and enjoyed some relief from one while present in the other, I did not have any such partition. My Aunt Thelma was my third grade teacher. My dad was an administrator in my elementary school. I saw them every day at school. In fact, Aunt Thelma drove me to school every morning and my dad drove me home in the afternoon. In between was an entire day of teachers, administrators, cafeteria workers and support staff who were all family friends. People who knew everything about me and about my family, who often came to my home or me to theirs. This was not simply the school community. P.S. 143 in Corona, Queens—just down the block from the Dorie Miller apartment complex and walking distance to Shea Stadium— was the proverbial village that had more than just a hand in raising me.

My earliest memories of childhood are actually of kindergarten at P.S. 143. It was 1960. Mrs. Cumberbatch was my teacher, a wonderful woman in her early forties (I guess. Do you really think a boy in kindergarten can accurately guess someone's age?) with horn-rimmed glasses, a big toothy smile and a voice that always went up when she said your name. Mrs. Cumberbatch had a face dotted with freckles across a warm chocolate brown complexion. The result was a countenance that was never threatening or intimidating, but always welcoming and reassuring. Perfect for kindergarten. Mrs. Cumberbatch was also the proprietor of a quaint little country resort in Poughkeepsie, in upstate New York, where my family frequently vacationed for summertime outside of the city. It was a beautiful, multi-acre property with a swimming pool, a horseshoe pit, swings and lots of games for the kids. There was a seemingly endless supply of good food, most of it fried or barbecued, and lots of late night noisy card playing for the grown-ups. Of course, the grown-ups included many of the teachers from our school who vacationed there too.

School's out. No, it's not.

COOKIE

I have two older brothers, David (the oldest) and Michael (the middle child), who are a year apart in age, but are five and six years older than me. Growing up, David and Michael were close and shared many friends, activities and childhood experiences and memories. I was the baby that was never old enough to do the things that they did. As far as they were concerned, if I was around that almost automatically meant that the fun was gone. Because of the age difference, it also meant that David and Michael were done with elementary school and gone as I was just starting. So, they were never part of my elementary school memories or experiences. Good. My school memories were all my own.

At home, Mom was getting her masters' degree in Education at night from Hunter College. Before she was married and started a family, Mom attended Hunter College High School and Hunter College. Hunter College High School is a special school for intellectually gifted students, located on the upper east side of Manhattan and managed by Hunter College. Hunter is publicly funded and there is no tuition fee. That's what made it possible for my mother to attend. Her parents could not have afforded virtually any tuition at all. According to the school's literature, "students accepted to

Hunter represent the top one-quarter of 1% of students in New York City, based on test scores." Hunter has been ranked as the top public high school in the United States by the Wall Street Journal.

My mother's path to Hunter College High School was not without its own complications and challenges. As a child growing up in a crowded railroad apartment on St. Nicholas Avenue in Harlem, Mom was a precocious over-achiever. She made Phi Beta Kappa Society in elementary school and skipped a grade. In junior high she was a consistent honor roll student. And when she learned about Hunter College High School and its reputation for excellence, she knew she simply *had* to take the test for admission. Mom took the test and of course she passed. But life is never that simple or that easy. When the letter from Hunter arrived at Julia Ward Howe Junior High School 81 in Harlem, the school's principal, Miss Lawson, was incensed. This little colored girl had gone off on her own and taken this test without the principal's knowledge or endorsement. What's worse, she skipped a day of school in order to take the test. The nerve of this little colored girl!

Miss Lawson told my mom and my grandmother that Rita had skipped school without proper permission and would be marked as a truant for that day. As a result, Miss Lawson would not sign the paperwork that would allow my mom to transfer to Hunter's eighth grade. My grandmother was very demure and proper. She was not one to "cause a fuss" or create controversy, so she did not fight the principal's decision. My mom was stuck at JHS 81 for another year. So, Mom waited until the next year and took the test again. And again, she passed. Again, the letter came to the school and my grandmother was summoned to the principal's office. And Grandma, while waiting on a bench outside the principal's office, overheard Miss Lawson proclaim to someone, "Dammit. That Thomas girl got into Hunter again." This time Grandma would not be intimidated by the principal. This time the paperwork got signed and my mother went to Hunter College High School and then to Hunter College.

Ann Lawson, the principal at Julia Ward Howe JHS, stated years later at a Waldorf Astoria dinner given for her 25th anniversary in education, that she considered herself "a missionary for Negro children." She took pride in the accomplishments of her students and even kept a special file of all the girls she helped get into Hunter High School. What I have learned—what my mother learned—is that some white people just loved to open the door for bright little Black children so that they may attend a high quality school.

And they absolutely hate it when you attempt to walk through that door on your own.

In some respects, my childhood—and in particular my education—would follow a path similar to my mother's. Attending a prestigious high school on Manhattan's upper east side was a gift, but sometimes a hard gift to accept. It came with certain challenges and dislocations for a young Black girl from Harlem. Some memories were bittersweet. When I was a freshman at Amherst College, one of my writing teachers was famed poet Sonia Sanchez. Professor Sanchez became a mentor and muse in my early college days. Professor Sanchez—or "Sister Sonia" as most of her Black students called her—frequently cooked elaborate feasts for her students in her home, a cozy little cottage on the edge of campus. We would hang out, read poetry and talk politics. Often, other professors would drop in to join our salon. On one occasion, Sonia led a road trip to Harlem, where we had lunch with Gwendolyn Brooks (the first African American to win a Pulitzer Prize for poetry) and a private dinner with Louis Farrakhan.

One day in class, as a writing exercise Professor Sanchez told me to close my eyes and open my mind. And then she stuck an Oreo cookie in my mouth and said, "Okay, now write about that." And so, I did. And the result was a poem about my mother and about her memories of attending Hunter High School.

HYDROX

Crunchy, crumbly and too sweet for me
Recognized the taste right away,
Those cookies my mom ate all the time
When she was young
But not anymore

Don't think she ever liked them,
But she ate them all the time
When she was young
But not anymore

Her mother packed them for her every day
Along with a little homemade sandwich

And sent her to school downtown on the subway
Because that's where the good schools were

The girls downtown called her "Cookie"
'Cause that's what she ate every day
The girls uptown called her "Oreo"
'Cause she always ate her cookies with the girls downtown

Mark Robinson, 1974

Although my mother was pursuing her Master's degree and her teaching certificate, she already had a successful career working as an executive at Time Magazine and did not have any plans to leave. It paid well and was fairly glamorous. Mom started out in the secretarial pool at Time. She learned to type at Hunter High School and continued to perfect her skills both at college and practicing on a small used typewriter at home. Her speed and accuracy left the other secretaries in the dust. Anything my mom set her mind to do, she was going to do better than anyone else. That was my mom. My mom wasn't motivated by a traditional sense of professional ambition. Power and prestige were never her goals, although she was driven to be successful and to have a better life for herself and her family. Mom was driven more by perfectionism. She was always striving to be better, to do better. And she was always working to instill these same values and standards in her sons.

After about a year in the Time Inc. secretarial pool, she was chosen to be the supervisor of the secretarial pool, training and overseeing all the other gals. And not long after that, she was plucked from the pool and assigned as executive secretary to Larry Laybourne, Time's assistant publisher. A few years after that, she became executive secretary to Henry Luce III. "Hank" Luce was the publisher of Time and the son of the founder of Time Magazine. She worked for the most powerful man in the company. In the 1960's, she had a job that most young Black women could scarcely imagine. She had no intention to give that up. Besides, my mom was just too loyal to ever consider quitting a job. But education was important. It was a calling. And since Mom loved to teach, she used the basement of our house and organized remedial classes in English and history for kids in our middle class Black neighborhood. I use the term 'remedial', but the lessons she taught were far more advanced than anything that was happening in our school classrooms.

On Saturday mornings, when most kids would be out playing ball or riding their bikes or watching cartoons like Top Cat or Huckleberry Hound or The Flintstones on TV, my brothers and I, along with about a half dozen other neighborhood kids, were in the basement brushing up on schoolwork with my mom. It made my mom very popular with neighborhood parents. And it made my brothers and me very unpopular with the neighborhood kids who were unlucky enough to spend their Saturday mornings in our basement classroom. Nobody cared that it made us better students or improved our grades. Not us kids. But no one would ever say anything against our mom. Not to our face. That was a law of the streets and it was absolutely inviolate. But as intimidating as my mom could be sometimes, she absolutely loved kids, so it was hard for anyone not to love my mom right back. Mrs. Robinson was one of those moms that the kids in the neighborhood genuinely liked, but also knew never to mess with, never to talk back to, and never to let her see you doing something you shouldn't be doing.

I had teachers that treated me like family. And family that gave me homework.

School. Home.

This also posed something of a problem on the school playground. For most kids, if something happened in the schoolyard; you had an altercation with another kid, you said or did something you shouldn't have, you didn't listen when you should have, stuff like that, the offense would have to rise to a certain level of seriousness to justify school officials sending a note home to your parents. 90% of the stuff that happened in the schoolyard would be handled by a stern, chastising remark from a teacher or a para, and perhaps a five minute "time out." Hardly anything was bad enough to warrant a note home to your parents. But when your dad worked in the principal's office at your school, it didn't matter how slight or minor the offense. Dad would find out about it. And Dad, being a man of honor and integrity, and someone that most of the other school workers looked up to, had to make it clear to everyone, that there would be no favoritism or special treatment when it came to his kids. Oh no. We had to live by a higher standard. Zero tolerance.

That was a hard thing for me growing up. I spent a lot of years afraid of and distant to my dad. My dad wasn't mean. He was never violent. He skillfully managed a balancing act where I don't think that he ever struck any of us kids, yet still managed to convince you that it was possible. And there were times when his sternness could seem unforgiving. If you did something wrong, he would remind you of a similar offense you had committed six months earlier. He had a memory to rival any computer system. Just as every kid lived in fear of the "permanent record" that every school professed to keep on each child, my dad maintained a detailed set of ledgers on his three boys in his head.

Home. School.

My dad never knew his father. When his mom became pregnant, his father left. He left his wife, he left New York. To this day we can find no trace of him. And my dad's mother passed away from tuberculosis when he was only six. He was raised by two aunts who showered him with love, but who nevertheless were an incomplete substitute for a boy who wanted a mother and a father. My dad grew up with love and support and attention and guidance, but also with an acute awareness that he didn't have parents the way other kids did. He had to learn how to fill that space on his own. Most people when they first become parents are not fully prepared. But at least they have the ability to copy what they have witnessed growing up. Most people can "fake it 'til they make it" and figure out what kind of parent they're going to be. They can remember what mom or dad said or did when a particular situation presented itself and call upon that memory as needed. My dad didn't have that cushion, that reference point. He couldn't ask himself, "What would Dad do?"

And so, in spite of the fact that my dad was an extraordinary man and human being who was respected and admired by us kids and by family, friends and co-workers, he was still a work-in-progress as a parent. I know that he did a simply awesome job of raising my two brothers and me, but I had very little awareness and appreciation for that until I became a parent myself and began to realize the journey my father had traveled. We didn't do a lot of the traditional things that fathers and sons do together. We didn't play ball or catch. Raised by two aunts, sports was never his thing growing up. It wasn't his thing now as a father. It never became my thing either. Sure, I regularly played touch football or punch ball with friends in the streets of my neighborhood. But I never joined or played on any team, in school or out. And there was never any professional sports team that captured my interest or my loyalty.

In elementary school, my dad and I saw each other every day, although preferably from a distance. If a kid in school was sent to see my dad, it was never a good thing. It meant the kid had been bad. And the last person he wanted to see was my dad. And if I had been sent to see my dad during school hours, it was definitely not a good thing. But our time together, our quality time, was in the car ride home each afternoon. In the summer of 1963, after I completed first grade, my family moved from Corona to St. Albans, a new neighborhood many miles away. No more walking to and from school. I rode home in the car each day with my dad. Dad would ask how my day went at school. And because he was there, and because he knew everyone and everything, there was no faking an answer. There was no superficial small talk. We actually talked about the day and got into everything. My life was an open book. And each afternoon in the car, we would read along together.

The other indelible part of my car rides with dad was the radio. There were no tape decks or CD players back then, only the radio. My dad was a huge fan of jazz, so the car radio was always tuned to WRVR, the jazz station based in Manhattan's famed Riverside Church. Ed Beach was the host of a show called "Just Jazz" and my dad and I cruised to the songs of Ella Fitzgerald, Nancy Wilson, Sarah Vaughn and Stan Getz, Dave Brubeck, Stanley Turrentine, Ramsey Lewis and the Modern Jazz Quartet. And if Cal Tjader came on the radio, my dad couldn't resist biting his lower lip and doing a little dance in his seat as we drove. Even though in later adolescence I would go on to embrace my own taste for Motown and rock and the music of my teen years, the car rides with my dad established my musical foundation and a lifelong love of jazz. More importantly, I learned that my dad didn't just enjoy music, he understood music. He could break down a song and a melody and tell me what to listen for, how to critique music in a way that eventually transcended genre. As I said before, I spent a lot of years afraid of and distant to my dad as I grew up. But those car rides home each day during my elementary school years were our private, special time. A treasured time.

And then one day the unthinkable happened. It was time to graduate from elementary school. Like any kid, I was not just eager to grow up, I was in a hurry. But this was a dramatic—and traumatic—transition. I was heading off to a new school where I had absolutely no family connections, no support network, no one to share my day with. I know that my elementary school experience was pretty unnatural and uncommon, but this was a monumental adjustment for someone going into sixth grade.

When I first started kindergarten at P.S. 143, my family lived in Corona, Queens. We lived on 111th Street, just 2½ blocks from the school. Back then, my grandmother would walk me to school. It was our neighborhood school. But by the end of my first grade year, my family had moved from Corona to St. Albans, practically on the other side of Queens. We had a terrific little house in Corona, on a quiet, friendly street, but it was my parents' "starter home." When they first bought the house on 111th Street, it was just mom and dad and my oldest brother David. But the family had grown since then. Now Grandma and Grandpa lived with them too, having left their apartment in Harlem to help take care of us kids while Mom and Dad went to work. There was also Mom's uncle Harold, who had lived with Grandma and Grandpa. And of course, there was now also my brother Michael and me. There was also my mom's sister Hyacinth, who was attending City College during the day. So, things were a little cramped. My parents were now comfortably part of New York's Black middle class and they could afford more. And they definitely needed it.

St. Albans was a community with an important history. In the 1930's, 40's and 50's, successful Black athletes and entertainers had the money to afford to buy nice homes and nice places to live, but communities in New York City, the nicer communities, were not receptive to integration. It didn't matter how much money you had, you still could not buy a home in an upscale white neighborhood. Period. That's what made St. Albans special. This was an enclave in South Jamaica, Queens where affluent Blacks had their own community. While most of the surrounding neighborhoods had ¼ acre and ⅛ acre lots, St. Albans offered ½ acre lots with sprawling 4 & 5 bedroom homes. Back in Corona, the sidewalks had 10-12 foot tall saplings that were planted in little plots of dirt that were four feet square. In St. Albans, the sidewalks had a continuous ribbon of grass that stretched the length of the street. And the trees were oaks that rose 40 or 50 feet and occasionally formed an arch, adjoining the trees from the opposite sidewalk.

This was one of a small handful of neighborhoods in the city where Black New Yorkers who had any money came to live. St. Albans' ascendance as a Mecca for jazz musicians began in 1923 when Clarence Williams, a successful musician and entrepreneur from Plaquemine, Louisiana, purchased a home and eight lots at 171-37 108th Avenue. Anticipating the increasing popularity of jazz in the north, Williams moved to New York with his wife, singer Eva Taylor, in 1923. Desiring open spaces reminiscent of his upbringing in the Louisiana delta, Williams made his home in St. Albans. He would be the first in a lengthy line of jazz musicians to come to this unique neighborhood in southern Queens.

St. Albans, and in particular the subsection known as Addisleigh Park, was home to a whole host of Black celebrities and jazz legends, including Count Basie, Ella Fitzgerald, Mercer Ellington, Fats Waller, James Brown and John Coltrane as well as sports legends Jackie Robinson and Joe Louis. When my parents moved to St. Albans in the summer of 1963, they purchased the home that had belonged to Lena Horne, although they did so against the forceful objections of my grandfather and his sisters. My grandfather's sisters had been incredibly successful entrepreneurs since the 1940s and now owned a real estate firm (among other things). Sisters Camilla ("Aunt Cammie") and Keturah ("Aunt Kitty") felt that my parents would be spending beyond their means and before long the bank would take back the house because they couldn't keep up with the mortgage. That was probably not a real threat and my parents knew it, because Aunt Cammie and Aunt Kitty sat on the board of directors of the bank too. Allied Federal Savings Bank in Jamaica, Queens was one of New York's first Black-owned banks and was a significant source of support to many local businesses and residents. Allied later merged with Carver Bank and under the Carver name became the largest Black-owned bank in New York. Aunt Cammie and Aunt Kitty had a much more modest house in mind for my parents, one of their own listings of course. My parents—God bless them—completely ignored Grandpa and his sisters.

In our family, no argument was ever more important than the bonds of family, so no one stayed angry for very long. My parents bought Lena Horne's house and my grandparents came along and lived with us as well. Both my parents worked, so Grandma and Grandpa watched over my brothers and me. Our new house became the family's geographic anchor, with the rest of my grandparents' children all buying homes within minutes of us, and that physical proximity continued for decades.

My mom had a favorite expression, a quote from a poem by Robert Browning, *"A man's reach should exceed his grasp/ Or what's a heaven for?"* She knew that the house that she and dad bought would be a financial hardship, but for them, that was the point. They were reaching for something. And by reaching for it, they made it possible. That was the lesson they taught us at every chance they could. It also turned out to be a lesson they taught their siblings, because they all bought homes in the same community. That closeness defined our family.

As a marketing and tourism promotion, the Queens Historical Society published the Queens Jazz Trail Map which featured the actual addresses of various jazz legends and included our house! One morning my grandfather was looking out his bedroom window on the second floor of our house and saw a crowd of people, all with cameras, taking pictures of the house. My grandfather, who was in his 90's, started yelling for my mother, "Rita, what are all these white people doing in front of the house?"

The Jazz Trail map was published sometime in the late 1990s, a long time after I had grown and moved away. But I don't think that my parents liked the experience. I don't think that their privacy was ever seriously disrupted, but it was a strange feeling nevertheless.

I should probably spend a little time talking about my grandfather. He was, after all, one of the most remarkable men I have met or known in my entire life. Calvin Thomas was born on the island of Tortola in the British Virgin Islands. If anyone would like to know where on Tortola my family came from, they need only to look at a map. There is a section at the east end of the island marked on the map as "Thomas Land." That's my family. If you have ever flown to Tortola, you have arrived on a smaller, adjacent island called Beef Island. It is the only part of Tortola that is actually flat enough to build an airport. The rest of Tortola is very steep mountain terrain. My grandfather's family used to own Beef Island, until one day the BVI government decided to take the island by eminent domain (a process by which the government acquires private land to be used for the greater good of the community) so that they could build the airport. The government told my grandfather's father, "Here is a check as compensation for the land. You can either cash the check, or you can spend the rest of your life fighting this in court. But you will lose." So they cashed the check.

My grandfather was the seventh of eight children, and the only boy. Every one of his sisters was a trailblazer and a person of incredible accomplishment, so Grandpa grew up with a genuine respect and appreciation for women as complete equals and partners, despite having grown up in a very traditional British Caribbean culture. He was an enlightened man before his time. He came to the United States in 1924, at the age of 18, along with several of his sisters. Grandpa made his home in Harlem, while a few of his sisters settled in the greener, more residential borough of Queens. Grandpa seemed more at home in the heart of Harlem's West Indian community. With his sisters, Camilla and Adina, as well as other family members, he played an important role in the formation of St. Paul's Methodist Church and in the founding of the Allied Federal Savings Bank (now Carver Federal Savings), both in Jamaica, Queens.

But what Grandpa was best known for was his role as founder and life-long member of several organizations; The Royal Sachem Social Club, The Dawn Social Club, The St. Thomas Cricket Club and The British Virgin Islands Benevolent Association, with which he was affiliated for over sixty years. He served as its first president, its last president and for many of the years in between, despite his frequent protestations that they should elect someone else. Through his work and leadership of these community organizations, he helped find jobs and places to live for the new arrivals from the Virgin Islands. He helped purchase books and supplies for schools in the British Virgin Islands, helped fund the restoration of churches and schools damaged by storms and hurricanes. His organization purchased the first x-ray machine in the Cottage Hospital in Tortola. These were Grandpa's values and they were unshakable. You took care of family and you took care of your community. The success of any individual was dependent upon the success of the village. This was how he built and raised his family.

Grandpa was employed by the Horn & Hardart Company as a Commissary Foreman, not at their famous Automat, but at corporate head-quarters, and remained a faithful and tireless worker until his retirement in 1968. In the early years, when my mother and her brother and sisters were growing up, Grandpa's salary was pretty modest. The household budget was pretty tight, nothing at all like the comfortable, upper-class lifestyle that Grandpa had known growing up in Tortola. It was often a struggle. But Grandpa was confident that he and his family would make their way in the world, and that every day would be better than the day before. And Grandpa and Grandma showered their children with love and inspired them to aim high and believe that they could accomplish anything. Absolutely anything.

I think that my mom and her siblings were convinced that if their dad believed it, then it must be true, so they never second-guessed their ambitions.

Every week, Grandpa would bring home a shopping bag filled with Horn & Hardart pies and pastries and treats. My grandmother never learned how to bake because she never needed to. There was always something delicious for dessert in the cupboard. In fact, the first time that Grandma attempted to bake an apple pie—very late in life—she cut up a single apple and placed it in the crust and put it in the oven, expecting the apple to rise and fill the crust. I owe my sweet tooth to Grandpa.

Grandpa passed away in 2003, at the age of 97.

LUNCH MONEY AND FRENCH CLASS

Technically speaking, now that we lived in St. Albans, P.S. 143 was no longer my neighborhood school and I should have transferred to another school close by. But my dad worked at 143, so I was permitted to stay. Instead of walking to school with my grandmother each day, now I rode in the car. The reason that all this is important, the reason that it makes a difference is that when it came time to graduate from elementary school and move on finally to a new school, I was in a completely different school system than my elementary school classmates. Instead of moving on to sixth grade in a new school along with all my friends, I was moving on to a place where I didn't know a single soul. Considering the artificial cocoon I had been existing in, I was terrified.

My school year in my completely new school, in my completely new district, got off to an historic and eventful beginning. It was September of 1968 and just as school was about to begin, the New York City teachers union went on strike. This was the historic clash with the local administrators of the minority school district of Ocean Hill—Brownsville in Brooklyn. The clash and the beef may have been local, but the teachers strike was citywide. And the strike lasted for 36 days, creating major disorientation and confusion everywhere. Furthermore, the tensions that were fomented by the teachers strike also seemed to exacerbate the distrust and disconnection of Blacks and whites throughout the city. The white communities were growing intolerant of the endless demands for civil rights and integration.

The Black communities were growing impatient with promises and compromises that never seemed to result in actual progress. And because of the strike and the issues it represented, the teachers were more or less automatically on one side of this divide. Black and brown school children were often the victims—intended and unintended—of this hostile antipathy.

Surprisingly, despite all the turmoil and anxiety stirred up by the strike, my sixth grade year at I.S. 147 ("Intermediate School") in Cambria Heights, Queens was a pretty good and fairly uneventful year. Once the strike was over and the classroom routine was underway, I have no special stand-out memories of that year. There was none of the stress that I anticipated upon entering a new school.

That would come soon.

I.S. 147 was an intermediate school, an odd entity within the New York City school system. An intermediate school covered only the sixth grade. It was neither an elementary school nor a junior high school. It was a short stop in between, designed to address classroom size and to offset school overcrowding in some of the city's school districts. The logic of the configuration was a bit complex and although it did result is smaller class sizes, it also meant that students were constantly changing schools, undermining continuity and the important ability of school teachers and administrators to get to know their students well. Politically, it was a compromise that never entirely satisfied or pleased anyone. Educationally, it was an experiment that was previously untested and ultimately proved to be more failure than success.

That would come for me the following year. After I.S. 147, I moved on to J.H.S. 59 in Springfield Gardens, another school, another neighborhood, and another break from the friends I had just acquired at 147. At the time, I wondered why none of my new friends were coming with me to J.H.S. 59, but were going to other junior highs instead. It seemed odd and unfair that for two years in a row I was being yanked forcibly from the ground and replanted someplace else. What kind of plant can grow roots or bear fruit under these inhospitable conditions? What I didn't realize at the time was that my parents were actively engaged in a game of chess, strategically moving my piece across the board in an ongoing effort to ensure that I was placed in the school that offered the best educational opportunities for me. Even if it presented me with my own peculiar set of social and psychological challenges. I could have gone to the same junior high as my other friends. I could have gone to the same junior high as my two older brothers, but J.H.S. 59 had received better ratings and better test scores. The smart move was to place me there, and so calls were made. Strings were pulled. The chess piece was moved across the board.

J.H.S. 59 may have been a better rated school, but it wasn't the partner school for I.S. 147, as I have just explained. It was never intended to be the place that those students migrated to for one very obvious reason; J.H.S. 59 was a 6-7-8 grade school. It already had a sixth grade. And the students from that sixth grade moved on to seventh grade with all the same friends. The teachers and administrators knew these students; their names, faces, personalities and their transcripts. Me; none of the above.

And so, when I arrived at 59, everyone had friends. Except me. Everyone knew the teachers. Except me. I know that I sound like I'm whining about something that really shouldn't be that big a deal (get over it, kid) but bear with me. I'm leading up to something.

J.H.S. 59 was also different in another unexpected (at least for me) way. At both P.S. 143 and I.S. 147, the student profile was more or less 50/50 or 60/40 white and Black, a relatively even mix based on the demographic profile of the areas. All in all, a pretty good thing. My school friends growing up were also a balanced mix of white and Black because, after all, that's just the way it was, and I don't think that any of us kids really gave it much thought beyond that. Everybody was cool with everybody else, but to us that was a given, that was the default mode. At 59, however, the student profile was more than 90% white and less than 10% Black. The school was bordered on three sides by St. Albans (where I lived), Rochdale and Laurelton, all in the southeast corner of Queens, just before the Nassau County line. At the time I was in school there, Rochdale was more than 90% white and less than 10% Black. Laurelton, just on the other side of Springfield Boulevard, was the opposite, more than 90% Black and less than 10% white. J.H.S. 59 sat restlessly between them. It might as well have been an outpost in the Demilitarized Zone along the 38th Parallel.

Rochdale was a village made up almost entirely by an enormous cooperative housing complex. Rochdale Village was an attractive community covering 122 blocks designed to provide residents with a park-like, suburban setting inside the limits of the urban South Jamaica part of Queens. When construction was completed in 1963, it was the largest private cooperative housing complex in the world. Although the developers touted Rochdale as a model of mixed race housing, the reality was that none of the units were being offered to Black families. After months of demonstrations and protests, New York City government stepped in and eventually 10% of the apartments were occupied by Black families. A decade later, in the 1970s, "white flight" took on unstoppable momentum and it wasn't long before Rochdale became almost entirely Black. But back then, when I was in school, this was supposed to be a neighborhood where working class white families could "get away from" minorities.

My parents—never afraid of being pioneers—probably saw this attribute as a plus and a reason to send me there. Perhaps it is a bit of prejudice, but most Black parents would perceive a predominantly white school as an opportunity for their child to receive a better education. White schools got better budgets, and better books and supplies. White schools got better teachers. White schools expected their students to succeed. White schools were part of a system designed to provide "better" education. And education—in our house and many others—was the key to upward mobility, personal security and happiness. Education would be the armor to protect me from all of the hazards, challenges, impediments and predictable assaults that life would place in the path of a young Black man.

But J.H.S. 59 was different. Really, really different. The students there were entirely unaccustomed to interacting socially with Black kids or with Black people in general. For the kids, circumstances simply did not require it. For the adults, they had worked too hard and paid good money to buy nice homes in a nice neighborhood precisely so that they would not have to. A friendship with one of the Black kids at school was considered—at best—a kooky idea, a novelty, something you would do if you really wanted to stand out, make a statement. Some did. Most, however, viewed the idea as completely nonsensical; "Why the fuck would you want to do that? Are you one of them now?"

There was a girl in my seventh grade science class that year who refused to be my lab partner. "I'm not allowed to talk to people I don't know," she said. "I'll get in trouble." The teacher seemed to understand completely, so I worked alone.

I wasn't shunned in any overly dramatic sense. I didn't get the complete silent treatment or anything like that. The kids that I saw every day, the kids in my regular classes, were—for the most part—friendly. Friendly, but never friends. There was a palpable sense of disconnection and alienation, of being present, yet apart. I always felt as though I was engaging in small talk or pleasantries when we spoke, the way you would speak to someone you just met at a party. I was constantly listening to other kids talk about what they did together over the weekend or what they were planning to do. I was never invited. Never included. This was certainly not the first time in my life that I had experienced racism, but it was the first time that I was old enough to perceive it and recognize it for what it was. I was not the subject of any brutality or hatred. There was nothing about the experience that could ever be described as 'traumatic' or that would scar me emotionally. But it would—and did—leave a lasting impression that would begin to adjust my perception of the world around me. And for a 12 year old kid in the seventh grade, it sucked.

Each morning before school, all of the students would gather in the school yard for roughly 15—20 minutes before being marshaled into the building according to your grade and your class. That's when everyone talked about what they did or watched on TV the night before. That's when you asked which of your classmates finished their homework and who had the answer to the math problem that hardly anyone understood. That's when the guys stood around staring at the girls and the girls stood around talking and staring back. The morning schoolyard ritual meant that you didn't have to wait until lunchtime to coalesce into the usual cliques, you could self-identify and segregate right at the start of your day. I usually stood near one group or the other, trying to look casual, but rarely as an actual part of a group. Usually I would talk to one of the really nerdy kids, not because I was a nerd—I wasn't—but because they were equally grateful to have someone to talk to.

On this particular morning, while chatting it up with Ira, one of the nerdy kids, we were approached by two kids who weren't from our class. Two Black kids. I had gotten to know and become friendly with a few of the other Black kids at our school. There weren't that many of us and we were scattered across different classes. None were in any of my classes, so our opportunities to form friendships were limited. There was another new obstacle to forming friendships with some of the other Black kids at 59, one that I had not encountered before.

I am very light-skinned. Black folks come in nearly every possible shade and I happen to be near the end of the light spectrum for Black people. If you did not know me, you might assume that I was a Caucasian of Mediterranean descent. My family is West Indian and come from the U.S. and British Virgin Islands, places where the influences and roots are extraordinarily rich and diverse. That diversity is reflected in the broad range of skin tones represented by my family. Many people assume that I am bi-racial or perhaps a quadroon. I am neither. I am Black. Both of my parents are Black. All four of my grandparents are Black. All eight of my great-grandparents were Black. Beyond that I can make no assurances.

Being light-skinned had never been an issue for me before. I knew who I was and what I was. And anyone who knew me, knew who I was and what I was. I never had to explain myself or my identity before. The idea didn't even make sense. But this bizarre and unfamiliar world at J.H.S. 59 was different. The white kids knew for certain that I was not one of them, and if any had a doubt they would simply ask, "Are you colored?"

But the Black kids at 59 weren't too sure where I fit either. I wasn't from their neighborhood, over in Laurelton, or even anywhere close by. We didn't grow up together. And I was much lighter-skinned. My skin was closer to white than it was to Black. So, I was an oddity to them, one that was met with caution and skepticism. In the schoolyard I stayed with my class, which did not include any other Black kids. And because the Black kids were less than 10% of the total school population, it was easy for them to feel separate, isolated.

And so, on this particular morning, Ira and I were approached by these two kids. We both knew them, but we knew them differently. "You got my money?" one kid said to Ira.

"Yeah" Ira said, reaching into his pocket and handing him a few bills.

"You got money for me?" the kid turned and asked me.

"Why would I have money for you?" I asked, with a combination of confusion and schoolyard bravado.

"I'm just askin' if you got money for me. If you don't, you don't." He said while already turning to walk away.

Completely puzzled, I looked at Ira and asked him what the heck was that all about. Nervously, he waited until they had gone beyond earshot. "On the first day of school that kid came up to me and said that he doesn't get enough money from home, so I have to buy him lunch one day each week." Ira confessed.

"So, every week he comes to collect, and you pay him?" I said, amazed and bewildered. "That's just stupid. Why would you do that? Why would you give him your money?"

"Because he could kick my ass." Ira said exasperated. "I'm not stupid, you are."

I don't have any idea what my thought process was, assuming of course that there actually was a thought process, but while Ira was still talking I turned and walked away. I marched right over to the nearest teacher or school aide standing in the yard and reported on what I had just witnessed. I'm not sure what I expected. I guess I expected the teacher to go get Ira's money back, but she just told me to get inside and get to home room.

It turns out that the teacher did not go get Ira's money back. Instead, she sought out school security and told them what I had told her. School security snatched up the two kids and escorted them to the principal's office. A few minutes later, Ira and I were being summoned to the principal's office as well.

"Are these the two boys?" the principal asked.

"The two boys, what?" Ira replied, completely unprepared to give a straight answer.

"Are these the two boys who took your money?" the principal added impatiently.

"I don't know anything about this." Ira insisted unconvincingly.

"Yes, these are the two I saw." I interrupted from several steps away.

"Oh my God." Ira protested. "I can't believe you told them. Why did you do that? Why would you do that? This is none of your business." I did not know Ira very well, but I knew enough to know that Ira lived with fear as a daily companion. And right now, he was being assaulted by fear from every angle. He was afraid of what the two boys might eventually be able to do to him. He was afraid of what their friends might do to him when they found out. He was afraid of the principal and the school security officer who were doing their best to look and sound intimidating. And he was afraid of what his parents were going to say and do when they found out that he was giving away his lunch money and never said anything.

"This is serious, son." The principal turned away from Ira and looked at me. "Tell me exactly what you saw, exactly what happened."

"Nobody hit anybody, or anything like that," I said. "And nobody threatened anybody. He asked him for money and he gave it to him. That's what I saw."

"Is that what happened, Ira?" The principal now tried to look sympathetic as Ira nodded. "And why would you do that, Ira? Why would you give him money?"

Ira told his story, sometimes reluctantly, sometimes with a flood of details, and unburdened himself obediently to these authority figures. I'm not sure if it made Ira feel better or feel worse. Looking at Ira it was hard to tell.

I thought I understood what was happening in the principal's office that day. I thought I understood what was going to happen. The truth is that I had absolutely no idea. I could not have imagined the larger wheels that were being set into motion or who among us those wheels would roll over and barely notice the bump.

My parents raised me to resist being judgmental about people, to avoid labeling people as "good" or "bad". Because most people try to be good but don't always succeed. Often don't succeed. My parents taught me that most of the time when a person does a bad thing, it's because they failed to be good, not because they succeeded in being bad. And that was a very important distinction. It doesn't mean that it is ever okay to do a bad thing, but the action should not define the person, because then there is no path to redemption or to forgiveness.

In the principal's office that morning, I was helping to define two boys that I barely knew as "bad" in a way that was far more permanent and far more destructive and reckless than I could possibly imagine. I was just a kid obeying authority, as I was taught to do. That does not excuse my actions and I am not trying to make excuses. I did a very bad thing that day by failing to perceive the consequences of my actions. I did not simply "take part" in the call to justice being held in the principal's office. I had set it into motion. I cannot take it back and I cannot look back on my memory of that experience without feeling guilty and irresponsible. I was too young to understand that there is something called the school-to-prison pipeline, a system that grinds up young Black boys in order to perpetuate a permanent imbalance of power, a permanent racial status quo. But even then, something in my gut told me that I would forever regret my role and my choices.

I have.

It's possible that the two boys had preyed on several others in the school yard, that there were other kids who came to school in fear because of them. It's also possible that their entire felonious spree amounted to less than $5.00 in lunch money. I just don't know. But the school considered these two 13 year old boys to be a serious menace, so the police were summoned and—based upon statements from Ira and me—were taken to the police station where their parents would have to come get them. This surreal morality play did not finish its spiral into toxic bias and stratospheric overreaction until it played itself out weeks later in Queens County Juvenile Court with a ruling that authorized the expulsion of the two boys from school.

I never found out what became of those two boys. I never looked back or reached back. I just went on with my life. I am ashamed to say that I don't even recall their names. But in writing about them now, I can only believe that I caused them more harm than they could ever have caused me. I know that I was complicit in a system that was all too quick to dispose of them and all too willing to deny their better potential. It would be arrogant and absurd for me to claim that I was somehow made better by the experience. No one was made better by the experience. No one.

This all happened in late fall, early winter, so there was a lot of school year left to endure. It was 1968, later to be reported and remembered as "*annus horribilis.*" The mood of the nation and of the world was bleaker than a dirt-grey sky. King. Kennedy. War. Violent protests and even more violent police. Race riots. Me. Tiny, insignificant, unhappy me. I was now a pariah to most of the other Black kids at school. In their minds what I had done was foreign and treasonous and unfathomable. And although I did not share the same us-versus-them world view that they embraced, I understood it and I knew that they had every right to feel the way they did.

I had grown up in the 1960's as a middle class Black kid. At the time, I thought everybody did. At the time, I thought that my life experiences were not that different from any other Black kid. To be honest, at the time, I thought my life experiences were not that different from any other white kid. What the hell did I know? Apparently not that much. Sure, I understood that I was Black. And I understood that white people were "different." But up until now, that had never really affected me in a way that was personal to me. I can't say that I had ever really been hurt before by that difference. But the experiences of this year had changed all of that. I had grown up just enough to begin to see the landscape clearly and begin to recognize the contours and sharp edges of a geography beyond my own backyard.

As an adult, I know now that racism existed all around me when I was growing up. I know now that it was a time of wrenching upheaval. This was the mid-1960s, the climax of the Civil Rights era; a time when our country was—in so many significant ways—so completely different than it is today. But I didn't know that. I don't think that anyone can know that in the moment that they are living it. The present is never a moment in history while you are living it. It is simply the here and now. And for me, in that moment, there was no analysis or perspective or context. The "here and now" was simply a less happy time in my life.

The white kids at school didn't treat me any differently, which is to say, I didn't really matter to them at all.

As the year continued, I continued my efforts to persevere in school and my grades reflected that struggle. I had always been an "A" student before, although I honestly don't know what it means to be an "A" student in elementary school. I was always reading and performing several grade levels above where I was. I was always comfortable at school, but then, school was always a comfortable place. This was no longer true. I was no longer comfortable, and I was no longer performing well. My grades were a disappointment to me and to my parents. And this was perhaps the first time in my life where my report card was not a source of pride for my parents. I was approaching my thirteenth birthday, becoming a teenager; a time in every boy's life that should be filled with excitement, anticipation and exuberance. It was for me a time of loneliness, alienation, disappointment and despair.

But as sub-mediocre as my mid-year grades were, there was one particular grade that made my parents sit up with alarm. I was getting a "D" in French, with a comment from the teacher that if I did not improve in the spring, I would fail.

Fail.

My parents scheduled a parent-teacher conference and went in together to see my teacher. I did not accompany them. They wanted to be able to have a candid conversation with my teacher and speak openly about why I might be failing. Whatever they discussed, they would come home and share with me whatever I needed to know.

When they came home that evening I expected them to want to speak to me right away, to tell me what the teacher said, and to tell me what I had better do to straighten up and fly right. Or else. But talking to me that evening was not their number one priority. They were busy talking to each other. Whatever the hell had gone down at school that evening was something they needed to work out between themselves. And that was completely baffling to me.

When Mom and Dad did finally speak with me, in what was apparently merely an intermission in their own conversation, they asked me one question. "Did you know that you were in a second-year French class?"

"Uh huh." Of course, I knew I was in a second-year French class. I might be doing poorly, but I'm not stupid.

"But you have never taken French before." My mother argued.

"I know," I said, starting to feel like this line of questioning might be opening the door to some sympathy.

"So why are you in that class?" My mother pressed.

"Because everyone else in my class took first-year French last year, but I wasn't at 59 last year, so I didn't get to take it." I explained. "They would have to put me in a class with sixth graders for first-year French." As much as I hated French class, I could not imagine having to sit in a class with sixth graders. That would be totally awful and embarrassing.

"And your teacher knows this?" My mother asked. "Your teacher knows that you did not take French last year?"

"I guess," I shrugged. Seemed like an obvious question to me.

"Well, apparently not," my mother announced. "Apparently, your teacher had no idea that you had never taken French before. She was quite surprised to learn that. She thought you were just doing poorly, lagging behind the rest of the class."

I was dumb-struck. "What did she say?"

"She said, 'well that explains a lot.'" My father now spoke. "She said that explains a lot."

This was not the world that I knew and understood. Teachers are supposed to know everything. They're not supposed to be clueless and say dumb things. All my life, the teachers I knew were family and friends, and they were never dumb. They were never less than you thought they should be. But this was different. Part of me felt relieved that my parents understood that I was in a situation in French class that was over my head, that it wasn't all my fault. And if it was my fault, at least I had an excuse. But part of me also felt weird and uneasy about all of this. Does this mean the teacher messed up?

And if so, what am I supposed to do about this? What is the teacher going to say to me tomorrow? What am I going to say to the teacher?

That evening my parents came to the realization that J.H.S. 59 had not, after all, been a good school choice and that was their only reason for sending me there in the first place. Mom and Dad were more than just fully engaged passionate parents. They were educators. They knew precisely what it meant to be a good teacher. They knew how schools were supposed to operate. But they were deeply disturbed by what they observed that night. It was incomprehensible to them that a teacher would not know something as basic and essential as whether a student was in their first or second year of French. To them, that was simply crazy.

I suspect that my parents' misgivings about the school had been growing over time, especially after the drama of having to take me to Queens County Family Court to testify against two boys for a school yard crime. I never talked about friends from school, because I didn't have any. My mood and behavior had changed. It was easy to see that something was wrong. But that parent-teacher conference crystallized the issue and catalyzed their determination to take action and get me out of that school as quickly as possible. Mom and Dad were not people who agonized over decisions. They weren't the kind of people who spent time wringing their hands and second-guessing previous beliefs or decisions and they did not spend much time looking in the rear-view mirror at events in the past. That night, sitting at the kitchen table, my parents began making plans to send me to Dalton.

CHAPTER 3

WHAT WE WERE COMING FROM

RAYMOND SMALTZ

THE PROJECTS

I LOOKED UP THE TERM; "THE Projects" in the <u>Urban Dictionary</u> and here is how it was described:

> *"Usually a group of dirty buildings made for really poor/ homeless people to live in. Projects are dangerous, very dirty, filled with gangsters, drug dealers, pimps, hookers and such. The first set of projects made (Starrett City, made in 1963) were made for Blacks to live in, but over the years people of all races started to live in projects.*

What a crock! Actually, according to Wikipedia, the "projects" were an initiative by the city and state of New York, along with multi-millionaire developer Robert Moses, to provide low-income housing for families during the 30's and 40's. The strategy of the Federal Housing Administration was to build up suburban communities across the U.S. by providing affordable housing and mortgages to middle class families. That strategy, of course, did not include Black families. Redlining and housing covenants effectively kept Black families out of the suburbs. The government strategy for Black families was densely concentrated inner city apartment living in highly segregated sections of the city.

There are dozens of projects strategically placed throughout New York City and they're run by the NYCHA (New York City Housing Authority). My particular project, Robert F. Wagner Houses, consisted of 14, 16-story buildings and 8, 7-story buildings, a total of 22 in all. It had around 5,290 residents who lived in 2,154 apartments. The complex was 26.9 acres and each group of buildings had its own set of playground equipment for the kids. (Many a bloody elbow or skinned knee were acquired on the "monkey bars.") Wagner also contained a public grammar school, P.S. 80, and a junior high school, JHS 45. The Wagner Houses were named after four-term Mayor, Robert F. Wagner. They cost around $30 million to construct in the mid-1950's. Most projects even had their own police force; "Housing Cops" (usually the misfits of the NYPD were assigned to the project police authorities). These "Housing Cops" were supposed to provide security for each project, although we were never sure who they were actually protecting when we were growing up.

The projects of New York City spawned many multi-talented individuals over the years. Actor/comedienne/talk show host Whoopi Goldberg grew up in the Elliott-Chelsea Houses on the west side of Manhattan. Academy Award-winning actor, Louis Gossett, Jr., claimed the Coney Island Houses of Brooklyn as his launching pad. Even vilified Goldman Sachs executive, Lloyd Blankfein, was raised in Brooklyn in the Linden Houses. And one of my basketball heroes, Hall of Famer Kareem Abdul-Jabbar, known in the projects as "Big" Lew Alcindor, claimed the Dyckman Houses of upper Manhattan as his home. One of the more infamous boxers of this era, Mike Tyson, was terrorizing residents as a young man in the Albany Houses of Brooklyn. And one of the Bronxdale Houses' occupants was nominated and appointed to the highest court in the land in 2009—Justice Sonia Sotomayor.

Thomas Sowell, writing about New York's Housing Projects for the National Review Online, quoted a piece from the New York Times: *"These were not the projects of idle, stinky elevators, of gang-controlled stairwells where drug deals go down...these were public housing projects of an earlier era, when such places were very different from what we associate with the words 'housing projects' today."*

That's the world I knew growing up.

I was born in 1956, the same year the Wagner Houses were completed. At the time, my family lived near 116th Street and St. Nicholas Avenue in Harlem. My family did not move to Wagner until the early 60's. For my family, moving to 2370 Second Avenue, apartment #8H must have felt like the television program "The Jefferson's," since we moved from an older tenement building on the west side of Harlem to the brand-new towers in East Harlem, bordering East River Drive and adjacent to the Triborough Bridge. The Wagner Projects were also sometimes dubbed the Tri-Borough Houses because of their proximity to the bridge.

I was a middle child of my mother, Norma Beatrice Smaltz (her maiden name is Cole), but the first son of her union to Raymond Bailey Smaltz, Jr., also known as "Big Ray," making me Raymond Bailey Smaltz, III. This used to make me feel like royalty and the direct association with my father and grandfather made me feel unique. There were my older brothers Dwain Cole and Norman Franke before me, both of whom had different fathers, and my younger brothers Mark and Peter, with my sister Rachel as the last child of my parent's union. We three younger guys shared one of the 3 bedrooms in the "new" apartment. Dwain and Norman shared another and my parents had the final bedroom to themselves until my sister was born in '64.

Believe me, there was a lot of nonsense, noise and knuckle-headedness that went on between Mark, Peter and myself in that tiny room overlooking Second Avenue and 122nd Street. Our bedroom had one single bed for Pete on one side of the room and a bunk bed on the other from which Mark and I terrorized each other. On the top bunk of my personal fortress, I was officially the "purveyor of pandemonium." I never failed to come up with various ways to annoy our father, like jumping from the top of my bunk bed onto Peter's bed. A minute later, my father would storm down the hallway yelling, *"Now cut out all that racket, you hear me? Get to sleep, dammit!!!"*

One of my most memorable ploys was to convince my brothers to stuff dirty clothes, which were in abundance, into our beds to make it seem as if we were hiding underneath and then make such a racket, so as to force my father to come screaming down the hall, throw open the door and proceed to "read us the official <u>Big Ray Riot Act</u>!" He never had a clue in the dark that we were secluded under the bed, in the closet and behind the dresser, snickering to ourselves as softly as we could while he berated a bunch of dirty laundry. He was so pissed that it forced my mother to follow-up after his outburst, only to bust us when she discovered that, in response to answers to her questions, our voices sounded a little odd, prompting her to turn on the lights and discover our various hiding spots, which forced a snicker from her and belly laughs from us. We knew our antics would be recounted the next day by our neighbors because the entire 8th floor of the building could hear him, since my father had a booming voice (I am also blessed & cursed with) that never failed to carry through our windows, walls and probably pipes too.

Though we were a large family in a small three-bedroom apartment (eight of us in all) and poor, I never realized how much we didn't have, mostly because everyone else in the building was also struggling. The only difference between the neighbors and us was the number of kids in the family. If there were only a couple of kids, like my friend Ronald Tucker and his brother Vernon, or another grammar school classmate, Edward Rivera, and his sister, they had a little more than we had growing up. But my Mother never failed to prepare a hot meal for us in the morning during the winter months of school; and there was always something on the table that evening for dinner—even in our worst times as a family. And "hand-me-downs" were the way of the world for struggling large families like ours, especially with five boys (although my younger brothers certainly lucked out more than I did, because I meticulously cared for my clothes, which my brothers Mark and Peter were all too happy to share, whether I had actually out-grown the garments or not).

Over the many years of living at Wagner Houses, as many more families from all over the U.S. and the Caribbean came into the country, languages came and went on the floors of the projects. One moment, you could hear a family speaking Spanish to each other through the walls, while the next you could hear two people arguing with West Indian accents. Sometimes, you might even hear Yiddish being spoken, as many Jewish families took advantage of the new housing at the end of the 50's. The Wagner projects were relatively multi-cultural during that era, with a smattering of White residents throughout the development.

Wagner bordered a close-knit community of Italian-American families who owned many of the brownstone tenements that made up the area south of 120th Street and Second Avenue, stretching to the river and down to 116th Street. One of the most famous restaurants in our neighborhood was Patsy's Pizzeria, where it was alleged (you never heard it from me) that members of the different crime families frequented the establishment. While the Black and Hispanic families managed to co-exist with their Italian neighbors, it was only with the caveat from my mother, "...Now don't let me find out that you were hanging around that neighborhood!" If we didn't heed her warning and felt adventurous enough to go for an "icee" or some of Patsy's famous, turn-of-the-century oven-baked pizza, we did so with the full intention of "getting in and getting out!" Mostly, our projects were made up of hard-working lower middle-class and poor residents, some of whom subsisted on welfare, trying to feed their families the best they could.

One of my earliest friends was a Puerto Rican kid named Eddie Colon, who was maybe half my size, but had a tough-ass spirit and could play the meanest game of touch football, as we constantly picked up his limp body from countless unwanted encounters with the pavement. He lived down the hall from my family at 2370, attended the same public school in the neighborhood as I, and was even in the same class. We were like the comic strip characters "Mutt and Jeff" made popular at the turn of the century, but with an "Afro-Rican flavor" and inseparable for a time growing up in the projects. There was something about this very protective friendship that spawned much of my later behavior in school and on my athletic teams.

No one in my neighborhood had money for very much, so purchasing any equipment for different sporting activities was a pipe dream. If you were lucky enough to own both a football, a basketball, or a baseball, bat and glove, everyone wanted to be your friend. Early on as a kid, football was my favorite sport and the New York Football Giants were my heroes; from Charlie Conerly to Fran Tarkenton, Frank Gifford to Emlen Tunnell, Aaron Thomas to Bob Tucker and of course, free safety Carl "Spider" Lockhart and the wide receiver who created "The Spike"—Homer Jones! Crowding around our outdated, frustratingly inconsistent, Black and white television set was an afternoon ritual every Sunday, with my old man being the Giants' biggest cheerleader.

My Mother was the center around which things revolved in our tiny apartment. I wouldn't call her an overbearing personality, but she was by no means a "demure, shrinking violet" when she set her mind to achieving a goal for us as a family. She was a very handsome, fair-skinned woman, tall at 5'9" and smoked Salem cigarettes when we were kids, but dropped the habit "cold turkey" when she began to study the Jehovah's Witness faith. Unfortunately, my old man didn't share her same goals for our family and he had several negative traits that precluded accomplishment. He didn't respond to authority very well, which always made employment problematic and put an extraordinary amount of pressure on Mom. It also made for some epic screaming and yelling that would carry on for hours, sometimes days, until he decided to walk out of the apartment to escape Mom's "sharp-tongue" and see what the "latest number" was.

My father struggled to stay in one job or another. It was a constant battle between white folk's impression of him as this handsome, intelligent, strong, and powerful Black man; versus his lack of discipline, slickness and laziness. This put him in more than one challenging situation with his many employers. One moment he could be providing for his family's needs by bringing home exquisite cuts of meat from the Washington Beef and Supply Company on 9ᵗʰ Avenue, providing many a bountiful meal for six hungry kids, as he drove his truck around the city delivering precious beef to all of the major hotels and restaurants in New York. The next moment, he could be found sitting in his chair with a copy of the want ads in the New York Times, wondering when the next gig will reveal itself to him. Unfortunately, we never realized that some of those times he was bringing home huge cuts of veal, or skirt steaks, a couple dozen kosher beef franks or a pot roast—they weren't necessarily paid for, having "fallen off the truck." Well, expensive cuts of meat could only fall off that truck but so many times and then...well, you can guess what happened. So, my father would use his contacts within the Teamsters, which controlled the trucking industry, and slide over to driving liquor trucks around the city. This gave him a chance to schmooze many of the jazz and supper clubs—making him a "man about town" because he serviced some of the coolest bars with some of the coolest people.

It was hard to set goals for a poor growing family of eight in the projects in the 60's and 70's if you couldn't count on a steady income stream and Pop was always in and out of different jobs. I can't ever remember a time that we weren't under some kind of pressure to make rent for the month, to put enough food on the table for everyone, to buy clothes for all the boys and Rachel, to replace something broken in the apartment, and ultimately... to put three of us through private school. My mother would say, "we had enough dispossessed notices to paper the wall!"

Somewhere between my attending P.S. 80 and P.S. 96 in Harlem, the schools figured out that the "Smaltz boys" were a fairly bright lot, pretty well-behaved, while towering over most of their other classmates. We didn't have much, but my Mother always made sure that our clothes were pressed, neat and clean and that we had something in our brown paper bags to eat for lunch. Mom tutored the three younger boys by reading to us constantly. Our sister Rachel attended the very exclusive Park Avenue Christian Day Church for her pre-school years. When it came time for me to attend first grade at P.S. 80, they placed me in a 1 - 3 class, taught by Mrs. Stryker, since they didn't really know exactly where to place me, but by the next school year, I moved up to Mrs. Camper's 2 - 2 class, where my personality and love of reading began to take shape.

The author I loved as a child and who taught me how to read, was **Dr. Seuss,** also known as **Theodor Seuss Geisel.** It was always exciting to receive a brand-new Dr. Seuss book in the mail every couple of weeks, sealed in brown cardboard with my name imprinted on the label. I knew nothing of the old English-style poetic meters of "anapestic, amphibrach or trochaic tetrameter" that Mr. Geisel employed—I only knew I was receiving a special treat delivered by the mailman and enjoyed the stories and illustrations of this author's works. I couldn't wait for the next installment to arrive. Whether it was "One Fish, Two Fish," or "The Cat In The Hat" or "Yertle The Turtle," I was entertained for hours and taken away to a place far from the streets of Harlem or the noisy battles in my family's apartment. And through this journey of imagination, I was exposed to a world of fantasy and possibility and my appetite for knowledge never seemed to be satisfied. I saw the lengths my Mother went to see her children achieve. Although those books were relatively inexpensive—managing a household on a limited and inconsistent budget didn't allow for subscriptions to a children's book club, but Mom figured out right away the investment was worthwhile because once I had mastered each book, my brothers would also have their opportunity to be exposed to the wonderful styling's of Dr. Seuss.

Whatever basic skills and learning habits my first two teachers at P.S. 80 instilled in me, the teachers at the Joseph C. Lanzetta School, P.S. 96, took my overall development a step further. The two schools were within blocks of each other. My brother Mark and I embarked on the 2nd and 3rd grades with much anticipation and excitement. Not only was P.S. 96 a brand-new school that opened in '64 and an exciting new opportunity for us, but it also stimulated our creative juices in music, art, dance and theater. It was at P.S. 96 that I met Mr. Levy, a middle-aged gray-haired teacher who introduced me to music. Mr. Levy toiled endlessly with us poor kids from the neighborhood. He gave us the chance to experiment with different instruments and to learn musical form.

The "brass section" in the grammar school band was right up my alley, since I was one of the bigger kids in third grade, with an endless supply of "hot air." If Mr. Levy was short a French horn or trumpet player, he slid me over to that section of the band, in order to "get him over" for that particular performance. But I suppose that I enjoyed the trombone best. As a kid, I tried to listen to all of the great jazz trombone players that my folks had in our home. One of my favorites at age nine featured J.J. Johnson and Kai Winding playing a duet to "Yes Sir, That's My Baby." That duet never failed to thrill me every time I played it on our "hi-fi record player." Though we couldn't afford them, Mr. Levy trusted most of the kids in his class to take the school's instruments home so that we could practice over the weekends and bring them back on Monday for our classes.

Mr. Levy was an early musical mentor because of his appreciation for jazz. Even though we were learning traditional songs played by marching bands, Mr. Levy would often break into some Duke Ellington or Count Basie "riffs" when he wanted to have some fun at the piano. He was an amazing and extremely gifted man. He could play every single instrument from the piano to the violin, from the flute to the trumpet, not to mention the clarinet or the drums.

My 3rd grade teacher Miss Levy, no relation to my music teacher, taught the 3 - 1 class at P.S. 96 and was an older gray-haired Jewish woman who barely seemed to have enough energy to keep up with us. I was disappointed to learn she would be my first teacher at my new school because of how old she looked. I wondered who played this unfair trick on me and where did they live so I could throw an egg at their door. Our classes were mostly exercises in control for her. She was constantly trying to get our attention, banging her ruler on the desk. There were so many bright Black and Brown kids in that class, I think she just wasn't creative enough to keep up with our eagerness to learn. Miss Levy wasn't a bad teacher, just not very exciting or stimulating. And in order for me to grow in this new environment, I had to find other outlets of interest to occupy my frantic mind. Music was one activity and the other was art.

My Mother and oldest brother Dwain had the "artist's gene" in our family. Were it not for his enlisting in the Marines at 18, I believe Dwain could have received a scholarship to an art college or university and become a successful artist.

My interest in drawing took hold in 3rd grade. Futuristic contraptions were assaulting my mind and whenever I was done with my schoolwork, I would pick up a #2 pencil and begin sketching out the cars, space ships and personal vehicles of the future, spurred on by the different science fiction shows of the 60's. I was fascinated by "The Outer Limits" and later "Star Trek," and the epic superheroes of Stan Lee's Marvel comic books. I had sketched so many different ideas on paper that I had enough drawings for my own "one schoolboy exhibition." The school agreed to display my work on the main floor of the building. Each invention had detailed explanations, arrows pointing to the relevant part of the device. The art display was there for my parents to see when they came in for parent-teacher conference. It had to have been a great source of pride for them both; I know it was for me.

In 4th, 5th and 6th grades an entire new world was opened to me through the guidance and counsel of Mrs. Grollman, Ms. Cohen and Ms. Petrocelli; three very different, attractive, white women teaching "some of the best and brightest" Black and Hispanic children in the public school system in East Harlem. They created an environment for me to grow academically and socially, by taking me under their wings and exposing me to all the books, music, art and culture that wealthier kids took for granted. Along the way, I was introduced to two wealthy women who would ultimately lay the foundation for me to enroll at The Dalton School.

It was Miss Cohen who exposed me to the "Young People's Concerts," conducted by Leonard Bernstein, the late Music Director of the New York Philharmonic Orchestra. Miss Cohen would come up to East Harlem in a taxi, pick me up in front of my project building. She or her fiancé would then transport me downtown to Lincoln Center, where we would enjoy the concert. After the concert, Miss Cohen would bring me to her family's apartment for a traditional Jewish dinner on the West Side of Manhattan in the 60's, and then bring me back to Wagner Houses.

Talk about culture shock! I was just a 9 or 10-year old kid from the projects. My mother always made sure to dress me in a clean, pressed shirt and tie, looking my best, as I embarked on my excursion "downtown"—but I was nervous the entire time as I pressed my nose against the car or taxi window.

I watched the tenements, bodegas and the winos in front of the liquor stores give way to well-dressed women walking into and out of luxury high-rise buildings with doormen in the front. Finally, the majesty of Lincoln Center came into view, with its expansive plaza and hundreds of people scurrying around before entering. We convened in the spacious, grand foyer of the Alice Tully Hall and took our seats in the middle of the row. Bernstein was a charismatic conductor, hair flying with every movement of his baton. He introduced the children in the audience to Shostakovich, Copeland and Ives, along with a little bit of Armstrong and Ellington. You could tell he took great pleasure in speaking to children—that he really enjoyed teaching and performing the music for the curious, wide-eyed kids of all colors from the city.

Before 4th grade at P.S. 96, I never knew what the term "teacher's pet" meant. I was in Mrs. Grollman's class that year, and my interest in my studies was heightened by all the extra attention I received from Mrs. Grollman and her family. Their commitment to me made a huge impact. With six kids in the family, we were all scrambling for attention from our parents. So many times we had to go to bed discouraged by the realization that our parents had little or no time for any one of us unless you screwed up, and then the refrain was, "…wait till your father gets home!" That's what made the attention of the Grollmans so special.

One of the other advanced students in the class was Maria Velez. She was a bright Puerto Rican young lady from the neighborhood. She was also very cute with a little mole on one of her cheeks. Maria and I shared a love of reading and we shared the same classes through 4th, 5th and 6th grades at P.S. 96. We were the standouts of Mrs. Grollman's class and were always the representatives for the school spelling bees, math quizzes and other challenges from other grades in our school or other schools in the neighborhood.

WOOLWORTHS

My first, real lesson about racism was taught to me by my Grandmother, Edith Cole when I was just 10 or 11. She was my mother's mother, a slight woman with sharp features, extremely fair-skinned, who could easily have been mistaken for a white woman, until you actually took the time to talk with her. Then, you'd understand what a fiercely proud Black woman she was; very protective of her people. Back then, everyone who was Black considered themselves "colored," and that's how my grandmother referred to Black people. My grandmother never hesitated confronting a white person if she felt she was being wronged because she was Black. My first lesson on racism was taught to me at, of all places, a Woolworth's lunch counter!

In February 1960, at an infamous Woolworth's in Greensboro, North Carolina, four young Black male students from North Carolina A&T sat at the counter waiting to be served lunch, knowing full well that Blacks were prohibited from being served. Segregation within the Woolworth chain forced Blacks to wait endlessly and then have to stand to eat their food. This protest by these students began to grow in the town of Greensboro, eventually forcing the storeowner to close his doors because of a bomb threat, even with police stationed outside and within the store. The North Carolina A&T student's actions sparked other sit-ins and economic boycotts around the state and ultimately across the entire south—desegregating many stores and public places along the way. But in 1966, even cities like New York weren't shielded from white people who thought that Blacks shouldn't be sitting or served at any counter at any Woolworths. A valuable lesson that I would learn the hard way.

My Grandmother took my younger brother Peter and me down to the Woolworth's at 86th Street on the Upper East Side. Peter was six or seven and I was ten. The neighborhood, known then as "Yorkville," was predominantly Irish-American, and its residents were notoriously biased against any people of color frequenting the stores or shops in the area. Just a few years later, I would become very familiar with this area because it was where I would attend a certain private school.

My Grandmother was picking up a birthday cake she had ordered for one of us kids. We entered the store and she sat Peter at the counter. She told me to mind my little brother while she went to check on the order. Soon afterwards, a white woman with a couple of her own children dragging behind her wanted to sit at the counter. She became agitated because my brother had taken a seat that did not allow her and her two children to sit together. With anger and venom in her voice, she ordered me to take my "little nigger brother off the stool," so that both her children could sit beside her.

In my neighborhood, Black folks called each other "nigger" as a matter of course, using the derogatory term in endearing, friendly banter between friends. We felt we deserved the right to acknowledge one another in that fashion. It wasn't a staple of my vocabulary, because my mother rarely used it. My father was much more liberal with the word. But this was the first time I was ever called a "nigger" by a white person and this was my first venture downtown in a public place where I was left alone to manage a situation that I was not prepared for whatsoever. My other excursions downtown were almost always supervised with one of my teachers from school or another family member. I was completely naïve when it came to any direct racial confrontations.

I became angry, but I was paralyzed as to what to do in this unfamiliar situation. My instincts told me, "don't turn this into a bigger confrontation." I slowly guided my brother Peter down off the stool so as not to create a scene in the store and upset our grandmother. Then, as my brother and I stood behind the stools we once occupied like two little forlorn souls, my grandmother returned to the scene with a look on her face that I'd only seen on a couple of occasions, but never anything like this. Her eyes were like two tiny slits behind her glasses, which made her absolutely menacing for a woman only 5' 2" tall. Out of nowhere, she let out a yell at this woman that still sends chills up my spine today, "How DAAAAARE you remove MY BOYS from their stools! WHO DO YOU THINK YOU ARE?! You think just because they're colored they can be pushed around, just like that?!"

The white woman had a stunned and incredulous look on her face, because she couldn't fathom why this tiny woman, who she probably perceived as "being white," screamed at the top of her lungs at her! She never realized that the "two little colored boys," were her blood and Grandma Cole was "a lioness protecting her cubs." All this puzzled and frightened white woman could do was to squirrel her two kids away as she scrambled out of that Woolworths, away from my grandmother's wrath. As I watched everyone in the store watch the commotion, Edith Cole turned her wrath upon me and scornfully reminded me of what I was tasked to do before she left to check on the cake. Her voice was barely a few decibels lower than her prior storewide performance, so that everyone watched as I hung my head in shame, knowing that I failed my responsibility. It was embarrassing, but a valuable lesson taught to me by my Grandmother. The civil rights struggle in America had come to another Woolworths' counter and I vowed that I would never—EVER—be taken advantage of like that again.

That incident, at the tender age of ten, at the Woolworths in New York helped me understand how I fit in the context of the civil rights movement across the country in the 1960's. My awareness of the struggles of African-Americans, or "colored folks," as my Grandma referred to us, was shaped by the struggles of my elder family members, who tried to deal with the subtle and not-so-subtle racism in New York City.

CHAPTER 4

1968 & 1969

M OST PEOPLE CONSIDER AMERICA'S WAR on terror since 9-11 to be a unique time in our history, a time when the threat of possible acts of terrorism hangs constantly in the air, creating a feeling of being constantly on high alert. But this moment and these feelings are not unique. There were times in our recent history that were actually much worse. Most people look back on the late 1960s as a period of radical cultural transition, but they don't realize (or don't recall) that it was also a moment in America when very bad things seemed to be happening all the time.

The late 1960s and early 1970s were considered the "Golden Age of Skyjacking." Between 1968 and 1972, more than 130 commercial airliners were hijacked in the U.S. That would work out to an average of almost 3 hijackings every month for four years. It would, except for the fact that 82 of those hijackings occurred in 1969 alone. 82 hijackings in one year. The acts of terrorism became so commonplace that the phrase "Take me to Cuba" became a comic punchline. Americans were scared to death to get on an airplane.

From Ray

In 1967, my younger brothers and I witnessed the riots in Harlem first-hand. As we peered through our windows onto Second Avenue, we saw store-fronts broken into, and gates and windows smashed, as angry groups of local residents indiscriminately ransacked shops all around the neighborhood. Then we heard the blaring of multiple police sirens and the fire-cracking sounds of shots being fired, as the cops hoped their presence might deter the civil unrest. In the end, 25 stores were looted in East Harlem and three people killed. Tensions between Whites and Blacks grew worse with each passing day.

In the summer of 1968, the whole country seemed to be coming apart at the seams. Earlier that year, Dr. Martin Luther King, Jr. was assassinated in Memphis while organizing a march for striking sanitation workers, and Robert Kennedy was murdered in Los Angeles while campaigning for the Democratic Presidential nomination. And three students were murdered on the campus of South Carolina State University.

In February of 1968, students from South Carolina State University, a historically Black college, conducted a series of protests against a segregated bowling alley in the nearby town of Orangeburg. On February 8, students lit a protest rally bonfire at the front of the SCSU campus. South Carolina Highway Patrol Officers quickly arrived on the scene and without warning or provocation began firing rifles, shotguns and revolvers into the crowd of around 200 protesters. Twenty-seven people were injured; most were shot in the back as they were running away, and three young Black men were killed. Samuel Hammond, Henry Smith were both SCSU students. Delano Middleton was just a student at the local Wilkinson High School. Middleton was shot while simply sitting on the steps of the freshman dormitory awaiting the end of his mother's janitorial work shift. Delano's older brother Duerward was in New York City, where he became the first Black faculty member of the athletic department at the prestigious Dalton School. Duerward "Dee" Middleton became a trusted friend and mentor to the young Black boys about to enter Dalton.

Nine SC Highway Patrol Officers were tried for the murders, but they were acquitted without much fuss or fanfare.

In the summer of '69 the SDS (Students for a Democratic Society), a political protest group, morphed into the Weather Underground, a domestic terrorist group that embraced violence and criminal acts as a legitimate form of political protest. Their favored tactic was the planting of bombs in public buildings, including the U.S. Capitol. Demonstrations were replaced by demolitions. A peaceful political organization transformed itself into a ruthlessly violent terrorist group in the blink of an eye.

We cannot say that all of the things going on in the world affected us directly or even indirectly, but there was more turmoil and uncertainty in the world around us that summer than at any other point in our lifetime. It is hard to imagine any aspect of the world around me that wasn't undergoing major change, but it was a transition into . . . what exactly?

So, what was going on in the world that summer? Some events were positive, lifting the spirits of everyone and promising that something better was waiting around the corner. This was the summer of Apollo 11 and man's first landing on the moon, fulfilling the promise made by President Kennedy just eight years earlier. The entire world watched Neil Armstrong take his first steps onto the moon's surface and utter those historic words. In that moment anything seemed possible. In that moment it seemed like all of us might fulfill our dreams. In that moment of optimism, you could believe that it was possible to wash away the stains of blood left by the assassinations of Robert Kennedy and Martin Luther King Jr. the year before.

The national mood was lifted further just a few weeks later by a music festival in upstate New York. Promoted as "An Aquarian Exposition: 3 Days of Peace & Music", it was held at Max Yasgur's 600-acre dairy farm near the hamlet of White Lake in the town of Bethel, New York. The festival came to be known as "Woodstock" even though the town of Woodstock was actually 43 miles away. 500,000 young people showed up for a weekend of some of the greatest music of a generation. And despite torrential rains, no one's spirit was dampened. There was no violence. It was a golden moment in time. It was lightning in a bottle.

From Mark

Ironically, literally the weekend prior to Woodstock I was in virtually the same geography for a weekend getaway in the New York Catskills with my mom and her best friend Jeanne Maillard. I was a favorite and frequent travel companion of my mom's and often accompanied her and my "Aunt Jeannie" on fun trips. This weekend we took a bus to the Concord Hotel, the largest of the resorts in the Catskills "Borscht Belt." If you have seen the movie "Dirty Dancing", you have a pretty good sense of the Concord Hotel and the experience.

Saturday night we got all dressed up for dinner in the Concord's grand ballroom, where comedian Jan Murray would be performing after dinner. It was a lesson in etiquette and sophistication. Not my first lesson, but an important reinforcement nonetheless. I think my mom was mindful that I would be entering Dalton in just a few weeks and this would be a good opportunity to test drive just how much couth I really had. Mom allowed me to order whatever I wanted from the very fancy menu and I ordered Steak Tartare, having absolutely no idea what it was. Of course my mother knew that, but decided to see how I would handle the situation. When my plate arrived, I was mortified. I was being served chopped raw steak with a raw egg yoke atop. Not only had I never eaten anything like that, I had never heard of anyone else eating anything like that. It stared back at me, daring me to eat it.

Recognizing my apprehension, my mother smiled at my dish and said, "I think they did an excellent job preparing your dish. I think you're going to love that." Aunt Jeannie winked at my mother and politely suppressed a laugh.

After only a moment's hesitation, I thanked the waiter and began to eat my Steak Tartare. And I finished it. I can't say that it is my favorite dish, or even one that I eat regularly, but I have ordered it a few more times over the years, always remembering that night. My mom was extremely proud of the way that I handled the moment, not causing a fuss or a problem and being open to trying something unfamiliar and exotic. My mother traveled all over the world in her job for Time Magazine. She often encountered situations—and meals—that were unfamiliar and exotic. And she knew that the ability to handle yourself gracefully and adventurously was the mark of a truly cosmopolitan person.

In addition to the Woodstock Music Festival that took place that summer in upstate New York, there was another very different music festival happening much closer to home. The Harlem Cultural Festival would later become known as "Black Woodstock" for evoking certain parallels to the rock fest. The Harlem Cultural Festival was a series of music concerts held in Mount Morris Park, north of 120th Street on Harlem's east side to celebrate African American music and culture and to promote Black pride and Black consciousness. It was an effort by the city to attempt to restore some semblance of positive community spirit after the devastating riots the year before. Every Sunday from June 29 to August 24, the concert series drew crowds of up to 100,000 across the generational spectrum. Performers included Sly and the Family Stone, Stevie Wonder, Nina Simone, Gladys Knight, BB King, the Fifth Dimension, the Staple Singers and comedians such as Moms Mabley and Pigmeat Markham. Nina Simone sang "Mississippi Goddamn" and then debuted a brand new song, "Young, gifted and Black" which wouldn't be recorded until three months later when she went into the studio in October and released the song the following February. Simone wrote "Young, Gifted and Black" as a tribute to her late friend, Lorraine Hansberry, author of the play "A Raisin in the Sun", but the song went on to serve as an anthem to the nascent Black Pride movement. The song captured the spirit of the festival and also the essence of the transition from an outwardly focused civil rights movement to an inwardly focused Black pride movement.

The New York Police Department refused to provide security for the concert series, in spite of the fact that New York Mayor John Lindsay was a featured speaker at the festival. The police were no fans of their liberal mayor and wanted as little to do with the event as possible. Consequently, private security for the festival was provided by the Black Panthers, who ensured that despite the blistering summer heat and the massive crowds, there was never an incident nor any trouble at the concerts. After the devastating riots of the previous summer, there was a palpable and unmistakable sense of a Phoenix rising from the scorched scars of Harlem streets. People were determined to stand back up and try again. And so, the decision to employ "our own" to look after "our own" became a metaphor of self-reliance, of taking back dignity.

The festival was the first of its kind for scale and for its significance to the Black community. Nothing like this had ever been attempted before, possibly because Black cultural pride had not been this vital and robust since the Harlem Renaissance four decades earlier. The Harlem Cultural Festival was both a catalyst and a reflection of a major re-awakening of Black pride, Black nationalism and Black culture in the summer of '69. And just like the Woodstock festival in upstate New York, even if you didn't go, you were touched and affected by the mere fact that it happened. Even if you didn't go, you recognized that you were now part of a different conversation. You could feel, almost literally, the ground shift beneath your feet and you looked around at the landscape to see how it had changed.

The summer of '69 moved so fast. There was never any time for reflection or perspective. There was never any time for the dust to settle so that anyone could get a good hard look at the landscape. The only thing you knew about the new landscape was that it wasn't finished changing.

And the biggest change in our lives was about to begin.

CHAPTER 5

ENTRY INTO DALTON

MARK ROBINSON

I REMEMBER THE DAY OF MY interview at Dalton. My mother brought me into Manhattan on what seemed like an endless combination of buses and subways. I remember thinking that I would never be able to figure out which trains and which stations were the right ones. Everyone moved so fast and with no thought for anyone else. I was convinced I would never be able to make the daily journey to school by myself. It was too complicated, too unfamiliar and yes, too scary.

When attending IS 147 and JHS 59, I rode the New York City bus from my home each day to school, using a standard New York City issued student bus pass. There was no bright yellow school bus that came right to the end of your driveway, that carried only schoolchildren, and went directly and only to the school parking lot. That typical suburban American experience did not apply to New York City school kids, not even in relatively suburban Queens. We took the city bus and rode alongside adult commuters on their way to and from work. That also meant that you almost never got a seat on the bus. The ride was almost always crowded, and it was simply unthinkable that a kid might enjoy a seat while an adult—any adult—was still standing. If you managed to get a seat, you gave it up to the first adult who needed one. The bus driver didn't know what stop was yours, and didn't care. That was your responsibility. Pay attention and pull the cord that rang the bell when your stop was approaching.

After getting over the fear and intimidation of being a "big boy" who rode the bus by himself to school, it became a relatively simple and stress-free experience. The stop where I got on the bus was just a block from my home and the stop where I got off, along with a dozen or so school friends, was just a block from the school. By the time I had been riding the bus for two months, it seemed like something I had done my whole life.

But getting from St. Albans, Queens, to the upper east side of Manhattan was an odyssey of an entirely different magnitude. I would need to take the bus each morning literally to the end of the line, to the very last stop at 169th Street at Hillside Avenue, where all of the other bus lines terminated in a chaos of onrushing commuters and where you had to be certain you were boarding the right bus. And when I got off the bus, I was still at the beginning of my journey. I would then board the subway, something I had never ever done alone before.

I look back now at my daunting commute to Manhattan as a thirteen year old and think about my own children. I cannot possibly imagine allowing Sean and Lily at age thirteen to travel to New York City and ride the subway alone. Just the idea of it fills me with anxiety. I don't consider myself an overly protective parent, but the mere idea of sending my kids to ride the city subway alone to school every day would be more than I imagine they could handle. And yet, I suppose, necessity makes the impossible possible. When you have to do it, you just figure out a way and you just do it. Sometimes not having a choice can be very empowering. I am sure that sending their thirteen year old child off to school in Manhattan, riding the subway alone, made my parents a pair of nervous wrecks. But they got over it because they had to. And so did I.

Of course, it was not as simple as just boarding the train and riding it to school. That would not have been enough of a challenge. This was way more complicated. At 169th Street, I took the E train to the Queens Plaza station (careful not to confuse it with the Queensboro Plaza station, which had different trains going to very different places) and transferred to the EE train which crossed the East River into Manhattan and arrived at the 59th Street Lexington Avenue station. At 59th Street, I got off the train and rode two escalators to switch to the Lexington Avenue train line and board the 4, 5, or 6 train to go to the 86th Street station. At this point it was just three short blocks to walk to 89th Street and The Dalton School. All in all, on a good day the trip took roughly 90 minutes each way to complete. Unfortunately, the New York City transit system didn't always have "good days", especially in the cold and snowy winter months, when you could count on adding an extra 30 minutes to the trip. For the first month or so I had my route written out on a piece of paper in my pocket and I referred to it regularly to keep from getting hopelessly lost. Eventually the daily commute became routine. You can get used to just about anything if you keep doing it often enough.

But just because you can get used to something, doesn't mean that it's okay. Getting used to it doesn't mean that it doesn't create an extra burden or create extra challenges. The typical minority student at Dalton lived much further away from the school than the typical white student. That meant a longer commute. My own commute was—on an average day—about 90 minutes each way; three hours a day. That's a lot. That meant less time for homework, less time for after-school activities. Less time to be with my friends. It also meant getting up earlier every morning and being more tired when you got to school. This last point is one that has received considerable scientific study in recent years and has been identified as a major contributor to teenage stress, depression and reduced academic performance. If you are a Black boy sitting in class looking the slightest bit drowsy, you have opened the door to an entire spectrum of biased perceptions and interpretations by teachers and school administrators. Is the curriculum material simply over his head? Is the boy depressed? Is he surly and inattentive? Is he acting out? Is he on drugs? Everyone starts making assumptions, and those assumptions can have long term—or even permanent—implications for your future as a student.

Gregory Thompson, a New York attorney who was also once a minority student at an elite New York private school, wrote this about the obstacles created by those long commutes.

"Two hours of commuting is rough on a child: it takes valuable time away from study and sleep, and it makes it vastly more difficult to maintain strong friendships with classmates outside of school. It is hard on parents in early years, who must take the child to and fro. This distance also puts parents far out of the social loop of information flow among parents: the kind of talk, gossip, and information sharing that helps give parents a more complete, inside view of what is really happening at the school, and what a child has to do to prosper."

I spoke with many former classmates while researching for this book. A few of the women I spoke with provided a unique perspective on the difficulties of commuting to school on the subway when you are a 13 or 14 year old girl traveling alone. Strange men, creepy men, are constantly exploiting the crowded spaces of New York subway cars to press up against you, rub up against you, brush their hand against you, leer at you and say horribly inappropriate things. It is bad enough enduring that experience when it happens. It can be truly demoralizing when you know you must board the same subway train every day, no matter what. That commute was one of the reasons that it was so much harder for some of the Black girls to continue attending Dalton.

KITTENS AND CATS

On this particular day I was coming with my mother for my admission interview at Dalton. It was not my first time visiting the school. My older brother Michael was currently a senior and had been attending Dalton for three years after spending his freshman year at Stuyvesant. I had been to see Michael perform in a school play, to compete in a fencing tournament (I always thought it was the height of sophistication that a high school had a fencing team) and to sing in the glee club. This, however, would be my first visit to Dalton 'for me', for my own needs and purposes.

The Dalton School is located at 108 East 89th Street, between Lexington and Park Avenues, nestled between luxury high-rise, pre-war apartment buildings with uniformed doormen on Manhattan's tony upper east side. The sidewalk is well-shaded, lined with mature Japanese Gingko Biloba trees and hybrid, thornless Honey Locust trees, where local residents would walk their apartment-sized, expensive purebred dogs and Caribbean nannies would push classic-styled Kensington baby prams made with black nylon taffeta. (It would be reasonable to assume that these nannies that you saw all the time were caring for the young children of working mothers and fathers, young urban professionals, that nannies were necessary because both parents worked. But the truth was that in the late 1960's most of these moms did not work outside the home. Frankly they did not work inside the home either. They simply had nannies to care for the children and housekeepers to care for the oversized apartments. That simply was the way it was.)

Dalton's location somehow managed to be both completely cosmopolitan and yet still somehow a world apart. Dalton's front façade was enclosed by a ten foot black wrought iron fence and gate that never gave the appearance of keeping anyone in or anyone out. Instead, the fence was merely a convenience for students to lean against, usually while smoking a cigarette, or for draping your deep blue canvas Dalton bookbag while you spent time with friends. At intervals that seemed to be literally whenever the school wished, East 89th Street would be completely closed to automobile traffic so that Dalton's younger students could play safely in the street.

The administrative offices were located on the second floor of Dalton's twelve story building. Although only one floor up, everyone took the lobby elevators to the second floor, where the doors opened to a long corridor illuminated by track lighting that focused on artwork displayed on the walls and on white pedestal cubes at irregular intervals. The ivory colored carpeting was deep enough to absorb almost all of the sound from the offices, creating a hushed tone of discreet busy-ness. The hushed atmosphere of the second floor was a very deliberate counterpoint to the manic clatter and pace of the rest of the school building, when someone called one of the offices on the second floor, the phones did not ring. They purred like kittens. Really. It was a little other-worldly.

The second door to the left was the Admission office and Mrs. Cameron was the Director of Admission. Agnes Theodora "Teddy" Cameron was a slender woman in her early forties who wore her hair short in a late 1960's modern professional style that revealed just a hint of grey. This was a woman who would never contemplate hair coloring. I don't actually know much about Mrs. Cameron's background, but she struck me as someone who could easily have been a neighbor of the Kennedy's on Hyannis Port, someone who enjoyed spending time outdoors, probably had athletic older brothers and was the product of a highbrow New England upbringing. She wore pearls and tweed and it all seemed completely natural and unpretentious on her.

Mrs. Cameron greeted my mother and me with genuine warmth and after a few moments of introductory conversation, she directed my mother to have a seat in the ante room while she invited me into her office for my interview. I know that there are a lot of elements to the admission process; applications, financial disclosure forms, admission exams. But I don't really remember any of that. All I remember is the interview with Mrs. Cameron.

While the corridor of the second floor was brightly lit in white and ivory, the inside of Mrs. Cameron's office was the opposite. The room was a cocoon of polished mahogany bookcases with books in nearly every space and nook. The room was lamplit and intimate. Her desk was covered in folders and papers but did not seem the least bit disorganized or disheveled. But it wasn't neat either. It was simply 'relaxed.'

She began our conversation by talking about my brother Michael, a senior at Dalton who had done very well at the school. I wasn't aware of it at the time, but my brother Michael had been a member of Dalton's very first class of male high school students. Dalton had been coeducational in the lower grades for a number of years, but had only very recently admitted boys into the high school. More importantly, Michael had been Dalton's very first African American male student. Although it was not discussed openly—and certainly not with us in any open way—it was a very, very big deal. Michael was a mile marker in Dalton's history.

Michael did very well at Dalton. He fit in comfortably in Dalton's academic and social ecosystems. That is not to say that Michael did not struggle at first, or that he did not face both resistance and rejection in the beginning. In some respects Michael's challenges were far greater than my own when it was my turn to attend Dalton. Being "the first" meant you were constantly surrounded by people—some well-intentioned, some not—who had absolutely no experience interacting with Negro boys. Many weren't sure that they wanted to. That goes for teachers, administrative staff and fellow students. Even Dalton's janitorial staff and elevator operators were white, mostly immigrants from Eastern Europe and from communities whose experience with Black people was either antagonistic or non-existent. And they surely did not know what to make of us. After all, to most Dalton students the janitorial staff were all but invisible, just like their domestic staff at home. And these workers understood their place in the social order. But they did not know how they were expected to treat Negros, especially Negro boys. There were no rules for this, spoken or unspoken.

But as the Marine Corp adage goes; Michael improvised, he adapted, and he overcame. And he did it better than most. Consequently, my entire Dalton experience, from the admission interview through all my years there, was spent either in my brother's shadow or measured by its contrast to his prior tenure. I don't blame or begrudge my brother. He wasn't the one constantly throwing this up in my face. He wasn't around. He was off at college. But all my teachers knew Michael. They loved him. The administrators knew Michael. And if that wasn't enough, even my classmates had a connection to Michael. At least half a dozen of my classmates had older siblings that had been in the same year as Michael and they were all old friends. Michael had been to their homes.

There were three words that I heard constantly through all my time at Dalton; "How's your brother?"

And those were the three words that began my conversation with Mrs. Cameron. She wanted to know if he and I had talked about my application to Dalton. She wanted to know if he had expressed an opinion to me. Her tone was neutral enough that I could not tell if she was trying to find out if Michael thought highly enough of Dalton to recommend it to his brother, or if Michael thought highly enough of his brother to recommend me to Dalton. In fact, Michael had wished me luck and then promptly dismissed the wish with a wave of his hand saying, "I'm sure you'll get in." But I didn't tell her that. Instead I told her that he merely asked me to share my impressions when I returned home from the interview.

I don't recall most of the questions that Mrs. Cameron asked me that day. I'm sure many were standard interview questions. Some were standard "Dalton" questions (these were questions that resulted from Dalton's rarified status as an elite and exclusive academic institution). And some were questions carefully chosen to evaluate the admission of a Negro boy to the Dalton School (carefully crafted psychological questions). The one question that has stayed in my memory, however, was the one question that seemed to make the biggest impression on Mrs. Cameron. She said, "Mark, if you could be an animal, any animal at all, which animal would you choose?"

"I think I would be a cat."

"And why is that?" She smiled at what was a fairly pedestrian answer to her question, probably already beginning to form an opinion about my aptitude and potential.

I had no preparation for this interview. I didn't know what questions might be asked. And I certainly had not given any prior thought to why I might want to be a cat. We had never owned a cat and I didn't particularly like cats. We owned dogs. I liked dogs. But the words just popped into my head, coming from no place in particular. "Well, for starters, I would not want to be any animal that people typically consider to be food. While they are alive, we don't really treat them like living creatures. We just treat them like a product for our consumption. That can be pretty awful. So that eliminates quite a lot of choices."

"Okay." Mrs. Cameron nodded her head.

"And I would not want to be any animal that people wore as clothing, whether feathers or fur or leather." I thought for a moment. "I'm not saying that I don't wear leather, or anything like that. I just wouldn't want to be the leather. So that eliminates a bunch more choices."

"It does."

"I wouldn't want to be some rare or exotic animal because many of them are at risk of extinction. The others are caught and put in zoos. That doesn't seem like a happy life. It isn't a life that I would choose for myself."

"I understand. So, you would want to be a pet."

"Well, yes and no," I said, still thinking through what was on my mind. "Birds and hamsters live in cages. Fish and turtles live in tanks and bowls. It's like a zoo, only smaller." I took a deep sigh. "Basically, there's only cats and dogs."

"So why not a dog?" Mrs. Cameron asked.

"I love dogs. I love my dog Max." I admitted. "But people impose a lot of expectations on dogs. Dogs are supposed to be obedient and loyal. Dogs are supposed to play with us whenever we want. Dogs are supposed to guard us and protect us. It just seems like we ask an awful lot, but we don't do that with cats. If we have a cat for a pet we don't ask the cat to be anything except be a cat and maybe to be our companion. But we accept the cat just the way it is. That's what I would want; to be accepted just the way I am, not how someone else wants me to be."

"Well," Mrs. Cameron said. "That's a pretty terrific answer. Thank you. I guess someone has asked you this question before." She smiled.

"No." I shook my head. "Never."

At the risk of gross over-simplification, that's how I got into Dalton.

I am pretty sure, however, that there is no standard or uniform path to the admission process at Dalton. And that is probably both a good thing and a bad thing. I think it is a good thing because uniformity rarely results in the equality and fairness that it was intended to achieve. Standardized systems are often based upon assumptions that ultimately prove to be erroneous. Standardized systems presume that minority students don't perform as well on standardized tests. The system is inherently self-rationalizing and self-justifying, so it presumes that the fault lies with the students rather than with the test methodology.

A flexible process allows the school to recognize and evaluate each student as an individual, and hopefully enables the school to preserve and nurture some aspects of that student's individuality once they matriculate. Without that flexible, idiosyncratic process, minority students, different students, students such as myself, probably never would have been admitted to Dalton.

But there is also a bad side to flexibility in the admission process, especially in the context of an elite private school such as Dalton. Every year, Dalton receives thousands of applicants for admission. Most of these applicants come from households and families very much like the people already attending the school; white and wealthy. And what happens when wealthy white parents see an element of flexibility in the admission process, they see an opportunity to bend the rules—and the entire experience—in their favor. Many wealthy parents (in fairness, not all) approach virtually every situation with the expectation that things should "go their way," that there is absolutely no reason that they should not get whatever it is that they want. And this is never more true than when wealthy parents are dealing with situations and challenges that impact the well-being and the future fortunes of their children.

And so it is fair to ask the question, "How many students were admitted to Dalton because their parents were able to bend a flexible admission process in their favor, because their parents possessed wealth, privilege, influence and resources that were far beyond the reach—or even the imagination—of my parents, or the parents of other minority students? I cannot answer that question. Perhaps not that many. But I seriously doubt that the number was zero. However, many there were, no one ever questioned whether they belonged at Dalton. No one ever doubted they possessed the intellectual ability to keep pace with their classmates. The school did not reflexively assign them to remedial classes before even bothering to evaluate their academic skills and capabilities. No one ever suggested that their mere presence at the school might lower the reputation and prestige of Dalton.

So why did they for us?

I used to think that most of my white classmates at Dalton were so much smarter than me. I used to think that they had a much easier time in the classroom than me. That was the common belief. That was the atmosphere at Dalton. That was the shared mythology. But years later, when I went back for an alumni reunion, many of my classmates opened up and told stories of their academic struggles at Dalton. I was completely taken aback by this huge reveal, that many of my classmates felt overwhelmed by Dalton's academic rigor, barely maintaining acceptable grades, and that several of them had been threatened—more than once—that they might have to leave Dalton if their grades did not improve. This was a revelation.

This would have been a perfect opportunity for schadenfreude, but that wasn't what I felt. Part of me did feel angry. Part of me did feel that this was a secret they shared with each other but kept from me and from the other minority students. We spent all that time worrying that we weren't good enough. We spent all those years allowing personal insecurities to convince us that perhaps we didn't belong. Feeling less than. Feeling as though at any moment someone would tap us on the shoulder and ask us to leave. But the truth was that we were all the same. We really were. And once I got past my initial anger, I realized that their secret was not a collective secret. It was an aggregation of individual secrets, each one of them simply hiding their own private insecurity and embarrassment, each one desperately protecting their own emotional vulnerability. And, perhaps most important, their candid admissions now were a gesture of intimacy and trust.

I could not be angry at that.

My brother Michael, who attended and graduated from Dalton before I had arrived, had a somewhat different story of his path to Dalton. Not at all the same as mine. Even so, his path was predicated on our parents' unwavering commitment to giving their children the best possible opportunities. I am sure that all parents want their children to have a better life than their own, to go further, achieve greater. Our parents certainly rose to that challenge and did what they could to kick away every obstacle in our path. It's hard

Mark Robinson & Raymond Smaltz, III

to imagine that anyone could have done more than our parents did to make our possibilities limitless. As a parent with children of my own, I continue to marvel at what my parents accomplished. It was 1963 and my parents had just moved from their crowded little house in Corona Queens and bought the house and property in St. Albans where the legendary Lena Horne had lived. My two older brothers had graduated from elementary school in our old neighborhood and were ready to start junior high in their new neighborhood.

My two older brothers, David and Michael, attended a different junior high school than I did. They both attended Linden Junior High (JHS 197) in the Hollis section of Queens because there was no junior high in St. Albans. Linden was brand new back then, built in 1960. It was barely three years old when my brothers were there. Michael remembered that he was there when he heard the news of President Kennedy's assassination. That was how he established the timeline in his memory. The edifice of Linden Junior High was classic late 1950's pre-fab institutional architecture; built for the lowest construction bid with no aesthetic considerations and no expectation that the building would last more than 20 years. And so, even though the building was new, it probably began to show wear and tear and feel worn almost immediately.

In the early 1960's Linden Junior High had a 60/40 ratio of Black students to white students, although white flight had already begun, and the ratio would slide each year thereafter. Michael recalls that he and David would ride the city bus to school every day with "the twins", Ronald and Roland Johnson, who were identical twins that lived a block away from us. Ronald and Roland had older sisters, Marlene and Darlene, who were also identical twins and attended Linden. According to Michael, "The sisters were badass and, from my perspective, well-respected in the school by other students. Whether it was true or not, I always assumed we flew under their protection at 192." Apparently, some of the other kids at Linden were a lot tougher than my two brothers, but with the protection of the Johnson sisters—real or perceived—there was never a problem. Well, except for that one time when one of David's friends was bullying Michael and knocked his schoolbooks to the ground, somehow also tearing his shirt. Michael punched the kid and that was quickly the end of it.

I recently came upon a New York Times article from June of 1970 with the headline, "Slaying of a Classmate Brings Violence Home to Queens

School". This was, of course, long after David and Michael had left Linden, but the article talked about the school's history of poor performance and student discipline problems. By 1969, almost half of the students who began 7th grade in September were no longer there by the end of the school year in June. Most were not reading at grade level. The school was failing and so were many of its students.

Linden Junior High was where Michael and our older brother David began to diverge academically. Michael was placed in an advanced students program (SPE, which stood for "Special Progress Enrichment"), with more challenging and stimulating classroom work. David was in a regular class. This also had the effect of surrounding them with two entirely different cohorts of classmates. The SPE students were isolated from the rest of the student body for most of the day. And this tended to reinforce the academic differences.

Despite working a full time job at Time magazine in Manhattan, our mom spent a great deal of time coming to school for frequent parent-teacher meetings that she requested, both for Michael and for David, trying to ensure that the school did its best for both of her sons. I suspect that some of the teachers and school officials did not understand why she pushed so hard. A year older than Michael, David had graduated from Linden and moved on to Francis Lewis High School in the predominantly white Fresh Meadows section of Queens. Francis Lewis was a good school with good teachers, but that also became its overwhelming problem. Francis Lewis— so much in demand—was and still is the most over-crowded school in New York City. Its enrollment of 4,100 students exceeds it proper capacity of 2,300 by 176%. Even a good school and a good student gets crushed under this pressure.

Navigating bureaucracy is rarely in a parent's skill set. Our parents were no exception. Despite the very best intentions, our parents didn't always know the right choice or how to make a complicated and uncooperative system give them what they needed. Unfortunately, my oldest brother David, being the first of three sons, was usually where the parental learning curve was steepest and at his expense. If there were ever any lost opportunities, they were lost for David. At the time, Francis Lewis seemed liked a good choice. At that moment, it may have been the only choice. In hindsight, however, David's opportunities might have been greater somewhere other than Francis Lewis.

Mom was determined to find something better for Michael, so she went to the Linden Junior High guidance counselor to arrange for Michael to take the test for admission to Stuyvesant High School in Manhattan. Stuyvesant is a tuition-free New York City public school that offers significantly accelerated academics for the city's most gifted college-bound students. Admission to Stuyvesant involves passing the Specialized High Schools Admissions Test. Each November, about 30,000 eighth and ninth-grade students take the three-hour test to get into Stuyvesant. Approximately 900 to 950 applicants are accepted to Stuyvesant each year.

The Linden guidance counselor strongly discouraged our mother from registering Michael for the admissions exam. This was not because he doubted Michael's ability to perform well on the test. The counselor considered Michael to be one of their prized students. But the counselor had a different vision for Michael. He asked, "Why give up the chance for Michael to be a very big fish in a small pond? At Stuyvesant Michael will be just another fish in a very big pond."

Our mother was firm and resolute. "My son's future is not your decision to make. He will take that exam." Mom wanted her kids to dream big. Michael recalls that when he graduated from Linden, Mom wrote in his JHS memory book a quotation from a poem by Robert Browning about Italian Renaissance painter Andrea del Sarto: "Ah, but a man's reach should exceed his grasp/ Or what's a heaven for?"

Michael took the exam, and of course he passed and was admitted to Stuyvesant the following year. Stuyvesant was indeed a very big pond, with a freshman class of roughly 750 students. The original Stuyvesant school building on First Avenue and 15th Street in Manhattan was built in 1905 and was 60 years old by the time Michael attended. He remembers the deep depressions in the internal stone stairs from over half a century of student footsteps. The building was so massive that when Stuyvesant moved to new facilities in 1992 the original building became the home of four separate high schools.

Stuyvesant was academically and intellectually rigorous and Michael enjoyed the quick pace of learning. Michael saw himself living up to new potentials, and a path forward became both more vivid and more ambitious. But Michael didn't love Stuyvesant. Not the way that he would soon come to love Dalton. The bigness of Stuyvesant was definitely daunting. Stuyvesant also placed greater weight academically on math and science disciplines, while Michael's passion was for the humanities. Stuyvesant was an acceptable but imperfect home.

And so, when Dalton cast its recruiting net late in the spring of Michael's freshman year at Stuyvesant, Michael responded to its siren's call. Dalton planned to begin accepting boys into the high school for the very first time in its history, and it was now scouting the city for New York's best and brightest boys. Most of that scouting was easy. There were sufficient boys in Dalton's middle school grades who—historically—would have been required to leave the school after eighth grade. Now those boys could stay, and their wealthy parents would be very happy. Problem solved.

Well, almost.

This was the mid-1960s. Our country was changing rapidly. New York City was certainly at the forefront of a lot of that change both politically and culturally. Dalton's new headmaster, Donald Barr understood how important it was that Dalton not only preserve and protect its legacy as a beacon and bastion of progressive education, but that it move quickly and boldly to stay a step ahead of the elite private school competition. Barr wanted Dalton to be the talk of the town. And part of that talk would be the admission of Black boys into Dalton's high school.

Dalton recruited Michael as though he were a star athlete, which of course he was not. But he was a star. In 1965, only 1% of Stuyvesant's students were Black. Michael was part of the 1%. And as an added bonus, Michael came from a family that knew Dalton, a family that was part of Dalton's history. The likelihood of successful assimilation into the Dalton community was very high. Michael didn't even have to take the required entrance exam. Dalton apparently wanted him that badly. His future, his Dalton future was clearly on the horizon.

In Michael's defense, he was not 100% allergic to sports. He recalls, "I was certainly not the greatest athlete in the world. I couldn't catch a baseball, and I was miserable at basketball, and knew nothing about soccer, three big sports teams at Dalton. But I was coordinated and pretty adept at some sports—like skiing, and later fencing. I was on the Freshman fencing team at Yale. But anything with a ball kind of threw me." Growing up we used to play punchball in the street near our house. Punchball is a classic New York neighborhood streetball game. Everyone from Sandy Koufax to Colin Powell fondly remembers playing the game as a boy. It's baseball, but without a pitcher, a catcher or a bat. The batter tosses the ball into the air and then punches it like a volleyball. The ball is a tennis ball-sized pink-colored rubber ball, usually a Spaldeen or a Pensie-Pinkie. We played in the street and bases could be anything from a hydrant to a parked car. During one game, Michael was running backward, attempting to keep his eye on the ball. Unfortunately, Michael turned around as the ball sailed over his head, just in time for his face to encounter the front end of a parked car. Michael didn't get the ball but ended up chipping a tooth. Mom was not at all happy.

"WHICH ONE IS THE COLORED BABY?"

My brother Michael attended Dalton before I did, but it was actually my oldest brother David who was a Dalton fixture long before either of us. My brother David was Dalton's first Black baby. But before I can explain that, I have to talk about Dalton's first female Black student, my Aunt Milly. Actually, she was Dalton's first Black student of either gender, at least in the high school.

In the post-war late 1940's, America was getting back on its feet and struggling to rebound economically. Expensive, elite private schools still had their reliable enrollment, but alumni and parent donations and school endowments were seriously anemic. Dalton's financial problems had begun well before the war and simply continued to weaken and cripple the school as time went on. Dalton founder Helen Parkhurst was a notoriously poor financial steward for the school, having no reliable sense of budget management. She also tended to make decisions unilaterally, without regard for the checks and balances of her staff or the board of trustees. In the late 1930s Parkhurst launched the "New Milford Experiment" with the intention that faculty and students would spend a month together on the rural property she somehow acquired, communing with nature. The farmhouse, dormitory and land also happened to be located near her own country home in New Milford, Connecticut. The experiment was a very expensive bust.

In 1942, Dalton declared bankruptcy with a debt of $91,764.65. Under the leadership of board of trustees president Richardson Wood (editor of Fortune Magazine), the school conducted a thorough investigation of its finances and subsequently asked for Parkhurst's resignation. In her place Dalton's board of trustees approached Charlotte Durham to become the school's new headmistress. Durham had been a teacher at the school and rose to become Parkhurst's right hand in running the school. The board of trustees told Ms. Durham that if she declined their offer to take over as headmistress, they would simply close the school for good. She accepted.

Even with its new headmistress, Dalton had reached a financial low point. Dalton's future—and therefore also its legacy—were in jeopardy. Richardson Wood and the trustees turned to the U.S. Department of Education for grant funds and desperately needed financial relief. As the story goes, the government said "Sure. On one condition." Dalton would need to shed its lily-white exclusivity and begin admitting Negro students. A few years earlier, in 1944, the school had begun "an experiment" and admitted 10 Black students to the Lower School, enrolled among the three, four and five-year-olds. The strategy was to integrate at the youngest—and therefore least controversial age—and gauge the reaction of the school's existing white parents. Dalton remained ready to pull the plug on the experiment at any time if the PTA response had been negative. According to Susan Semel's book on the history of Dalton;

> In all, only four families directly affected by integration left Dalton that year; two explicitly stated that it was "because of the Negroes."

And yet, in spite of the absence of any significant negative response to the integration experiment, Dalton waited almost five years—and only under pressure from the federal government—before integrating the high school, where it really mattered. Finally, after exhaustive debate, deliberation and hand-wringing, in the fall of 1949 Dalton admitted two Negro girls into the Class of 1953. My aunt Millicent "Milly" Thomas (and another girl named Regina Mason) became Dalton's first African American students in 1949. Two decades before my brother Michael, Aunt Milly had been a mile marker in Dalton's history. Quite literally, she changed the complexion of Dalton. My family, through fate, good fortune and random circumstance were integrally intertwined with the past, present and future of Dalton.

In the spring of 1949, my Aunt Milly was attending JHS 81, Julia Ward Howe Junior High School at 120th Street between 7th and 8th Avenues (renamed Adam Clayton Powell Blvd and Frederick Douglas Blvd in the 1970s), just a few blocks from her apartment at 60 St. Nicholas Avenue.

Julia Ward Howe was the poet, author and abolitionist best known for writing the Battle Hymn of the Republic. This was the same school that my mom, Milly's older sister, attended just a few years earlier. And Miss Lawson was still the school principal. This time, however, circumstances were different. This time proper protocols were followed. One day a bunch of white-gloved ladies from Dalton came to Milly's school and met with the guidance counselor. They were looking for the school's best and brightest and the guidance counselor identified Milly as a student who should take the test for admission to Dalton.

"I was asked to take the test along with a few other students," Milly recalls. "I didn't really know what it was for." After Milly took the test, she was brought to Dalton for an interview. "My mother and I were invited to come to Dalton, which wasn't that easy for us to get to. And I met the headmistress, Ms. Durham and sat for an interview with her. It was really quite pleasant."

"They told my mother that they wanted me to attend Dalton." Milly recalls. "They told my mother that Dalton was a very fine school where I could receive the best education, which of course was very important to my parents. But my mother said that we didn't have any money to pay for private school. They told her 'Don't worry about anything. We are offering Millicent a full scholarship. All her expenses will be paid.' So, of course, my mother said yes." In the fall of 1949, Milly became a freshman at Dalton.

Back then, in addition to the traditional academic curriculum, Dalton had a program that taught the girls of the high school how to be good mothers. A passage written by Helen Parkhurst in the book, <u>Dalton Remembrances</u> explains the program as follows:

> *In 1926 I came to the decision that if there was ever an oppor-*
> *tunity under right conditions, The Dalton Schools should have*
> *an infants' nursery as an integral part of the Secondary school.*
> *Years of experience trying to help young mothers understand*
> *their babies had led me to believe that many difficulties could be*
> *obviated if a training in motherhood could be given to young girls*
> *between the ages of fourteen and eighteen.*

But in the spring of 1951, when Milly was a sophomore, there was an apparent shortage of babies for the Dalton nursery. Lots of eager high school girls, but not enough babies. Milly told Miss Armant, the school nurse who ran the program, that her older sister Rita (my mother) just had a baby in December and she would ask her sister if she could bring the baby to school for a few hours each day. I am not sure if Miss Armant was delighted by the offer, or if she simply did not know how to say no politely. But in any case, the nurse told Milly that if her sister was willing to let the school borrow her baby, they would take very special care.

What followed was buzz throughout the school that there was going to be a colored baby in the nursery soon. Sure, most people at Dalton—students and teachers—had met colored people before. That was no big deal. But hardly anyone had ever seen a colored baby up close before. This was a source of almost endless anticipation through the halls of Dalton, until finally the appointed day arrived, and Milly's sister Rita brought in the colored baby, my oldest brother David.

Black people, of course, come in every possible shade of skin color. This is true even within the same family. It is certainly true in my family. But if you are white and it's 1951 and you haven't really met a lot of Black people, you probably don't know this. So, when students and teachers began to "just happen past" the school nursery in what soon turned into a steady parade, just about everyone whispered with a puzzled expression, "Which one is the colored baby?"

My brother David, like me, isn't merely light-skinned. He's damn near white. And to confuse matters more, David had twinkling green eyes. None of the Dalton students or teachers could pick out the new Black baby in their midst. That became the source of endless confusion and curiosity and conversation.

And that's how my brother David became Dalton's first Black baby. In fact, he was something of a celebrity at the school. Milly even carried David through the arch on Arch Day, a beloved Dalton tradition celebrating the end of the school year and the progression to the next grade.

One of the things that amazed me the most from Aunt Milly's recollections of Dalton was the fact that many of the teachers that she had while she was there were still teaching at Dalton a whole generation later. Milly's house teacher was Madame Ernst and she studied Latin with Lauralee Tuttle and art with Aaron Kurzen. Milly sang in the school chorus under the direction of Harold Aks. This was not the beginning of their teaching career when Milly studied under them, nor was it the end of their careers when Michael and I were their students. These men and women and others like them spent their entire adult lives teaching at Dalton. Their loyalty and bond with the school was the stuff of classic movie storytelling. I asked Milly if any of the teachers at Dalton ever made her feel unwelcome or treated her differently. She reassured me that this was never the case. Her memories of Dalton were all positive, happy memories.

Milly remembers that at Christmas time the Dalton chorus would go to various places around the city to sing carols and she somehow convinced Mr. Aks to bring the chorus to her parents' apartment building at 60 St. Nicholas Avenue (a fortuitous address) to perform Christmas carols. It was an adventure for the other students and quite a treat for the residents of the building.

Milly recalled another experience from her years at Dalton that mirrored recollections of my own and of several of my Black classmates. It seems to be an experience that most of the Black students at Dalton, at least from my time and before, can share. Like any typical teenage girl, Milly went to a sleepover at her classmate Jane Dubin's home. Jane's father was a State Supreme Court judge. When Milly arrived at their home, a maid (an older African American woman) answered the door and instructed Milly that she would have to go around to the service entrance. (While retelling the story, Milly looked over at me with a wry smile and said, "My own people.") The problem was that Milly had no idea what to do. She didn't know what a service entrance was. She had never been anywhere that had a service entrance. It took a fair bit of explaining and negotiating before Milly eventually made it inside her classmate's home. Remember, this was not the south. This was not Mississippi or Alabama, or even Virginia. This was New York City. This was supposed to be the most liberal and progressive city in America. New Yorkers have always looked down their noses at places that have separate Jim Crow entrances for Negroes. And yet here it was, not an extraordinary exception, but a common occurrence on the upper east side of Manhattan. If you were a little Negro girl attending Dalton, you soon got used to this.

CHAPTER 5

ENTRY INTO DALTON

RAYMOND SMALTZ

HIGH SOCIETY COMES TO HARLEM

"WHAT'S A ROLLS ROYCE SILVER Shadow doing parked outside 96?" Actually, I had no idea what model Rolls Royce this was at 10 or 11 years old, but television hipped me to the unmistakable logo on the front of the grill and that told me everything I needed to know about the person inside the vehicle—THEY WERE LOADED!

During my 5th and 6th grade terms at P.S. 96, several wealthy women from New York's upper-crust society volunteered their time and made the trek uptown to East Harlem, with the expressed purpose of introducing the brighter school kids to accelerated reading and math lessons. For these wealthy women, it was their way of giving back to those less fortunate, as well as identifying several gifted or advanced children who might have what it takes to succeed in the specialized schools in the city, possibly even gain entrance to exclusive private schools throughout the metropolitan area.

During the 50's and 60's, many well-intentioned people from all over the country, all walks of life, white and Black, descended upon cities, towns and hamlets in the deep south to volunteer, to assist with voter registration drives, and to march alongside civil rights activists and clergy. In some cases, these volunteers sacrificed their lives—all in the name of equal rights. Up in the northeast, a different kind of experiment was taking place. Educators at my public school as well as others, began identifying gifted kids from "ghetto neighborhoods" so that these Black and Brown children might diversify some of the predominantly white private schools around the city. Two wealthy white women in particular, Eleanor Stock and Mimi Levitt, became "spirit guides" for my mother and me; guides who individually challenged my mind by giving me all the attention I ever wanted. These women gave me the opportunity to grow intellectually while assisting my mother and pointing her in the right direction to my further education.

Mrs. Stock and Mrs. Levitt would come to the school and take my classmate, Maria Velez and me out of regular class and walk us down the hall to an empty room reserved for our sessions where we could read and discuss books not on any public school curriculum; "Great Expectations," "Ivanhoe," and "The Great Gatsby" were just a few titles. We were being infused with a wealth of knowledge that we weren't going to receive by sitting in class with 25 other kids. Throughout this process, Maria and I became friends and rivals—always casting glances at each other to see who figured out what before the other. Sometimes we would compare notes afterwards, but most times we attempted to outdo each other. Sometimes other classmates were brought into the group, but Maria and I were the focus of Mrs. Stock and Mrs. Levitt.

My mother developed a friendship with both women that endured long after my graduation from grammar and private school. For me, one of the true treats of this relationship was being chauffeured around East Harlem by Mrs. Levitt's driver in her Rolls Royce Silver Shadow. Whenever there were parent-teacher nights, these women would be a part of the review process along with my regular teachers.

Mrs. Levitt persuaded my mother to have me tested at the Northside Testing Center on Central Park North. I scored high enough on the Center's test to merit attention from the better schools of New York City. The results also gave my Mother the extra incentive to apply to a number of private schools, including Collegiate, Buckley, Trinity, Riverdale, Ethical Culture and The Dalton School. With financial help from her grandparents, my mother managed to put together enough money to complete all of these applications, moving us one step closer to her goal: putting me into one of the best schools in the city.

As graduation from 6th grade at P.S. 96 approached, it was assumed that one or the other of us would receive the Joseph C. Lanzetta Award for Best Student at the end of the 1968 school term; Maria Velez or me. All of the teachers were being as coy as they could. No one wanted to let the cat out of the bag. But I believed I would beat out Maria. I may have had a little school-boy crush on her, but my ego pushed those feelings aside!

Finally, assembly day came—my last and final day at P.S. 96. When my name was announced in front of the entire school as the recipient of the Joseph C. Lanzetta Award, I began to choke up. I realized that this was going to be the last time I was going to see my friends and my teachers. Ms. Petrocelli, who always pretended to be tough and unmoved by most things, sat dabbing at her eyes with a handkerchief as I walked down the aisle. I began to tear up with the realization that the walls of this school that had once protected me, nurtured me, and comforted me, were now going to be a memory; replaced by a completely different and foreign environment and an entirely new set of challenges and experiences.

I had visited Dalton before, while I was still in 6th grade. The experience was mind-blowing for a twelve-year old. Dalton is a magnificent structure that appeared to soar up into the sky. The school sits regally in the middle of 89th Street between Lexington and Park Avenues., It has a black wrought-iron gate protecting the front of the school like a moat protects a castle, letting all who approach know that you must have business here or turn away. To me, this place seemed a world away from the nearby Woolworth's store, the site of my worst childhood experience. But, in reality, that Woolworth's was not far at all.

A counselor showed my mother and me around the school. There were flashes of blue everywhere—blue blazers on the boys, blue pleated skirts on the girls, and blue book bags with a yellow "D" emblazoned on the front. Back then, the school still maintained a dress code for students. I was turned off by the dress code at first because I rarely had to wear any jacket to school unless it was a special occasion. Even then, it would require some financial magic on my Mother's part to purchase a new suit or jacket. But, near the end of the tour, the counselor mentioned that the dress code was ending the following fall and a huge smile came across my face. I remember my mother being disappointed in the dress code lapsing, but she could tell by my enthusiasm that I liked what I saw.

Dalton was magical and intimidating at the same time. The counselor showing us around the school pointed out the science classrooms with their laboratory sinks and burners; the library on the 9th floor where the huge shelves of books were wonderfully flooded with beams of light through windows from both sides of the huge room, and the frenetic lunchroom with students milling around, jumping in front to grab their meal. I knew after walking through the school, seeing the kids of wealth rush around in completely different directions (no single lines anymore with the shortest in the front and the tallest in the back), I knew this was going to be the place for me.

"YOU'RE NOT IN THE PROJECTS ANYMORE, SON"

Walking through the doors of The Dalton School on my first day of middle school was one of the most nerve-wracking experiences of my entire life! How would this poor Black kid from East Harlem be accepted in this predominantly white private school? My Mother had no words of wisdom for my first day other than to make sure that I put my best foot forward. But that didn't inspire confidence as I took that bumpy bus ride downtown or as I watched kids arriving in taxis or being dropped off by private cars or by their nannies. Talk about "not being in Kansas anymore"! East Harlem was a loooong way behind me, and I was now officially, on my own.

I remember entering through the giant front doors and just standing for a moment. Kids and adults scurried around me in the lobby, headed to parts unknown. Some screamed and screeched at each other because they hadn't seen each other since the spring. They wanted to catch up on how their classmates were and how they spent their summers, or checked out their new school bags along with their wardrobe, straight from some fancy designer. I can't recall how I was dressed on my first day, but I do remember being very self-conscious. I was a young Black man, standing almost six feet tall, with a short afro, and I carried a bag for books that didn't quite fit in with those of my classmates. Later, I would eventually purchase one of the famous blue Dalton bags with the yellow circle and an old English style "D" in the middle, even though it sure as hell didn't hold half of the books I would need for my classes. I was then introduced to the concept of a "house" for the first time, where the students checked in with their house advisors, who made sure everyone that was assigned was present and accounted for and after a brief gathering, we were off to our individual classes. This was the first time I wasn't in one room for an entire school day—what a concept!

For the most part, the Dalton community helped me in my introduction to the school. I think that part of their interest, or curiosity, was due to my being so new and so completely different. I suspect that they were also sizing me up in comparison to the few other Black and Hispanic students who were there. Even though there were a few of us in my grade, I almost always ended up the lone person of color in a class.

Some of the other Black students, like Jay Strong and Kenwood Dennard (otherwise known as "Woody"), were already entrenched in the community. Only two Black females were in my grade: K.K. West and Carol Chaderton. They seemed inseparable.

My last name seemed to be a real point of interest for many of the students who understood Yiddish. S-M-A-L-T-Z, had everyone—student, teacher and parent alike, describing the origin of my moniker and what it meant. If I heard one more comment about how it meant "chicken fat" or if someone called me "Schmaltzy" one more time, I wasn't going to be able to account for my actions.

There were, however, several students who went out of their way to befriend me. Steve Postell, whose family lived right down the block on 89th Street and Lexington Avenue, was simply a cool dude who loved playing the guitar and listening to the Beatles. Another early comrade was Jeff Gates, who was a pretty good athlete with a mischievous streak. He and I shared several classes together. But the person who really went out of his way to make me welcome was Geoffrey Stern. Geoffrey had red hair and a face full of freckles. He had a wiry build similar to that of my old Puerto Rican buddy from the projects, Eddie Colon; and he wore a set of braces that caused him to talk with a lisp that made him hard to understand when he got excited. After meeting his two older brothers, Michael and Ronald, at school, Geoff invited me to his home to meet the rest of his family. I remember that Michael and Ronald would acknowledge me every once in a while if I saw them in the halls; but back then, high school students didn't mingle much with us so-called "middle school meatheads."

Socially and culturally, Dalton was like nothing I'd ever experienced before. The wealth of my schoolmates was staggering, and their rebelliousness was constant. Dalton students constantly challenged authority within the school and in their own homes. And they appeared to get away with almost anything. I knew, however, that their freedom of expression wasn't my reality. I came from a strict background and my mother would not have tolerated a challenge to her authority at home. So I watched my classmates, I observed their behavior and I laughed. Other times, I just shook my head.

Eventually, I found a way to become a part of the social scene at Dalton. The middle school kids at Dalton would get together for school sanctioned parties on a Friday or Saturday night. At these parties, there would be soft drinks and food and music. My musical tastes proved to be very different from my classmates. I wasn't listening to much Hendrix, Rolling Stones or Beatles as a kid growing up. Instead of tuning into the top-40 music stations WABC-AM, or WMCA-AM in New York with white jocks like Cousin Brucie, Dan Ingram, or Harry Harrison, I was listening to the "Super 16", otherwise known as WWRL, located at 1600 on the AM dial. WWRL featured the best Black DJ's of that era, like Eddie O'Jay, Gary Byrd, Jerry Bledsoe, and of course, the ultra smooth baritone of Frankie "The Love Man" Crocker. These were the cats that had me begging my parents or grandparents for some spare change to buy the latest single by Aretha Franklin, Otis Redding, Sam and Dave, Motown and my all-time favorite performer—the amazing "Mr. Please, Please" himself—the hardest workin' man in show bizness… Jaaaaaaaaaaaaaaames Brooooooooooown!

Watching my new white classmates dance at these social functions was another example of cultures clashing. At first…it really was painful watching them try to find the rhythm to their own music, much less a Motown, or Stax tune. And it was brutal on my feet when I tried to dance to a "slow jam" with one of the young ladies from the middle school. But they were my new classmates and I wanted to fit in and make it work, especially since I LOVED to dance. I wasn't a trained dancer, but as the artist "Jazzie" from the group Soul II Soul once said, "…a happy face, a thumping bass, for a loving race." That was me when one of my favorite songs was played. Anything with James Brown or Sly and The Family Stone caused me to lay down my best imitation of James Brown, which I used to practice at home, even performing a split or two at the appropriate time for the right tune. It took me quite a while, but as the parties in school and outside increased, I began to enjoy the sounds of Steppenwolf's "Magic Carpet Ride" or "American Woman," hits by Cream, featuring Eric Clapton, like "Sunshine of Your

Love" and "White Room," "All Along The Watchtower," by the late, great Jimi Hendrix, and of course, songs by The Beatles. As long as they sprinkled in a little bit of Otis, Sly, J-B and Motown…I was straight. I even remember accepting the challenge of dancing to the entire seventeen-minute, vinyl side two of the Iron Butterfly rock classic, "In-A-Gadda-Da-Vida," with Gwen Feder. They really should have handed out towels from the gymnasium for those marathon tunes!

I struggled as a student my first year at Dalton. My grades that year were far from outstanding. I managed, with the help of wonderful teachers like Mrs. Shmurak, who was very patient with me in her biology class and always gave me the extra time I needed, to stay afloat my first semester. I even dabbled in a little bit of art with Mr. Kurzon, who thought I had some ability. With my focus on schoolwork, however, my musical and artistic interests were largely abandoned after my first term at Dalton. They wouldn't really revive until I entered high school.

My history teacher, Mr. Ahearn, had a full beard that he would stroke throughout the hour and if you didn't concentrate hard enough during the lesson, you'd be transfixed and put into a catatonic state. But the teacher who meant the most to me, who treated me as a son, who inspired me and gave me the drive to do as well as I could at Dalton, was Monsieur Volel. Not surprisingly, Monsieur Volel meant a great deal to both Mark and me.

From Mark

> *Yves Volel was a tall man, about 6'3", with a husky, muscled build and an erect posture like the mast on a sailboat. He would have been an imposing, intimidating figure if not for his irrepressible smile and ceaselessly welcoming demeanor. Although Mr. Volel was not an easy teacher—his expectations for his students were very high—he had a reputation as a compassionate teacher. He would tell struggling students, "I cannot let you fail. It is my job to help you learn. If you fail, then I fail. So, we will win together." And every student left his class feeling cared for.*

In his native Haiti, Yves Volel was a graduate of the Academie Militaire d'Haiti and an officer in the Haitian Army before he gave up his military career to become an attorney and civil rights activist in Haiti. It was Mr.

Volel's activism that created confrontations with the regime of Francois "Papa Doc" Duvalier and led Mr. Volel to flee Haiti in 1965 and come to New York, where he soon began teaching at Dalton.

Yves Volel taught me introductory French in 7th grade, but he also taught algebra, trigonometry and probably could've taught calculus if he wanted to. He was that intelligent and that talented as an instructor. He was quick to say to me that I reminded him of his children, because he and I were of a similar skin tone and I was probably around the age of one of his sons. I've often thought that was the reason he took so much interest in my well being at school. He was a source of support for me during my early studies in Introductory French and Geometry at Dalton. If you were fortunate enough to have been a student in any of Monsieur Volel's classes, you quickly learned that his heart was as large as his frame and he made himself available to any and all students.

Although Yves Volel was a colorful, passionate man, to his students, he was Atticus Finch, the most decent and upright person we had ever known. I cannot speak for all of my classmates, but unquestionably among all of the minority students at Dalton, he was the kind of person that we all wanted to grow up to become. He was an incredibly important role model for the minority students. Dalton had a handful of teachers of color within the faculty, but Mr. Volel was the only teacher of color in the traditional academic disciplines. The others were fine teachers; artists and athletes, but Mr. Volel was a scholar.

From Mark

Students were always naturally curious about the private lives of their teachers, and never more so than with Mr. Volel. Students loved his stories about Haiti, about fighting the oppression of Duvalier's corrupt government. This was the 1960's after all. Protesting against the government was practically our religion.

Being the obnoxious teenagers that we were, we would occasionally exploit our knowledge of Mr. Volel for our own advantage and convenience. If we were supposed to take an exam that day, someone would say, "We'd rather talk about Duvalier and what's happening in Haiti." And Mr. Volel would begin talking and the exam would get tossed in the trash. It worked virtually every time.

During those classes, Monsieur Volel would get a little glint in his eye and his mind would wander, sparked by something that triggered the memory of one of his experiences under the brutal dictators Papa Doc and Baby Doc Duvalier. He'd pause, look up to the ceiling, and give an elaborate and detailed account of some aspect of the life he left in Haiti. Sometimes the students just looked at each other and tried to figure out, "where the hell was he going to this time?" But I suspect that it was a defense mechanism for Mr. Volel to help him cope with having left his family, wondering which of his family members would next be persecuted under the Duvalier regime.

Mr. Volel told those students who got to know him well that he was constantly being followed and watched by members of Duvalier's brutal Tonton Macoutes paramilitary force. He used to explain to us in his English laced with accents of his native "patois," that he was constantly watched by Haitian agents in New York. Like other students, I pooh-poohed his "secret agent stories" until one occasion when he and I were alone in one of our classrooms. He showed me the Colt .45 pistol he carried in his briefcase for his protection from his enemies, just in case he needed it. I always wondered if the other faculty or administration at Dalton knew Monsieur Volel "was packin'" all those years. No one heard it from me, because I intensely protected his privacy.

From Mark

For someone who never liked math and was never especially good at it, I learned quite a bit in Mr. Volel's class. I learned about the omnipresence of geometry in nature. I learned that the shape of an object dictated how it worked. But the greatest impact of Mr. Volel's teaching was that he taught me the value and importance of intellectual curiosity. Yves Volel was constantly sharing with his students something new he learned, something that he found interesting. I remember, he was so incredibly excited when Mazda first came out with their rotary engine cars. I think he spent a week talking to the class about it, and about the geometry of rotary engines. He created (and I believe he patented) his own design for windshield wipers based on the principles of geometry, and he explained to the class why they would work better. He was excited by the world and always learning from it.

In 1986, the people of Haiti rose up and revolted and Jean Claude Duvalier fled the country. Even with Duvalier gone, the corruption and governmental abuses remained. The people of Haiti were still suffering under dictatorial oppression. Shortly thereafter, Yves Volel returned to Haiti determined to fight for his people. He formed the Christian Democratic Party and announced his candidacy for president of Haiti. On October 13, 1987, Yves Volel went to police headquarters in Port Au Prince to demand the release of a political prisoner. On the steps of police headquarters he held a brief press conference, speaking to a handful of reporters, including print and television cameras. Moments later approximately eight plainclothes policemen began firing and killed Yves Volel instantly. The police then promptly confiscated all of the cameras and film from the press. Afterward, the Chief of Police issued a statement that Mr. Volel was attempting to stage an assault on the police station to facilitate the escape of a prisoner. The police were merely acting in self-defense.

It is so easy to believe that violent acts of inhumanity and corruption such as this could only happen in places like Haiti, but that world exists for us much closer to home. It is the world where South Carolina state troopers can open fire on a crowd of students and murder a young high school kid waiting to walk his mother home from work. It is the world where Ferguson police and New York police and Chicago police and Baltimore police murder Black men and no one is accountable. Haiti is not a world away. It is our world.

When I learned of Yves Volel's tragic and untimely death in Port-au-Prince in 1987, I was very emotional. Monsieur Volel had always spoken of and anticipated his death, but he was never afraid of it—just mindful of the fact that if it was to be: his soul was prepared. "Tu me manques beaucoup, Monsieur Volel…"

"In Dulci Jubilo"

One of my earliest Dalton middle school memories was walking on the second floor of the school, where once you entered, it was as if you were entering a reading library—ominously quiet and when you walked down the hallway. It was imperative to not make any noise whatsoever. The second floor was where the main administration offices were housed; the Deans of the Middle and High School, the financial office, the executive assistants to the administration heads and finally, the Headmaster's office. But on this occasion of walking through the solitude of the second floor, I was drawn to the sound of wonderful, melodious voices that emanated from behind a door nearly halfway down the hall. The sound came from one of the entrances to the auditorium balcony next to the projection room. This totally piqued my curiosity, so much so, that I couldn't resist opening the nearest door to observe the voices I was drawn to. When I poked my head into the darkened balcony, the light from the hallway illuminated the section of the balcony to reveal several rows of students, including several members from the football and basketball teams. And standing before them at the railing was this middle-aged, white man with tufts of gray hair on either side of his bald head, wearing a pair of wire-framed glasses, with an annoyed stare because I interrupted his rehearsal. He shouted at me to close the damn door and I didn't hesitate, as I high-tailed it away from the balcony, and off the second floor! What I had witnessed was the school chorus' *Madrigal Group*, featuring the best singers from the larger school chorus, as they prepared for the annual Dalton Christmas Pageant.

I loved music, especially rhythm and blues, jazz and soul from the albums my family collected from the 50's and 60's, as well as what I listened to on the radio which back then, was the only source for hearing the latest music. I also missed the brass instruments that I enjoyed playing at P.S. 96, but once I entered the Dalton middle school, there was no time, or money to pursue that interest any longer—it was all about doing well in my studies. But, now that I was in high school, I was eligible to join the singing chorus, which wasn't going to cost any money to join and which met only once, or twice a week for an hour. I did some singing in public school as a young man, spurred on by our music teacher and our school singing group even performed at a Home for The Aged on Fifth Avenue. At one of these events, there was a photographer for the New York Post who was chronicling our school group of Black, brown and white kids performing in a predominantly white Jewish senior facility. One of the photos he snapped, which made the front page of the paper, was of a young, Black male student wearing a yarmulke on his head and a shawl around his neck, singing a Hanukah song for the patients. That was me. I had forgotten that the picture existed until my mother cleared out belongings of my grandmother after she passed away in 1990 and found that clipping in one of her many scrapbooks.

When Dalton had auditions for the chorus freshman year, I wanted the opportunity to sing like those upper-classmen students I heard that day in the balcony, so I joined several of the other Black students who were upperclassmen like Shelly Anderson, David Burns, Carl Simmons, for the chance to become a member. Since the school chorus was open to the entire high school, it was one of those very rare school activities where students of all colors participated together and engaged each other on a regular basis. I would wager that many of those members of the school chorus would admit that were it not for the choral group, they might not have ever had any social interaction with students of color beyond the classroom.

Leading the school chorus and the Madrigal Group was a very special man who dedicated most of his life to teaching music and conducting choruses simultaneously at both the Dalton School and Sarah Lawrence College in Yonkers, NY for almost 50 years. Harold Aks began his college education at Brooklyn College until he was drafted into military service and was a weatherman in the Army Air Corps during World War II. When his enlistment was over he finished his degree at the Julliard School and earned his Bachelor of Music in conducting in 1948 and one year later, he was leading a chorus of young women at the Dalton School, a prestigious all-girl private school in 1949. A few years after that, he began conducting the girl's chorus at Sarah Lawrence. It wasn't until the passing of Harold Aks in 2000, that I discovered something even more unusual about this man—at the same time he was conducting for the Dalton School in the late forties, he was also conducting the Interracial Fellowship Chorus in New York City, which had as many as one hundred and fifty members who toured around the city and sang in different churches and concert halls. A January, 1955 New York Times article acknowledged this group of singers under the leadership of Harold Aks during one winter program, "...There are many things that could be singled out in the performance, but perhaps the most impressive was the masterly way in which Harold Aks, the conductor, traversed the great curve of the work." Imagine, this man was conducting an interracial chorus throughout New York in the 40's and 50's. During that period, it was fashionable for white audiences to listen to Black jazz musicians in the nightclubs that flourished all around the city; in the Village, Midtown and Harlem, with the sounds of Dizzy, Bird, Miles, Basie, and Ellington, but I am certain that there were many who questioned Black people singing Handel in the great churches of the metropolitan area. Mr. Aks was unafraid and undaunted, a pioneer on so many levels.

To my knowledge, he never turned down any student who wanted to sing in the school chorus, no matter whether they sounded like a bird, or a bullfrog. He was about the music, the teaching, and the fellowship. He exposed us to the incredible works of Bach, Handel, Mozart and many other great composers, as we learned to sing these classics in multiple languages. When the student chorus was unruly, he would bang his baton on his music stand and yell at the top of lungs, but always followed it with the playful trembling of his lower jaw, as if he were going to blow a gasket and then break out into a big smile. If you arrived to the basement early enough, you could sometimes catch him breaking into a jazz riff, as he played some of the music of his favorite jazz pianists like Oscar Peterson, Errol Garner, or Thelonius Monk. I was thrilled to try and guess which standard he was playing as he entertained us prior to our rehearsals and before he eventually handed the grand piano over to Elizabeth Smith, the choral and madrigal groups' dependable accompanist.

Of course, students had to audition for the school Madrigal Group because these were the privileged performers to sing background for the Dalton Christmas Pageant every year, as well as other special concerts Mr. Aks would arrange during the school term. The pageant featured the music of the holidays sung a capella and included *Carol Of The Bells*, *In A Manger*, *Hark! The Herald Angels Sing*, *Adoremus Te* and *In Dulci Jubilo*, which was the piece that we opened and closed the pageant with each and every performance. The singers weren't in the audience, or on the stage for the performance; we were in the balcony which was closed to the general public so that there were no distractions during the event. I like to think that our voices emanating from "up above," gave the selections an almost angelic sound and I suspect that Mr. Aks knew that as well.

My audition for the Madrigal Group freshmen year was a harrowing and nerve-wracking experience. I was never so nervous during any football, or basketball game than I was for this occasion. One-by-one, I watched members of the larger school chorus put their egos on the line to prove their worth in front of Mr. Aks, in the hopes of being selected a member of this elite chorus. I think by the time he got to me, sweat had formed on my forehead and it was all I could do to focus on his commands, but he calmed me down with one of his trademark jokes before he put me through the scales and I was able to match his notes with my voice. We didn't find out until later in the week, or the following week if we made the Madrigal Group and when I was informed that I had been selected as a member, it evoked an immediate sense of pride and accomplishment within me. This was odd considering the new militant stance I had begun to embrace to protect myself from the white establishment at the school. But with Mr. Aks, his enthusiasm toward the students, his absolute love of teaching, his dedication to inclusion in the school choral group, were all inspirational acts of love on his part and you couldn't help but be drawn in to share those experiences.

CHAPTER 6

FRIENDS, DATING AND THE DALTON SOCIAL EXPERIENCE

MARK ROBINSON

M Y FIRST EXPERIENCES AS A Dalton student were in "house." Most schools had homerooms; that place you went first period of the day and spent 20 minutes with a group of students and a teacher whose responsibility it was to keep track of you, both in the literal sense of daily attendance and in the broader sense of how you were doing in school overall. But Dalton didn't call them homerooms, they called them houses. This made them seem more like a family gathering and less like an institutional construct. At least that was the intention. And at Dalton, each house was encouraged to embrace its own quirkiness and idiosyncratic identity. Dalton, after all, embraced every opportunity to keep traditional educational norms and practices at arm's length. This was driven by Dalton's Montessori philosophy and by the marketing of the Dalton "brand", which justified the private school's very high tuition.

House—more specifically, Miss Hellman's house—was where I met and made my first friends at Dalton. It is always difficult being the new kid who enters a world where the rest of the kids all know each other. Friendships and histories are firmly in place and you are this seedling trying to penetrate the hard-packed soil so that you have a chance to take root. But at Dalton, this challenge is magnified exponentially. The Dalton School begins pre-kindergarten and continues through 12th grade. By eighth grade, kids haven't simply been friends for a couple of years. They've been friends for their entire memories. What's more, as I mentioned before, roughly one in three students has an older sibling or even a parent who attended Dalton, meaning that some friendships have been passed down like a legacy. There was absolutely nothing that someone like me could do to play catch-up in that race. You knew you were hopelessly defeated before you even tried.

Dalton offered no welcoming process, no on-boarding mechanism. The culture of the school, the social ecosystem, was designed to support insiders, not outsiders. If you were new to the school, you had better figure out fast how to become an insider, or at least how to behave like one. No one in the Dalton world, not administrators, not faculty, not students or parents, made any meaningful effort toward proving a support system for anyone who was not a "native born" Daltonian. The well-being of such individuals was never a priority, never a concern.

And so, as a survival mechanism, I put a great deal of effort into making friends during my first months at Dalton. My parents probably thought that I put more effort into making friends than into making grades, and they were probably right. I didn't flounder academically. I held my own. But I didn't exactly soar either. There were four other Black kids in Miss Hellman's house; two boys and two girls, and that was pretty unusual. Most of the houses in Dalton's middle school had no Black kids in them at all. The few that did had only one or two back students. Miss Hellman had five. There was Kendall (K.K.) West, Rose Marie Garcia (technically, Rose Marie wasn't Black, she was Puerto Rican. But she was one of us.), Paul Driver and Jay Strong. And me.

Despite my best intentions, initiating a friendship with Kendall and Rose Marie was pretty much beyond my social skill set at the time. As an eighth grader, I had never been on a date with a girl. I had never kissed a girl. Any girl who was waiting for me to initiate any social interaction was going to be waiting a pretty long time. I wasn't entirely inept. I wasn't a dweeb. I was charming and had a decent personality. And I am told that I was rather cute. But I lacked the self-confidence, especially in the new world of Dalton, to make the first move with any girl. That would change in time, but not in eighth grade. And so, although I was friendly with Kendall and Rose Marie (who I thought was especially sweet), it was never more than that. And sadly, both girls left Dalton after eighth grade.

The other Black boys in Miss Helman's house were Paul Driver and Jay Strong. Both Paul and Jay had already been at Dalton a very long time. Paul entered Dalton in the third grade. Jay entered Dalton's nursery school at three years old. Dalton was the only school he had ever known. His Dalton classmates had been his lifetime friends. They saw Dalton and experienced Dalton in a way that I could not possibly imagine. Their frame of reference was as foreign to me as all the other new kids I met in my new school.

Paul Driver was always a bit of a wild child. Whether it was a strategic choice or an unrestrained impulse, Paul always favored whatever action drew the most attention to him, preferably in a manner that shocked. Paul's persona always gave the impression that he did not study very hard or put a lot of effort into getting good grades, but I suspect that Paul's academic and intellectual gifts were greater than he ever let on. In all the conversations between Paul and me, I never felt smarter than Paul. He might say something crazy, but he never said something stupid. I think that Paul understood very well the lowered expectations of Dalton teachers (and students) for Black boys and so he simply gave the public what they wanted. Of all the Black kids at Dalton, Paul seemed to me to be the one who most knowingly gave Dalton the middle finger, usually with a wink and a smile, and still somehow managed to prosper there and see it through to graduation. But for my own sensibilities, Paul walked a little too close to the third rail for my comfort, so he and I never really became close.

Jay Strong was a very different personality. As open and unguarded as Paul was, Jay was the opposite. Jay always seemed to have an invisible yet impenetrable wall that he stayed behind. Jay had a wry or sardonic commentary about everything. His wit and his intellect were razor sharp, but I always felt that its primary purpose was to keep people at arm's length, to never let anyone too close. And because Jay succeeded in these efforts, I never had any understanding of why he was so guarded and removed. Although we were friendly, we were never friends. Digging out my old eighth grade yearbook and looking back at our photos, I realize that Jay never signed my yearbook, probably one of the few classmates who didn't.

While writing this book and discussing our Black classmates, I was asked if I thought that perhaps Jay—who had been at Dalton since nursery school—felt that the Black kids who were arriving in middle school were invading the turf that he had all to himself for so many years. That's probably an impossible answer to know. If I ever get the chance to ask Jay that question, I'm not sure he would know the answer either.

Jay also performed in several of the school's theatrical productions and had a real flair for comic timing and stage presence. Many years later at a reunion of our class, I saw Jay again and learned that he was now a comedy writer and a professional stand-up comic. I could not imagine a more appropriate career. At the reunion I spoke mostly with Jay's wife who told me all about what Jay was doing. I was very happy that Jay had found someone to share his life with and with whom he could be close.

I look back at my first year at Dalton and my recollection is that I made a lot of superficial friendships, but not really any deep or lasting friendships that year. There was one guy, Willie Scott, who was one of the few other Black boys in our grade. Willie was small and small-framed, someone who probably was picked on more than a few times because of his size. But he was unhesitatingly friendly, quick with a smile and usually equipped with a good joke to share. I would often have lunch with Willie in the school cafeteria, but I don't think we had ever been to each other's homes or engaged in many activities outside of school. And after eighth grade Willie left Dalton and I lost track of where he went.

Carol Chaderton was the other Black girl (along with Kendall West) in our eighth-grade class. Carol wasn't in Miss Hellman's house, she was in Mr. Ahearn's house, so we saw each other less often. Like me, Carol was also from Queens, (she lived in Springfield Gardens), but she did not commute on the subway every day. Carol's mom was a teacher at a school on East 96th Street, so she rode to school in the car each day with her mom, an experience similar to what my dad and I had in elementary school. I imagine that Carol must have many treasured memories of those rides to school with her mom. Carol was a cute, skinny girl with boundless energy and neatly trimmed bangs and a twinkle in her eyes. Early in 1970, the Jackson Five released their big hit "ABC", and one of my favorite memories of Carol was seeing her go crazy dancing to that song after just acquiring the 45.

Carol had been attending Dalton since first grade and she knew the school and all of its occupants as well as her backyard at home. By ninth grade, however, that familiarity had begun to grow stale. At fourteen, none of us is the same person we were when we were six. In first or second grade, the kids at school are your most important friends. They are the people you see the most and with whom you share the most memories and experiences. By ninth grade, however, each of us begins to branch out, explore our worlds and discover new experiences with new acquaintances and new friends. For Carol, part of that exploration was the discovery that her world in school and her world outside of school were not entirely compatible. In fact, they might have been in conflict with each other. For Carol, the answer was to return to public school in her home neighborhood of Springfield Gardens, Queens.

Turning fourteen and the beginning of high school is a natural period of significant transition for most young people. The independence and maturity of adulthood inches just a little bit closer. The clarity of self-awareness becomes just a little bit sharper (although still elusive). We discover that our bodies possess hormones that are like hand grenades without pins. We change physically, emotionally and intellectually. Even when the world around us is completely calm, our spirits wrestle with chaos. But when the world around us is in chaos—as it most certainly was in 1968, 1969 and 1970—it is possible, perhaps even likely, to become as unmoored as a double-wide trailer in a Kansas tornado. That might explain why the minority kids who came to Dalton in middle school or later tended to stay at Dalton, while the minority kids who had been there since lower school now felt it was time to leave.

As I look back nearly 50 years ago, it isn't easy to remember the ordinary everyday feelings and experiences all that clearly. If I only had superficial friends that first year, who were those superficial friends and how did we come together? What did we do when we were together? Why did we like each other? Why did that change? In what ways did I change? It would be wonderful if I could call up the answers to all of these questions, if I could remember every detail instead of just a handful. But I'll have to settle for what I have and try to turn those few memories into a larger understanding of my life at that time. In recalling and sharing stories of my time at Dalton, and especially stories about school friendships, I am acutely aware of the stories of happy memories when friends came over to your house. These are often stories of precious moments remembered fondly many years later. In the five years that I attended Dalton, eighth grade through senior year, there's probably less than ten classmates whose homes I ever visited or was invited to. But that is probably a reasonable number. On the other hand, in those five years not one classmate ever visited my home, though many were invited, at least in the beginning. After a while, there really didn't seem to be any point. I suppose that you could make the argument that the parents of my white classmates at Dalton were appropriately apprehensive about allowing their child to visit a Black classmate who lived in a neighborhood known for poverty or drugs or crime. For better or for worse, Harlem did not have a good reputation in the early 1970s. It is not unreasonable for parents to be protective. But my family didn't live in a "bad neighborhood." We lived in St. Albans, in Queens. My parents bought the house that Lena Horne lived in. Lena Horne. Count Basie, Ella Fitzgerald and James Brown were my neighbors. It didn't matter. It just didn't matter. Not one classmate ever visited my home.

There are two traits in human behavior that on the surface might seem contradictory, yet somehow manage to coexist. I came to understand these things later in life as a marketing professional where it was my job to understand human behavior and use it to my clients' advantage. The first trait might more broadly be described as "tribal behavior", where for reasons of survival we tend to remain close to members of our own tribe or clan. This is equally true for whites and Blacks. While integration might be a goal of civil society, it is not necessarily an instinct of human behavior. In the context of American history, many of the attitudes and behavioral patterns of Black people today are the result of societal and sociological truths that span generations. Minorities in America are far more likely to actively seek out other members of their "group" than members of the majority. In 1997, noted psychologist Beverly Tatum wrote the book, "Why are all the Black kids sitting together in the cafeteria?" which echoes the question often asked by white classmates and teachers. We have learned that connecting with other members of our "group" can offer physical safety, political influence, emotional support (sympathy, empathy) and social common ground. For Black people, "sticking with your own kind" was also often a social mandate of the American majority. As a result, we place significantly greater emphasis and importance on connecting with our peers and spending time with them.

But there is another impulse that is equally true. This is a behavior most commonly observed among immigrants who come to a new country. Their instinct for survival; physically, socially and economically, is to bond with the incumbent power structure and establishment class. Historically, immigrants understood that in order to succeed in America, you must become "American." After all, if you are new to a community, there is no benefit or upside to allying yourself with the least empowered cohort, but every reason to try to become part of the tribe that sits on top. And when you are the new kids in school, you seek to bond with the establishment cohort.

These two impulses might seem to be in direct conflict with each other. And perhaps they are. But just the same I know that this is what we did—both of these things—as the new Black kids at Dalton. And if you wonder if this created cognitive dissonance for us, if this messed with our heads at all, the answer is most definitely yes.

In his 1903 book, The Souls of Black Folk, W.E.B. DuBois wrote eloquently and insightfully about the toxic impact of these conflicting impulses on the mind and soul of the Negro race. Imagine how much more fragile and vulnerable is the mind and soul of an adolescent Black boy.

> *"One ever feels his twoness—an American, a Negro; two souls, two thoughts, two unreconciled strivings; two warring ideals in one dark body, whose dogged strength alone keeps it from being torn asunder....He simply wishes to make it possible for a man to be both a Negro and an American, without being cursed and spit upon by his fellows, without having the doors of Opportunity closed roughly in his face."*

It's also easy—so many years later—to look back at my experiences at Dalton through the eyes of my adult self and attempt to apply a sophisticated understanding of myself and of the people around me. It's easy now to ask questions that an adult would ask, or to assume answers that seem obvious to me now. I also have the benefit of knowing how things turned out, of what the year-to-year progression looked like. But back then I was just a 13 year-old eighth grader who was grateful I got to school each morning without some grand subway misadventure, and got from class to class on time.

As an eighth grader, my understanding of who I was as an individual and as part of something greater than myself, was definitely a work-in-progress. For example, I have always had a recognition of myself as a Black person. And from the earliest ages I have interacted with people both similar and different from myself; Black, white, Hispanic, Asian, young, old, rich and poor. Growing up, those differences were details, specifics. They were never social or political distinctions. Those differences were never tribal or adversarial. But that awareness evolved over time as I grew up. My experiences at IS 59 made some of those differences matter in ways that made me uncomfortable. And that discomfort would eventually become integrated into the lens through which I saw the world and the armor I created when that lens perceived a possible threat.

In my first year at Dalton I definitely had some kind of connection to the other eighth grade minority kids. We spent time together, but not in any organized or purposeful way. We enjoyed each other's companionship. We all shared an amorphous sense of displacement from the main social body of the school. We all shared some vague sense of "otherness", some of us because we were new, all of us because we were different. But that connection that we shared had not yet coalesced into anything tribal or anything political. That came later, a little at a time, until one day it was all the way there. By then we were older, and the differences between "us" and "them" were the product of many shared experiences and not simply imagination or paranoia. By then the world around us had also undergone many changes and—to the extent that any high school teenager "comes of age"—we came of age during the close of America's Civil Rights movement and the beginnings of America's Black Pride movement. By the time we graduated, the Black students at Dalton were beginning to flex their collective muscles as a full-blown constituency.

As I mentioned before, because my dad had grown up without a father, he never had much of a sports orientation or experience. He never got to play catch with his dad, or talk about sports teams or their favorite athletes. I had grown up pretty much the same way. My dad's ambivalence to participation in sports had been passed down to me. So, when I arrived at Dalton, I had neither the prior experience nor the inclination to sign up for any team sports. This naturally surprised school officials who assumed that all Black kids had a consuming passion—and a natural gift—for sports. It wasn't until my senior year that I joined any sports. I signed up for Judo and for a time I was quite good at it. That was until I found myself in a match against classmate Adrian Van Larhoven, who was at least twice my size. Size shouldn't always matter in Judo, until it does. Adrian picked me up and flipped me like I was a rag doll. I hit the mat so hard it seemed to me that the building shook. More than 40+ years later, my back still vividly and painfully remembers that day.

One of the activities that I did join, however, was the middle school yearbook committee. I think I was recruited by the two girls who led the committee, Gwen Feder and Susie Wels. Gwen and Susie were both very outgoing social personalities; precisely the kind of people who should manage a yearbook. And also precisely the kind of people who were totally comfortable befriending one of the new Black kids in school and persuading him to join the yearbook committee. That included going to their homes after school and on occasional weekends to work on the yearbook. We became good friends that year and working on the yearbook became a useful window into learning more about my other classmates. Gwen and Susie made the effort to befriend me, and through them an invitation that granted me an entrance into the Dalton student world. By the end of that first year I no longer felt like a stranger at Dalton. I knew my way around. I knew the way things were. I could anticipate and interpret experiences and—to a limited degree—I could manipulate circumstances to my advantage, or at least to my comfort.

But familiarity is not at all the same as integration. Knowing the Dalton world, my peers, my teachers and my environment, did not make me one of them. I had a permanent guest pass, but I was nevertheless unmistakably a guest. You see, there was always this one simple, immutable practical barrier between true Daltonians and the minority kids such as myself. Money. Your identity as a school-age kid was defined by the things you could do, by the experiences that were possible for you, by your lifestyle. And lifestyle and life experience were fueled by money, lots and lots of money and the privileges it buys. For us minority kids, "travel" was what you did to-and-from school. For our Dalton classmates, "travel" meant going someplace fun for the weekend because all of the east coast ski resorts would be too crowded. For our Dalton classmates, "summer" was a verb.

In the mid-1980s, about ten years after we left Dalton, there was a television show hosted by Robin Leach called "Lifestyles of the Rich and Famous." It was a voyeuristic orgy of all the fabulous homes, cars, clothes and various goings-on of famous and not-so-famous wealthy. The show was a huge hit and remained on the air for over a decade. Americans seemed to be fascinated by peeking around the curtain to see the lives of the rich and famous. But for me and for the other minority kids who went to Dalton, we were familiar with this world from a very different perspective. For us, the rich and famous were just the kids in math class and the lunchroom. Sure, there was luxury and glamour to their lives, but there was also banality. On TV, "champagne wishes and caviar dreams" is a wonderful, exotic, ethereal dream. A fantasy. In high school, all of those things just become things that the other kids have that you don't. In high school, all of those things become just another brick in the load of teenage alienation.

There is a natural tendency among teenagers to be competitive, to try to one-up each other, sometimes in a good-spirited and friendly way, sometimes not. Sometimes there was the pungent whiff of Lord of the Flies in the air. But it didn't matter. On most metrics that mattered to us kids, there was simply no way for the Black students to compete. You couldn't out-dress them. Some girls had wardrobe budgets that were equal to other people's household income. And many of the guys were into conspicuously dressing down, overtly shunning the appearance of affluence. And when it came to "what did you do this weekend?" we didn't even bother to try. Even if you were very smart, you were never recognized as the smartest kid in the class. The teachers had their favorites and we were never it. Forget about trying to be better. It was hard enough just trying to establish your bona fides as a peer, as one of the group. And you never really quite made it. Some of the Black kids excelled at athletics (sadly I was not one of them). Ray Smaltz was a natural athlete who dominated the basketball court and the football field. But that is what Dalton expected of us. That's what they assumed we all could do. So, the achievement always had an asterisk that diminished its value.

There was one other thing that we could do that they couldn't, one other thing that—truth be told—could occasionally trigger a twinge of jealousy among the white kids. We could be us. There is just something about Black people when we are being confident and comfortable in who we are, when our joy is observable by others, that causes them to say, "I want what they're having." They love our music, our dance, our comedy, our culture. And they do their best to copy it. This is why there are ever-present, often unfortunate expressions of cultural appropriation.

Of course, there are also times when our observable joy leaves a bitter taste in their mouths because they simply don't understand how or why we could be happier than they are. Not even for the briefest of moments. Their belief system and value system demand that they have the preeminent right to happiness and the rest of us should enjoy the leftovers. Us being us was sometimes viewed as an assault on those beliefs and values. And so, us being us was frequently regarded as acting up, being disruptive and failing to adapt and assimilate.

I wonder, as a logic question; if we don't fit in at Dalton when we are happy and comfortable and self-confident, does that mean that we do fit in when we are unhappy, uncomfortable and lacking confidence? Or does it simply mean this is when Dalton is most comfortable with us being there?

I feel that I should pause for a moment in my description of the briar patch nature of Dalton to point out and make clear that I have very fond memories and had many happy experiences at Dalton. They are the reason that I have stayed connected to the school over the years since graduation. I loved Dalton. In fact, that is worth repeating. I loved Dalton. The problem—and the important truth—however, is that Dalton didn't always love me back.

One of the big events of eighth grade was the class trip coordinated by the teachers in the History department. That year we were studying American history and the class trip was planned to coincide with our study of the Civil War. A big part of the trip was a visit to the historic Civil War battlefields of Harpers Ferry and Antietam. My classmates and I were loaded into two chartered buses that took us from Manhattan's upper east side to remote historic sites in West Virginia and Maryland. Ironically, I think that our bus ride was more of a novelty for some of my well-heeled classmates than it was for me. Growing up, I was accustomed to annual bus trips to Montreal with my grandmother and her church lady friends. Those trips, long hours and hyper-organized touring with a busload of elderly church ladies was about as much fun as it sounds. I was optimistic, however, that the trip with my eighth-grade classmates and friends would be better.

I loved the idea of visiting the battlefields and standing on the ground where important history occurred. It was cool to point to places where soldiers charged and clashed and died, where General Stonewall Jackson sat astride his horse. It was a way of looking at history that was fresh (at least for me) and vivid and exciting. The Battle of Antietam occurred on September

17, 1862. Five days later, on the 22nd of September, and very much a part of the aftermath of this battle, President Lincoln issued the Emancipation Proclamation, immediately changing the nature and outcome of the war and altering the course of our nation. The Proclamation was a gut punch to the vital Southern labor force and opened the door to Black enlistment in the Union Army. The war between the states was no longer simply about suppressing an insurrection and secession, it became about redefining the values of the American people. But none of this was taught nor even discussed by our history teachers, not in the classroom, not on this special field trip. In our textbooks, slavery was merely peripheral to the important issues that brought about the Civil War. It would be several more years before I had exposure and access to textbooks that did not gloss over or whitewash the real lessons of our history.

With abundant resources and outstanding teachers, Dalton was doing a better job of teaching history than most schools in the nation. And yet, even with such a high bar, Dalton was doing a very poor job of teaching history.

Our eighth-grade history field trip spanned three days, with two sleepover nights. One night was spent in a fairly generic and nondescript low-end chain hotel. But the first night was spent in an old West Virginia hotel that was a sprawling Victorian design and was likely selected for the period atmosphere it evoked. We probably occupied the entire hotel that night. I think there were about 80 kids on the trip accompanied by a half dozen teacher chaperones.

That first night after dinner the teachers were tired and eager to unwind and relax, probably with alcohol that they could not consume in front of students. Erroneously, they assumed that we students were tired too. They grossly underestimated the stamina of the average teenager. For us, this was time to party—barefoot, jumping from room to room—and an unprecedented opportunity for hooking up. Some were couples that had already been "coupling" for a while. Some were couples who had planned for this away trip to be their big opportunity to take their torrid teenage love to the next step. And some were just adolescent hormones lit on fire and set loose to seize the moment. As an eighth grader, I hadn't even been on a date with a girl before, not a "date-date". But it became startlingly obvious that night and the next morning that a conspicuous number of my classmates had already rounded the bases and were heading for home runs. It was almost impossible to grasp just how much more "advanced" they were compared to me. I have no idea the degree to which affluence and privilege played a role in their sexual sophistication, but it seemed that the routine lack of parental supervision created situations and opportunities for teen romance that were simply not part of my experience. Ironically, most of the teachers, school administrators and parents probably assumed that the Black kids, in particular the Black boys, were "faster" and more sexually active than the "regular" Dalton kids. Perceptions based more on prejudice than any reality. After this class trip I never looked at certain classmates the same way again.

Toward the end of the school year, I did finally manage to ask a girl out on a date; a fellow eighth grader named Lorraine. She was not a traditional Dalton Manhattanite. Lorraine lived in Forest Hills and commuted to school from Queens just like me. Perhaps that was an element of our common ground that opened the door just enough for me to ask her out. As occasionally happens for some early teenage girls, Lorraine had an extremely well-developed body for a 14 year-old. Extremely. And she was pretty and sweet with long dark brown hair and—most important of all—she said "yes" when I asked her out. On our first date we went to the movies, a pretty standard choice for a first date, although I don't recall which movie.

Our second date was over the summer and the school year had ended. We took the subway to Rockaway Beach, which was absolutely the very opposite end of the subway line and seemed to take forever. I picked Rockaway Beach because we could get there by subway, because it was summer now and the idea sounded like fun, with the beach and the adjacent amusement park. But mostly, as a 14 year-old boy, I picked it because I was dying to see what Lorraine looked like in a bathing suit. And she was everything I imagined and more. We spent the whole day together and had a wonderful time. Our second date certainly left the promise of a third date. Perhaps even a relationship. Being a proper young gentleman, I took Lorraine home when our date was over. This was when I met Lorraine's parents for the first time. They were naturally curious to meet this "Dalton boy" who had taken their daughter on two dates. I was going to be the first "Dalton boy" that Lorraine brought home and there was naturally a degree of heightened expectation. There was also (I can only surmise) an element of parental pride that their little girl from Queens was fitting in well with the elites from Manhattan's upper east side.

When we got to her house, I think Lorraine's parents were planning to have me come in for a few minutes of getting-to-know-you conversation.

But when they met me at the door and saw immediately that their nice Jewish daughter from Forest Hills had been going out with a Black boy, plans changed. I was not at all what Lorraine's parents expected to see. I was not invited in. We said goodbye at the door with a chaste kiss on the cheek and a door that closed just a bit too quickly. When I called a few days later to ask Lorraine out for a third date, her mother told me she wasn't home. She never called back. When September came, Lorraine did not return to Dalton. Her parents transferred her to another school, probably one closer to home. Probably one with less risk of dating Black boys.

That was the last time I dated someone from Dalton until my senior year. After eighth grade, Kendall West and Rose Marie Garcia left Dalton. Carol Chaderton left after ninth grade. For the remainder of my high school years there were no Black or Hispanic girls in my class at Dalton. This created something of a social vacuum. Of course, one could always date someone a year older or a year younger, if you wanted to make a play for someone outside of your grade. But in many respects what grade you were in defined your social caste. It was pretty rare to see anyone venture outside their own grade.

In hindsight, I probably should have been more self-aware that inter-racial dating was still quite uncommon and unpopular in the late 1960's. Uncommon? Unpopular? When I came to Dalton in 1969, more than a third of the country was still up in arms that the U.S. Supreme Court had struck down anti-miscegenation laws only two years earlier. Inter-racial dating wasn't simply outside of the mainstream, it was illegal and deadly. The law may have changed, but hearts and minds still had not.

Forget about the segregated south, there were still plenty of neighborhoods in the five boroughs of New York where a Black kid like me was likely to get jumped and badly beaten simply for walking down the street holding a white girl's hand. Emmett Till might have been a decade earlier, but "progress" was still a work-in-progress for neighborhoods like Bensonhurst in Brooklyn, the Belmont section of the Bronx, Silver Lake on Staten Island or Forest Hills in Queens. Like a typical 14 year-old boy, I didn't pay attention to half the things I should have been paying attention to. I look back sometimes and wonder how a reasonably bright kid such as myself could have been so habitually oblivious.

Oblivious. For me, the absence of Black and Hispanic girls in my grade was a disappointment but was hardly a deal breaker. To me, a pretty girl was a pretty girl, regardless of skin color or background. And during my four high school years there were a couple of girls for whom I had a serious crush. They made my heart skip a beat. Unfortunately, they saw me more as a friend and not as a romantic partner, and so those crushes were one-sided and unrequited. I didn't go to my prom, neither junior nor senior year. I have no prom memories to look back upon. In all modesty, I was a pretty good looking guy back then. And I had plenty of friends. Things just never came together romantically in high school. Nor was there anybody in my neighborhood back in St. Albans, Queens. Everybody in the neighborhood was a guy, at least those in my age range. It was a romance desert.

During the summer between my junior and senior year, I was working at Dalton in a variety of capacities; day camp counselor, switchboard operator (those kindergarten telephone classes sure came in handy!) and admission office tour guide. One day a family came to the school to finalize paperwork for their daughter who would be joining the senior class in a few weeks. The family was Tony Curtis (the Hollywood actor), his third wife Leslie and eldest daughter Kelly Lee (from first wife Janet Leigh), along with three year-old son Nicholas and newborn son Ben. I was asked to give the Curtis family a quick private tour of the school and to share with them my impressions of Dalton as a student. Kelly was a terrifically pretty girl with a fluorescent smile and long blond hair, friendly and surprisingly unaffected given her family pedigree. She was Beach Boys California sunshine compared to her father's darker, brooding Hollywood aura. She was much more her mother than her father. Kelly was probably more than accustomed to moving from school to school and she apparently decided right there to latch onto me as her first new friend at her new school. When the school year started, she sought me out to continue to show her around, find classes, know where to hang out, etc. We were comfortable with each other and after a week or two I asked Kelly out on a date. We went to the movies (I think we saw the Three Musketeers), had fun and enjoyed each other's company. I had already met her family and they seemed to like me, so it was unlikely there would be another awkward encounter like the one with Lorraine's parents, years before. In fact, I think that one evening we ended up briefly babysitting Kelly's younger siblings, including Jamie Lee. This was by no means any hot and heavy romance, but it was nice. At least while it lasted, which was for about two to three weeks.

For Kelly, assimilating into Dalton was not a passive process, it was a campaign. Kelly joined the cheerleading squad. Between practices and attendance at games, Kelly's social time became cheerleading time. Kelly's new friends were either other cheerleaders or the athletes. I was neither. I was history. And for the remainder of senior year when we crossed paths I would get a bright smile and a warm hello and not much beyond that. On graduation day there was a reception in the school library after the ceremony in the theater. All of the graduates and their families were there. As I serpentined through the crowd, navigating my way toward a refill of punch with my empty cup in hand, I suddenly found myself nose to nose with Tony Curtis.

"Would you mind telling me where the hell you've been?" Tony Curtis delivered the question with as much flair and melodrama as any of his films. He was wearing a dark velvet blazer with a silk scarf tied into an ascot.

"Sir?" I said, completely puzzled and a bit back on my heels.

"This school year started with you dating my daughter. Then suddenly after a couple of weeks you disappeared. What the hell happened? Where the hell did you go?" He hammered me with questions.

"Did you . . ." I tried to figure out how to respond. ". . . ask Kelly?"

"I'm not asking her, young man. I'm asking you."

I'm not sure what he thought, but I was beginning to get the impression that he thought I had somehow rejected his daughter. Which was just crazy.

"I think Kelly just got to know other people. I mean, we're still friends."

"None of those other boys she brought home were half as nice as you. Not one." I think I got poked in the chest with his finger.

"Thank you, sir."

"What college are you going to next year?"

"Amherst College."

"Kelly is going to Skidmore. Not that far. Look her up sometime, will you?"

"Of course, sir."

And then, like a puff of smoke in a Houdini movie, he was gone.

I did kinda sorta keep touch with Kelly when she was at Skidmore. My good friend Cathy Fire was also at Skidmore and kept tabs on her, so to speak. But we lost touch with each other not long after that and only recently reconnected. The advent of social media has enabled us to communicate easily and fairly frequently. Indeed, Facebook has reconnected me with quite a few of my old Dalton classmates and has rekindled many friendships. Kelly and her husband live in Idaho, about as far away from New York City life as you can imagine. Our social media interactions bristle and crackle with typical political and ideological confrontation, somehow still managing to remain friends.

Dating a Black guy in high school.

Still today, the idea of a white girl dating a Black guy in high school remains a much bigger deal than our enlightened selves would like to acknowledge. As the parent of a Black son, I know that some attitudes and anxieties have progressed very little from 50 years ago. It is part of what I—as a parent—must be sure to explain to my son. The idea of a white girl dating a Black guy in high school continues to be a potent source of pre-judgment by others regarding the choices and virtues of the girl and the choices and preferences—and potential dangers—of the boy. So, imagine how much more social agita this kind of pairing could cause half a century ago.

Dating a Black guy in high school.

In 1969, this was unapologetically a bright red line even for many of Dalton's most liberal and progressive parents (Tony Curtis notwithstanding). Let them go to school together, but please God, don't bring one home. This was the recollection of many of our classmates in story after story. Almost every one of the young Black men who were in the high school at Dalton during this time had a romantic connection to one of their white female classmates at one point or another. And no matter how discreet the young couple attempted to be, or the lengths they may have gone to keep the relationship on the down low, people noticed, people judged, and people almost always had something to say. And when they had something to say, it was almost always said to the girl, because no one wanted to risk confronting the boy. That would have been politically incorrect. And that would have exposed the speaker's true feelings and attitudes when it was important to maintain a certain façade.

But there were also kids who thought, "Hey, this is pretty cool." And there were kids who thought, "What's the big deal? What difference does it make?" And there were probably just as many kids who felt this way as there were those who did not. There were always friends and allies at Dalton. We could not have survived if there were not. We could not have remained sane (to the degree that we did) if there were not. It is also fair to say that even the best of people at Dalton might not have known where they stood if we had not been there too. It is easy, after all, to have strong moral character if that character is never tested. Our presence there, the young Black boys of Dalton—at this particular moment in time—gave people a reason and an opportunity to find and embrace their better angels. It certainly wasn't something that we set out to do. We were not engaged in an overt civil rights movement to change the interracial social climate at Dalton.

But it happened, and it happened because we were there.

Even without the romantic connections, friendships were formed that never would have happened otherwise. Dalton tossed a rickety wooden footbridge across a racial divide and a socio-economic divide that enabled people on both sides of that divide to see a bigger and more diverse world than either side had imagined ever existed. Instead of seeing two dimensional images off in the distance, we interacted with real, three-dimensional people. A lot of people were permanently changed—hopefully for the better—by our presence at Dalton. And that includes parents, grandparents and a whole bunch of tight ass, white-gloved doormen on Park Avenue and Sutton Place, who suddenly had to be respectful to young Black boys and begin greeting us politely when we came to visit a classmate, and not direct us to walk around to the service entrance.

Because we were there.

My two closest friends at Dalton were Bill McGill and Cathy Fire. I met them both during my freshman year. They were both a year older than me and in the sophomore class, but still we found a way to spend a great deal of time together. Bill had just come to Dalton since his family moved to New York from San Diego, California where Bill's father had been the Chancellor of the University of California at San Diego. William McGill Sr. had accepted the position of president of Columbia University, a huge step up in prestige but also a huge step into the center of the late 1960's student anti-war rebellion firestorm as protests raged on the Columbia campus. Over the previous few years, the SDS (Students for a Democratic Society)

had conducted continuous demonstrations, sit-ins and building occupations on the Columbia campus. The university's outgoing president had proven himself incapable of forging a meaningful and constructive dialogue with the student protesters and unable to restore normal academic order to the school. The university trustees reached out to William McGill, who had faced similar challenges in southern California.

The move from suburban southern California to Manhattan, especially living in Morningside Heights in the middle of Harlem, was quite a radical transition for my new friend Bill, as was his adjustment from public school to elite private school. He was experiencing far greater culture shock than I ever did. Bill needed a friend as much as I did, and we gravitated to each other in spite of being opposites in several respects.

At school, we seemed to spend a tremendous amount of time smoking outside in front of the building. Bill was a cigarette smoker, as were most classmates at the time. I, on the other hand, started smoking a pipe in my senior year. Looking back on it, I cringe at the pretentiousness of the memory and I wonder what people thought of me at the time. But I really did smoke a pipe (take a look at my yearbook picture) and knew my tobacco. I didn't start smoking cigarettes until my freshman year in college. I was dating a beautiful girl from Louisville, Kentucky named Angela Cherry. She was the beautiful daughter of millionaire Wendell Cherry and she was a student at Hampshire College while I was attending Amherst. She drove an AMC Pacer, that odd little car that everyone mocked, but she loved. It was Angela who got me started smoking Nat Sherman cigarettes. Of course, no ordinary cigarette would have been satisfactory. If you were going to switch from a pipe to a cigarette, it would have to be something equally pretentious and obnoxious. I ended up smoking Sherman's from 1975 to 1985, when my wife Laura made me quit smoking entirely as a mandatory condition of having children.

Anyway, Bill McGill and I would spend lots of time outside in front of the Dalton building when we had free periods (when I wasn't in the darkroom) and we would hang out with Cathy Fire and with Cathy's friend Gita Mehta. Gita was the younger sister of Mimi Mehta, a classmate and friend of my brother Michael. (I believe I mentioned how that happened often.) Cathy was one of the cutest girls at Dalton, about 5'2" and roughly 100 lbs. and a scratchy, scraggly voice that did not match her face. She would have been great doing voice-overs for cartoons. Despite her size, she possessed more physical energy than Bill and me combined. Cathy would make Bill and me jog with her around the Central Park reservoir as her protection against molesters. By the time we made it around the reservoir—if we made it all the way around—Bill and I needed oxygen and a nap. Cathy was barely breathing hard.

Cathy and her family lived in an apartment on the corner of 79th Street and Park Avenue. I was envious of her 10-block walk to school. The first time I visited Cathy at home I approached the doorman and announced that I was here to visit Cathy Fire. He called upstairs and received clearance to admit me. As I walked into the building lobby, he directed me to a specific elevator and said, "You will take this elevator here." He wasn't particularly deferential, but he wasn't off-putting either; all business. I rode the elevator upstairs and the oddest thing happened. The elevator doors opened onto a small foyer with a single antique chair made of hand-carved wood and velvet cushions and side table with a Tiffany lamp. As I looked around wondering if I had gotten off on the wrong floor, a door to the foyer opened and I was greeted by an elderly Black woman.

"You're here to see Miss Cathy. Come in please, she'll be right out." I was led into a living room that certainly looked like a place where no one ever sat casually or did normal everyday things. A museum looked more casual and relaxing by comparison. The carpeting was so soft yet dense that it felt like your feet sank an inch when you stepped on it. There were no overhead lights. There was a table lamp near the Steinway grand piano. The rest of the illumination came from small lamps that hung directly over an assortment of large oil paintings that filled the room. All of them were quite good. Some of them were famous. It was a bright sunny day outside, but you could hardly tell from the heavy velvet curtains that covered all but a narrow vertical slit in the windows. I remember being overwhelmed by a voice in my head that screamed "Don't touch anything!"

A minute or two later, Cathy came bouncing into the room in a tee shirt and shorts, looking like perfectly normal Cathy, somehow oblivious and also perfectly at home in these extraordinary surroundings.

"Are you hungry? I make awesome grilled cheese and tomato sandwiches."

Still attempting to process my surroundings, I said, "There's only one door when you get off the elevator."

"This apartment is the whole floor", she said. "Isn't that ridiculous? Come on, let's get some lunch."

Cathy is one of the most effervescent people I have ever met. You can't help but feel happy and upbeat around her. But Cathy's family life seemed to be nothing but unrelenting darkness and tragedy. Cathy's dad was Sam Fire, a multi-millionaire who made his fortune factoring cash for the garment industry. (*Factoring is a financial transaction where one company purchases the Accounts Receivables of another company. This is commonplace in the garment industry, where the manufacturer must spend a great deal of money on materials, overhead and labor, long before they are able to sell their goods to a retailer. Another company—the "Factor"—comes in and offers to buy their Accounts Receivables, perhaps at 85 cents on the dollar. This enables the manufacturer to maintain critical cash flow.*) By all accounts, however, Sam Fire was not particularly interested in the more sentimental aspects of fatherhood. To say that he wasn't close with his children would be an enormous understatement.

I don't recall exactly when, but early in our high school friendship, Cathy's mom Viola died from cancer. Right in Cathy's early, extremely vulnerable teenage years. Not long after that, Cathy's oldest brother Hyatt committed suicide. Years later her other brother Philip "Sparky" Fire committed suicide as well. The deaths of her brothers hit Cathy like tandem sledgehammers. Cathy's family had more money than I could imagine, but money could not protect them from profound unhappiness. Cathy was—and still is, 45+ years after Dalton—one of my dearest friends, but there was never ever a moment when I was envious of her life. I learned from friends like Cathy and other classmates at Dalton never to envy their wealth. There were a lot of things about the very rich kids that were my classmates at Dalton that I didn't know or didn't understand. But one thing I did understand was that many of them—more than you would expect—were unhappy. It was very clear that money does not protect you from unhappiness. And sometimes it invites it.

As a result, I have always had an ambivalence toward wealth for myself. As an adult, I have always wanted to make enough money that I never had to worry about paying my bills or providing for my family. But never more than that. I wouldn't want it. I think I would be unhappy with it.

Most people assume that Black kids come from broken homes. Single-parent homes or dysfunctional homes of some kind. Yes, statistically, there are many Black households like that, but not as many as people assume. And it certainly was not true for me or my fellow Black classmates at Dalton. Every one of us came from homes with two parents that busted their humps for their families and made sure their kids had a better life and better opportunities than they did. Every one of us grew up in homes with very traditional values and fairly strict discipline.

Ironically, the same could not necessarily be said for many of our wealthier white classmates. It was pretty surprising to us how many of them grew up in dysfunctional households. I am not at all suggesting that this was true for all or even most of our classmates, but it was true for a lot of them. There were a lot of kids whose parents fell into a couple of different categories.

There were kids where the dad was an entire generation older than the mom. The kids were teenagers, but dad was in his sixties. Often this was the result of a second marriage. In any case, these dads were either too old to play an active role in their kids' lives, or they had already raised a previous set of kids and were simply not that into doing it all over again.

And there were kids whose parents were divorced. These kids spent their lives shuttling back and forth between parents based on elaborate custody arrangements. When these classmates invited you over to their home, you had to confirm which home they meant because they had homes at either parent.

And there were kids that had biological parents and also functional parents. The functional parent was usually a nanny, an older West Indian woman who—for all intents and purposes—raised the children. These kids had greater bonds and emotional attachments to their nannies than they did to their biological parents.

Like I said, money does not protect you from unhappiness. And sometimes it invites it. There are many people who might be quick to assume that the Black kids who attended Dalton at that time were naturally envious of their wealthy white classmates, that we coveted the things they had. Honestly, I can't think of a single Black classmate who ever expressed that sentiment, and I doubt that any of us ever felt that way.

CHAPTER 6

FRIENDS, DATING AND THE DALTON SOCIAL EXPERIENCE

RAYMOND SMALTZ

DOORMEN AND COUNTRY CLUBS

I CAN'T SAY THAT I HAD much of a choice when it came to the decision to attend private school, or with this dramatic upheaval in my life. I was expected to do my best, because my mother knew that if I could be successful in this environment, so could my younger siblings. And before I started classes, my Mother told me I had to put all of my focus on schoolwork and nothing else. She placed great importance on my making a good impression on the school and keeping up with my schoolmates. That warning also meant—NO ATHLETIC TEAMS!

Even though I never played any organized sports in public school, or with any outside youth organization, the prospect of playing on one or more of the Dalton teams was more than exciting for me. That is, until my Mom burst my bubble. She did make a deal with me, however, that if I got good grades during my first year at school, she'd "consider" allowing me to play on the middle school football and basketball teams once I was ready for 8th grade. That was the end of the negotiating process, meaning this was a non-negotiable deal and I had my marching orders for the end of '68 and the spring of '69. So, if I couldn't play on any of the school athletic teams,

I'd have to entertain myself playing touch football in Central Park, or in front of the school when they closed off 89th street between Lexington and Park Avenues during lunch, or in gym periods throughout the week. There was many a broken side-view mirror strewn along the pavement in front of Dalton by guys like me, Jeff Gates, Paul Driver, Nicky Blair, Doug Frank, Jason Ekaireb or little Louis Pacheco, a Hispanic kid who was almost half my size, but who also had a mischievous way about him. But out on 89th Street, even when we couldn't find a football and replaced it with a Frisbee, we'd have the same results. Of course, no one ever claimed responsibility for the carnage on the street and after a litany of complaints by residents on the block tired of paying for their damaged parked cars—we were basically asked to "cease and desist!" As for "Little" Louis Pacheco, I found him completely entertaining, as he taught me the fine art of folding a piece of paper into a small triangle for "finger football," as we did our best to shoot the triangle through each other's upright thumbs as if they were a pair of football goalposts.

As I mentioned earlier, I was practically six feet tall at 12 years of age, so I appeared a little older than I really was. And being the avid football fan that I was, I used to take on the older guys in my neighborhood on the weekend when they had their big touch football games. Those games would occupy the entire concrete field of Junior High School 45 on the property of Wagner Houses. The guys would be resourceful enough to find spray paint or large pieces of colored chalk, to draw their makeshift lines and mark the first down distances, as well as the out-of-bound areas. We would get out there and play from sun-up till sundown, or until one of the teams ran out of healthy players. Falling down on that hard concrete from a two-hand touch blow was a bitch, but if you wanted to play, you had better get up and not complain or you'd be embarrassed right out the park. I was even good enough to be picked for the big matches against other housing projects and brought home many a gash, cut or bruise to prove my mettle. Somehow, I just knew that playing on grass with equipment was going to be a hell of a lot more fun than suffering on the hard concrete, but it would have to wait. When it came to playing basketball, however, I wasn't quite as coordinated and would be flat-out embarrassed by the hard-core ballplayers in the projects. While I wasn't the last player picked during the summer months of '67, '68 and '69—the guys on the block weren't exactly fighting over me. But when I played during the Dalton gym periods, I really didn't have too much competition at my height other than David Sardi, who was even taller than I was in 7th grade, but was tragically uncoordinated. He was a one-man wrecking crew on the court, with the sharpest elbows in captivity and merited many an angry glare from me, followed by an occasional strategically placed elbow of my own.

I didn't comprehend the full extent of my athletic ability and how it would shape my time in school until near the end of the second term of 7th grade—we had an event called "Field Day," which was a Dalton tradition, held at the end of each term in the spring/summer at Riverside Park on the west side of Manhattan. Back then, the entire middle school would be let out of class, so that everyone could participate in various track and field athletic activities, where the 1st, 2nd and 3rd place participants in each activity: long jump, high jump, sprints, etc., would receive a different color ribbon. Unbeknownst to most of the middle schoolers, Field Day also allowed the team coaches to acquire a sense of the more athletic students in the various grades that they wanted to keep an eye on for their own middle school, junior varsity and varsity teams in high school. For me, it was a sort of "break out" moment because I won, or came in second place in several different events, including even beating my pal Kenwood "Woody" Dennard in a 60 or 70 yard sprint (Steve Postell was certain Woody was going to dust me). I ended my first Field Day at Dalton with numerous pats on the back and loads of attention—feeling pretty damn good about myself as I caught the eye of folks like Christa Quick, Doug Bessone, Duerward Middleton (who was one of a small handful of Black teachers in the school in '68 and would later become a tremendous mentor and ally), as well as Alan Boyers, the Director of Athletics for the school, as well as the Head Coach of the varsity football and basketball teams. Alan Boyers had a very particular and lasting part to play in my time at Dalton.

At the end of the school semester in the summer of 1969, I had a slew of invitations to hang out around the city with classmates, especially hanging out in Central Park, as well as being invited to the summer homes of wealthy families in the Hamptons. However, no matter how good I felt about my first successful year in private school, the reality of who I was and who I would become as a young Black man mingling with the upper crust of New York City, would unfold during that summer—like a cold slap in the face.

One such incident took place on Park Avenue, at the building of my classmate Stacie Winston. A group of classmates from our grade had a get-together planned for Central Park and we coordinated to meet at Susan's building before we walked toward the park. I remember turning the corner walking north on Park Avenue, and observed a short, unassuming doorman, hands behind his back standing in front of the building. I had a bag of lunch that my Mother prepared for me for the afternoon (what can I tell you—that was my Mom). As I approached, this short, red-faced man with glasses and a hat with the number of the building on it, impeded my path into the building and told me in an annoyingly nasal voice, "All deliveries are made to the back of the building!"

Then it hit me—this was another "Woolworths" confrontation. After giving up enjoying my vacation with my neighborhood friends and sweating through the entire summer of '68 preparing for private school, and completing my first year at Dalton keeping up academically with the "best of the best"—I was still a "NIGGER!" This incident would be my indoctrination to the world of the privileged throughout the wealthy dwellings of New York City, best exemplified by the dedication of each building's doorman to "keep out those who don't belong." This doorman's name happened to be Irving and he defiantly stood in front of the entrance of the building as he blocked my path. But this time, instead of freezing up in Woolworth's next to my little brother, I was determined to make this confrontation a memorable one. I loudly argued with him for the next ten to fifteen minutes as I insisted that I wasn't there to make a "goddamn delivery." This was probably Irving's first time confronting a Black man of my stature who refused to budge, so when I demanded that he call upstairs to the Winston household because I wasn't leaving until he did, he finally called up to the apartment. A very angry Stacie came downstairs to personally escort me to their elevator and up to her apartment. After that initial confrontation, Irving tried his best to be my "friend" whenever I showed up to visit the Winston family and he made it a point to go out of his way to acknowledge me. To this day, I still wonder what the hell the family told him to make him so damn accommodating.

I got another dose of reality that summer visiting my pal, Gregory Sloan and his family when they took me out to their summer home in Quogue for a long weekend. The ride seemed to take forever to the far end of Long Island, especially since up to that point in young life it was the longest car ride I'd ever taken. My family never owned a car except for an old, used Borgward that my uncle gave us, which was never made for a family of eight. That antique managed to get us to the beach a few times during a couple of long, hot summers, but my old man didn't look after the car at all and before we knew it, it was vandalized right in front of our building and eventually set on fire.

The grounds that the Stern's summer home occupied were amazing! According to Greg, the home was originally built in 1908 and once we hit the road that led to the house, it seemed to go on forever, like some rich estate in an F. Scott Fitzgerald novel. Before we even got near the house, we passed by several horses running around a huge pen. Each of the boys had their own horse, along with their own room, their own television and their own boat. Hell, if Greg had been old enough at the time, he probably would've had his own car, too! Greg didn't have a motorized boat like his older brothers Michael and Ron, but he did have a really neat Sunfish sailboat, that he patiently tried to teach me how to manage in the middle of Quantuck Bay. For me, it was a harrowing experience, because as much as I loved the idea of being out on the water, this Black kid from Harlem could BARELY swim. I didn't know the bow from the stern, or the mast from the jib, but because of either sheer stupidity, or bravery, I was determined to be of some use to Geoff in handling the sail and not getting knocked in the head with the boom when he yelled, "COMING ABOUT!"

After Greg finally trusted me enough with my pedestrian sailing skills to take an extended trip on the water, he and I sailed to the other side of the bay to a country club called the LaRonde Beach Club located in Westhampton Beach. There, we met up with a couple of his friends whose families also had tremendous residences all along the bay. It was like being on a Hollywood movie set. The club was exquisite with a fabulous swimming pool and luxurious beach chairs with wealthy women lounging around in fashionable straw hats, an assortment of sunglasses to rival a Saks Fifth Avenue display, being served mixed drinks in the late morning by cabana boys.

All of this wealth being flaunted was intimidating to me. More important, however, I was immediately made aware of the visual impact I made on the grounds by the turned heads and the "storm clouds" on the horizon in the form of several boys around our age. They approached my friend with menacing intent to try and intimidate him. We couldn't have been at the club more than 10-15 minutes before this occurred. No one openly used the word "nigger." Instead, they yelled at Greg for bringing me to the country club, told me I didn't belong there and why didn't I go back to where I belonged (which was going to be difficult because I couldn't sail by myself and I definitely didn't know how to drive).

All of a sudden, one member of this "LaRonde Beach Club Gang" tried to put their hands on Greg. Why did they do that? I've always hated bullies, I've always protected innocent folks that I was around from bullies and was filled with a rage that I could not manage or control. I pulled this idiot away from Greg, shoved him to the ground and a wrestling match ensued that was not going well for this assailant. My anger was palpable and even though these boys outnumbered my little Dalton sidekick and me, they weren't in any rush to be bleeding all over the pool area.

After the skirmish was broken up, no one from the club was remotely interested in Greg's or my side of the affair and we were unceremoniously ordered to leave under the watchful eyes of everyone at the club. We slinked off the property and through the front entrance, headed back to the Sunfish tied up at the dock. While the thought of *really* getting into a scrum with those punks crossed my consciousness, I was mindful of not bringing "all of my street" into the situation and didn't want to cause my friend any further trouble. He was already going to be knee deep in it once his folks found out. We never discussed what happened that afternoon when Gregory told his parents, but I barely fell asleep that evening in Greg's room thinking of what transpired earlier that day. Sadly, that incident ruined our weekend together and was a rude awakening not just for me, but for Gregory. Later in September, when school began again, and he didn't return to Dalton for eighth grade, I wondered whether our country club experience led his parents to find another school.

The country club confrontation, along with the "Wrath of Irving," and many other assorted smaller micro-aggressions in and around school, challenged my coping skills my first year at school and tempered the excitement that I once had prior to my attending Dalton.

Though my enthusiasm for the start of the school year was guarded, it did signal the fulfillment of the promise that my mother made to me regarding joining the school teams, as well as the beginning of my athletic career at Dalton. I passed all of my subjects with enough achievement that my

Mother gave permission for me to play football in the fall. So, the end of summer meant football practice on Randall's Island, located between Manhattan and Queens, connected by the Triborough Bridge. Randall's was a 25-30 minute walk across the bridge from my projects because the entrance to the footbridge was only a couple of blocks from my building. But even with the close proximity of the practice field to my projects, I was forced to ride the old, bumpy bus that took us from school over to the island for practice and then return to the school, passing my apartment building on Second Avenue on the way back to Dalton to shower. It seemed pointless to me and I vowed to figure out something to minimize my travel in later seasons, but those were the rules at the time.

When school started in 1969, it wasn't nearly the nervous exercise it was for me the year before. This time, I was eager to renew acquaintances with Dalton classmates, to walk through the halls of the building I had now mastered with a purpose and keen knowledge of where I was going and when I needed to be there. My new house was supervised by Dennis Phillips, who was a bit of a "pretty boy" history teacher at the school, causing all of the girls to giggle and squeal under their breath whenever he strolled around the halls of the school, or paced our house. I was the only person of color in my house. That was odd because another teacher, Ms. Hellman's house had several Black and Hispanic students in it; Jay Strong, Paul Driver, K.K. West, Rose Garcia and one Mr. Mark Robinson (the talented photographer of our class and who has been an inspiration to me since we reconnected in 2009). You'd think the school would've spread the wealth around a little bit more when it came to diversifying the *houses;* especially since the influx of Black and brown male students was still a relatively new phenomenon.

During this period, the girls at Dalton began to take an interest in me; although when cornered by any one of them, I was terribly awkward and shy. With all the after-school activities and parties I was invited to, there were many weekends when I would simply crash at Jason's after a school affair, or maybe someone else insisted I come spend the night at their place, so I didn't have to take the bus or subway all the way uptown after midnight. Of course, none of that would happen before a phone call home to clear everything with my mother. I remember being attracted to classmates like Martha Straus, or Allison Slon, and Jenny Jacobson, who were all kind of tall and cool to slow dance with because I was tall, but since I never had a girlfriend before attending Dalton, all of the "mating rituals" made me feel really insecure, as I clumsily attempted to woo a young Dalton lady. After many of these weekend affairs, I took an interest in one lady and soon discovered that many classmates believed we couldn't possibly be right for each other. In spite of all that, somehow, we were drawn towards one another.

Stacie Winston was an extremely bright, popular and diminutive young woman, who looked great in a pair of jeans, with a cute smile that was occasionally overshadowed by her braces on the top and bottom of her teeth. Back then, many of the female students at Dalton who wore braces weren't particularly attractive to me, but there was something different about Susan—something quite special. She was an "A" student. She sang and played the guitar and despite my initial experience of coming to her home with "Irving the doorman", her family greeted me with open arms whenever I visited.

Through whatever strange forces, the poor Black kid from Harlem and the popular young White girl from a wealthy Park Avenue family, found a common bond that forged a long lasting friendship that endures to this day. My mother never worried where I was going on a Friday evening or a Saturday afternoon during the fall and winter of '69, because while I was dating Stacie, she had the number to their home and trusted that I would act accordingly, and things would be fine. When it was late, she even let me spend the evening at their home on many occasions, where Stacie, with an occasional assist from her mother or younger sister, would make up a sleeping bag for me. Stacie's bedroom was literally the size of my parent's entire apartment and it was all very impressive to me because Stacie was my very first girlfriend and while we didn't exactly make a big scene or engage in much PDAD (public displays of affection at Dalton)—everyone knew we were an item. Stacie had already dated two of the other popular young guys in the middle school who I played football alongside, like Doug Frank, so her relationship with me raised eyebrows because of our races and the scornful way many viewed our connection.

While other students at Dalton had already had their first sexual experiences by the time they were entering their teens, Stacie and I never really got past the heavy petting stage, even though she'd end up with an occasional hickey on her neck that was questioned by all of her friends. But, at that moment in our young lives, the act of sex wasn't a huge priority—laughing together, sharing special moments and experiences together, and the occasional cuddling, was more than enough to sustain us. One of those special moments together was taking in a concert at Madison Square Garden in the winter of '69-'70. The musical lineup featured Grand Funk Railroad, the soon-to-be hot comedian Richard Pryor who was at his foul-mouthed best and a very, very tardy Sylvester Stewart, aka "Sly Stone," who was probably higher that evening than Pryor. The "contact" from the marijuana smoke wafting in the rafters of the Garden was incredible and even though neither one of us did any drugs (well, I can't fully account for Stacie, but I never smoked cigarettes or marijuana, or drank alcohol in school or during college), you couldn't help but get a buzz that night while digging the incredible sounds of some legendary rock groups. THAT was a real special night for both of us, as I stood on the floor and clapped till my hands were sore, as she stood on the seat beside me with one arm over my shoulder, as we enjoyed the amazing scene!

Everything that was happening to me seemed "too good to be true," and much to my ultimate dismay, it was. During the time Stacie and I dated, I was no longer invited to all of the same parties by the same students anymore. My school locker was vandalized with notes slipped in it about why I shouldn't date Stacie and should date my own kind—similar to some of the suggestions shouted at me from the Westhampton Country Club that summer.

I even caught a student (who to this day remains a mystery to me), stuffing a nasty note into my locker. It was this confrontation which tried my patience. I had enough and picked up this unfortunate student and violently threw him up against the lockers on the 6th floor while classes were going on. It took several school athletes in a nearby classroom to pull me off this sorry fellow. Afterwards I was summoned for meeting with the head of the Middle School, Mr. Casey. Fortunately, I wasn't suspended after that incident, especially since the note that was placed in my locker was read by Mr. Borger, who was one of the phys. ed. instructors at the school. He was an old basketball player who played with some decent Columbia basketball teams in the 60's and who would later scrimmage against the varsity athletes on weekends. He sat along with Mr. Casey and warned me about any future confrontations.

On another angering occasion, I had my coat stolen from my locker after I finished showering from practice and searched the hallway on the second floor, for someone from the school administration to plead my case. Mr. Barr, Dalton's Headmaster, happened to be in his office late that evening and listened to my plight. He loaned me the money for the taxi fare home, but I was unable to get a cab to drive me uptown on a rainy evening downtown (yes, trying to flag a cab in the city wasn't easy back then either). I was forced to walk from the bus stop back to my projects with no coat in the pouring rain, with only my book bag for any kind of shelter. I tried to explain to my Mother what happened with water dripping all over the kitchen floor, but her stern look told me all I needed to know about how to handle events like this in the future.

Finally, one evening when I was visiting at the Winston home, I accidently walked into the kitchen of Stacie's family, where her Grandmother uttered a racial slur about me and demanded to know why Stacie lowered herself dating me. Everyone around the table stopped what they were doing and turned to stare at me as I stood with a stunned and shocked expression. Once again, I was finding out the hard way that I was still nothing more than a nigger and had no special privileges—not even in this home. I remembered closing the door behind me as Stacie's mother, reprimanded the grandmother for her spiteful words. I wearily trudged to the beautiful Winston family living room, which featured an incredible grand piano on top of a sparkling white rug with the lights from the city shining in the background of the darkened room, as they illuminated the expensive paintings on the wall. I placed my head on top of my arm and I leaned forward, face down, on the piano—hiding my tears. This big, tough kid from the Wagner Houses, star of the football and basketball teams was severely wounded by a 70-year old grandmother. Stacie sat beside me as she tried her best to apologize and console me. She told me how her grandmother really didn't mean what she said, but I couldn't focus on anything around me, much less her words…everything in the room; from the piano, to the paintings on the walls, to Stacie's face, was blurred by my tears.

Our relationship was over, whether I wanted it to be or not. I could've dealt with the bullshit in school, those students who rejected our relationship were cowards and would never have confronted either of us face to face…as convicts used to say about certain prisons where they were incarcerated, "that was easy time," but I couldn't go back to the Winston home again. Knowing that certain family members didn't accept me would've been too much stress on me and too much stress on Stacie. Perhaps I was naïve about dating a well-to-do young white girl from Dalton. Things on the surface of our time together appeared uncluttered, but there were outside influences constantly gnawing away at the fabric of our relationship. The rest of that second semester was emotionally strenuous for me. Everything about Dalton took on a different note. Everything about other classmates' antics seemed trivial. I walked past friends that I would've normally engaged. I even adjusted my lunchroom schedule so that I ate alone. My time at Dalton would never be the same… again.

"Stand!"

Sly Stone was a poet of the 60's and 70's and the words to his smash hit, "Stand" spoke loudly to me. At one point in the song, he writes, "…There's a cross for you to bear—Things to go through if you're going anywhere." This line from his song meant so many things for so many people of all colors, but as a young Black man in the privileged world of Dalton, the words represented what I'd committed myself to, what I'd already suffered through in my short time there and what was yet to unfold. Either I was going to have to find a way to cope with the inequities, the pettiness, the heartaches, and the jealousies and the discrimination, or I was going to fail. As Sly wrote, "…You have to complete and there is no deal."

I made a promise to myself after breaking up with Stacie…I wasn't going to get involved with another white girl at Dalton—EVER! I wasn't interested in having to manage everyone's else's opinion of who I chose to date and why. It might have been a drastic solution to my situation, but it allowed me to deal with the pain of how much I still cared for Stacie, while still attending school together. I created a wall—a wall of security that would allow me to cope with the bullshit. If a few folks' feelings got hurt along the way, so be it—as long as they weren't mine.

Before the school year ended, Coach Boyers recruited those who he had plans for on the varsity football team the following season and we hit the weights religiously every other day as we gilded our bodies to prepare for the punishment we would face in the fall. In a few short months, I went from around 155 lbs. to 175 lbs., while maintaining, even increasing my speed. Some of the teachers and coaches got together on Saturdays with the varsity basketball team members and had some spirited full-court, balls-out, pickup games, which showcased some pretty good competition. Coach

Boyers supervised the entire day's activities, chose the teams and after the games were done, put us through some end of the afternoon line drills—just for good measure. He was old school before the term became a part of the national lexicon and enjoyed watching young men bent over in agonizing pain, as he prepared us for his "torture chamber" next season.

Lawrence Borger, the former Director of the Middle School, was a big man of at least 6' 6", and he played on Columbia's basketball teams of the late 60's and knew several of the players from those well regarded teams including former All-American Jim McMillian, who along with Rhodes Scholar Heyward Dotson helped the Columbia University team win the Ivy League title in the '67-'68 season. McMillian would later replace Hall of Famer Elgin Baylor of the Los Angeles Lakers and be an integral part of the Lakers NBA Championship team of 1971-'72. He and his former Columbia teammate Dotson, taught me some tough lessons on the court and even though I had grown to 6' 3" near the end of 8th grade, I was no match for the girth and slickness of these guys. I was also now banging bodies with Dalton's varsity players such as Kleon Andreadis, Pat McSweeney, Keith Brown, Steve Vlamis, the always chatty Jose Gomez and my school idol, Larry Stackhouse. Even Mr. Middleton brought his high-energy game to the fracas and taught some of the varsity guys a lesson about leaving him alone for an open jumper; as he talked smack going back up court. Guys like Geoff Lawrence, Curtis White and Rob Crichton, who all played that season on the junior varsity team, would soon become my teammates when the fall approached, but we competed every weekend together, all vying for playing time down the road. I relished the competition, enjoyed the camaraderie with my older classmates, as most of the guys forgot I was still a snotty-nosed middle-schooler and brought me into their circle. With my self-imposed exile from most of my middle school classmates, these guys made me feel part of their team, as well as part of the school and Coach Boyers couldn't help but notice.

The summer of 1970 brought about an opportunity to fill the void of friendships lost in private school, as I renewed and made "new" friendships from my neighborhood and Wagner Houses. The projects and surrounding tenements in East Harlem were riddled with junkies, dope-fiends and pushers, some of whom were Vietnam vets returned from the war, who all tried to make a dollar or to get a fix. While I attended Dalton in '68 and '69, a methadone clinic opened up right across the street, in-between our local barbershop and the corner drug store, which created a string of nodding patients all along the block for their daily dose. The aroma of "weed," "smoke" or "Mary Jane" (marijuana) could be scented in all of the surrounding blacktop courts where the guys played ball or simply hung out with no jobs and nothing else to occupy their time.

There was something else that I began to discover about my old neighborhood. If you went to a private or a specialized high school, your old buddies from the neighborhood now accused you of "acting white" or trying to sound like "white folks." I had a difficult time adjusting to "just hanging'" with some of the guys I used to play basketball and touch football with.

It was through a chance meeting with Shira Small, a young lady I had known from PS 80, that I would meet a teacher from Junior High School 45—right on my block, who would help me find a new purpose for my time away from Dalton. George Marchal, a white junior high school teacher from Dayton, Ohio, was an unlikely person to imbue young Black and Hispanic kids with a sense of pride toward their neighborhood, but he helped transform a decrepit old mattress factory on 122nd street, into a summer place where disadvantaged school kids improved their reading and writing during the summer months. He had a quick wit and a devilish smile in between puffs of his cigarettes. He played a mean, take-no-prisoners game of bid whist and even though he was a small, freckled-face man, he didn't take shit from any of the brothers in the neighborhood who tried to intimidate him. Once the community residents saw what he was trying to achieve for their kids—Marchal was officially protected. If you meant to do him any harm, it was at your own risk. He even had a photo spread entitled, "Summer On A Hot Block—East Harlem Neighborhood Tutorial Center" in the September 17, 1968 issue of **LOOK Magazine**. He and several of the block residents posed on the fire escape of the factory building that they cleaned up and turned into a place for learning. He recruited the brightest kids from his junior high school that went on to high school and college, as well as other high-achieving students from the neighborhood and he implored them to "give back" to their community. And this "Official Pied Piper of the Ghetto" recruited me.

My involvement with the Neighborhood Tutorial Center opened up an entirely new world for me, full of hope, friendship, compromise and self-satisfaction. The tutors, supervisors and students of the program, with Marchal as the head, became a "family" and they created a whole new focus for me. The NTC also allowed me to earn my own money for clothes and outside activities as well as purchase the books and materials I would need for the next four years of high school. There was no way that I could ask my struggling parents for any money. Seeing a check with my own name on it at thirteen brought a tremendous sense of satisfaction that was hard to describe (except when I noticed how much was deducted for taxes—DAMN!).

At Dalton, I had often witnessed my classmates disrespect their parents publicly. But none of that attitude was ever going to be tolerated in Norma Beatrice Smaltz's household. Once, in a momentary lapse of judgment, I complained to her about how poor we were and how we didn't measure up compared to my wealthy new classmates. Before I could finish my complaint, she slapped me with a force across my face that made my eyes hurt and wounded my pride. She let me know that she wasn't sending me to Dalton to bring back "attitude," and if I wasn't careful she'd remind me again that I was never too big to be disciplined. Well, in many ways, my new compatriots at the NTC were a constant "backhanded slap;" as they kept me honest on what we attempted to accomplish in our community, because none of us were any better than the other no matter the school we attended. We all pulled on the same rope for the betterment of the students we attempted to serve as well as save and it was their academic achievement we were committed toward.

Shira Small's older brother, Keith, became a close ally and true friend during my time at the NTC. Shira and Keith lived in the next building over from mine in Wagner along with their father. Keith was a couple of years older than me and also an honors student at Julia Richman High School on the east side of Manhattan in the 60's. He was extremely bright, very cool, and could "talk shit" while playing bid whist or spades with the best of us! We were inseparable as we toured Harlem and 125th Street together during the summer months. We checked out all the Afro-centric bookstores, especially Lewis Michaux's eclectic store on Lenox Avenue and 125th Street. Together, we bought every new album by James Brown, Curtis Mayfield, Isaac Hayes and all of the jazz artists featured on the CTI jazz record label in Wil's Record Shop near the corner of 7th Avenue. We attended concerts at the Apollo together and through our close relationship, Keith helped re-strengthen my ties with the troubled Black and Hispanic community of my roots, ever reminding me that here, no matter how bad circumstances were for our people, I would be welcomed. And it was up to young adults like us to help improve the environment. The summer of 1970 and the

Neighborhood Tutorial Center stirred a transformation in me that would redefine my commitment to my "Blackness" and how I would interact with the white students and administration of the Dalton School for the remainder of my high school years.

We teenagers, young adults and supervisors sweated our butts off in the old factory, coaxed and convinced these kids of our neighborhood that education was the ticket out of the ghetto and if they didn't buckle down and treat school seriously, they might succumb to be the very same junkies, prostitutes and pimps they saw every day on their way to school. Every kid had a one-to-one relationship with their tutor as well as other activities like trips to the various museums around the city, the zoos in Central Park and the Bronx, an occasional Yankee game in the bleachers at the old stadium and cook outs at a nearby state park.

Marchal was able to recruit several teachers from JHS 45 who provided an individualized lesson plan for each student and a guide for observing each pupil, so we could find new ways to motivate the disinterested or the disenchanted. We were even encouraged to visit the homes of every student, which sometimes had mixed results. Not every parent wanted to be told their child needed to eat something before they came to our program. Sometimes, in lieu of a home visit about a child's nutrition, we'd just reach into our own pockets and feed them ourselves, so we'd be assured a productive morning together until it was time for lunch.

By the end of summer, the results were near "miraculous" and every child in our program improved by several grade levels on the standardized reading and math tests provided by the local school board. I found a place where I belonged that summer—a place that was safe and nurturing, exciting and fun, as well as tremendously rewarding. I was now more emotionally prepared for my next semester at Dalton than I had ever been.

There were very few Black female students in the high school; which was surprising since Dalton was once an all-female institution. And the Black girls weren't being wooed by most of the Black boys because the boys, especially the star athletes, found it much easier to date or hang out with the white girls at the school. The Black high schoolers on the teams used to tell me, "they had to work too hard to get next to the sisters and it wasn't worth the trouble." So, bright, attractive young women like Lisa Peterson and Palestrina Patterson, who befriended me during my freshman year, ultimately left Dalton. Palestrina may have been dissatisfied with the overall social environment and the lack of attention from the brothers. Lisa said that after attending Dalton since lower school, she just needed a change.

One of Black female students was Shelly Anderson. She and I became friends through her family's connection with my Aunt Audrey Smaltz. Aunt Audrey was the longtime commentator for the Ebony Fashion Fair, which traveled around the country and around the world empowering Black women to be beautiful, stylish and classy. Shelly and her mother lived on the upper west side of Manhattan in a complex called Park West Village. Those of us Blacks who weren't so fortunate to reside there, called those Blacks who could afford to, "bougie." Shelly was a sophomore that sang in the school chorus with me. She was also one of the leading members of the Third World Culture Committee, engaged in many different Afro-centric and ethnic inspiring activities throughout the school term. Even with this busy schedule, she found time for acting which featured her in with many different school productions, and her easy-going disposition and friendliness enabled her to be easily welcomed into the social fabric of the school. Being from a "bougie" family probably helped a little bit too.

A particularly cute sophomore transfer who had a short stay at Dalton was Alana Weeks, whose father was a well-respected Black attorney in New York and her mother was well-connected socially in the city. Alana and her mom were members of the Jack and Jill organization, which according to their website "…is an African-American organization of mothers who nurture future leaders by strengthening children ages 2-19 through chapter programming, community service, legislative advocacy and philanthropic giving…." Back then, as far as we "poor Black folk" were concerned, it was just another group of "bougie negroes" who had a greater economic ability to control their own lifestyles and destinies, and enroll their offspring in the best schools in New York or around the country. Jack and Jill helped to place many young African American children like Alana in private schools. However, while her family was considered upper middle class, owning a beautifully maintained brownstone on 145th Street in Harlem, Alana was academically overwhelmed by Dalton and struggled during her short stay.

Even though she was a year ahead of me, we discreetly saw each other on several occasions outside of school, mostly because she didn't want to be seen hanging around a freshman. And although she thought I was "cute enough" to hang around, there was "the gap" socially and economically between poor and middle, to upper middle-class Blacks. Alana's mother, like Stacie's grand-mother in a different way, never believed I was good enough for her daughter because I didn't come from the proper pedigree. Oh sure, I got a few brownie points for being the nephew of Audrey Smaltz, who was well-chronicled in the New York social scene and fashion community, but it wasn't enough to overcome the obvious lack of wealth in my immediate family. And so, our relationship "fizzled out" before it ever really went anywhere during my fresh-man year. To me, it just appeared that finding someone to share experiences with and show my affections toward was a continuously, arduous and unpleas-ant exercise, full of obstacles that challenged my self-image as a handsome, virile young man from the projects and a student of an elite private school.

"You're Either Part of the Solution..."

Freshman year at Dalton was an awakening. I began to wonder how, why and where I fit into this social experiment that was private school. At the start of the semester, I was befriended by three upper-class students who helped to shape my understanding of the untold history of African Americans and Hispanics in our country and also opened my eyes to the inner workings of Dalton and how it just barely tolerated their minority students. Frank "Aswad" Sewer, Eduardo Padro and Jill Dickinson were all seniors at Dalton. They gave me a tremendous sense of pride and I began to gravitate away from most of my white friends from middle school whose penthouses, plush apartments and summer homes were once my personal playground. The three seniors helped strengthen my inner self for the more challenging aspects of Dalton.

They were the co-chairs of the newly formed Third World Culture Committee, which I joined as soon as I became a member of the high school. The Third World Culture Committee was formed at Dalton as a result of the influence of the Black nationalist movement and Black student unions that sprang up across America's college campuses and inner city high schools; much to the dismay of school administrators. Dalton had no curriculum for Black his-tory in America—just the part of American history involving slavery and how it was an important aspect of commerce in America's development. There was never anything that taught about the oppressive and cruel nature of slavery, or how it brought about the Civil War. There was no study of African-American inventors, writers, philosophers, etc., except for the standard struggles of Black figures like Harriet Tubman, Crispus Attucks, Frederick Douglass and of course, Martin Luther King, Jr. Greek and Roman history, the Renaissance and Restoration periods, the discovery of the New World, on through the establishment of the colonies and the American Revolution, the Civil War, the Spanish American war, the Depression and both World Wars in Europe and the Far East were all covered in great depth and detail. Black students at Dalton were calling for a part of their progressive liberal arts education to include aspects of Black and Hispanic studies and culture in the same way other academic institutions were being challenged across the country in the late sixties and early seventies. In the book, "Black Power—The Politics Of Liberation," Stokely Carmichael and Charles Hamilton made a powerful argument:

> *The concept of Black Power rests on a fundamental premise: before a group can enter the open society, it must first close its ranks. By this, we mean that group solidarity is necessary before a group can effectively form a bargaining position of strength in a pluralistic society. Traditionally, each new ethnic group in this society has found the route to social and political viability through the organization of its own institutions with which to represent its needs within a larger society.*

Sewer, Padro and Dickinson were determined to "close our ranks" and launch a student committee that would be the stimulus for building an inclusive academic curriculum. In his book, "From Black Power To Black Studies," the author Fabio Rojas, highlights this very movement:

> *Between 1966 and 1973, Black studies was a pressing issue on college campuses as a direct result of the civil rights movement, a rise in nationalist sentiment, and student mobilization. Groups such as the Black Panthers and chapters of the Student Non-Violent Coordinating Committee (SNCC) became prominent features on campuses and were at the front of the Black studies movement.*

I became fascinated with Stokely Carmichael's group, the Student Non-Violent Coordinating Committee and the Black Panther Party and their programs that aided the poor and the disenfranchised in the Oakland community and was ground zero for affiliates across the country. I felt a kinship to their community-based programs through my summer with the Neighborhood Tutorial Center. Not only did we supplement the education of the kids in our own community, but we fed them as well. And for many, that was either their most nutritious meal or quite possibly their only meal of the day. All of this Black pride and acknowledgement of the greatness of our race spurred me to let my Afro grow to its fullest (much like Angela Davis) and to wearing an army fatigue jacket like the Panthers (supplied by my older brother Dwain, who enlisted in the Marines and brought back some of his old gear). I grabbed anything he was willing to give me when he visited home from overseas and I decorated my jacket with the peace sign and Black Power patches on the front pockets and shoulders.

The formation of Dalton's Third World Culture Committee did not occur without controversy. Eddie Padro and Frank Sewer were called into Donald Barr's office to discuss the committee and their issues with the school. According to Eddie, Barr made it perfectly clear that he opposed the creation of this committee and thought it constituted an unwelcome and unwarranted militance toward the school. Padro and Sewer pleaded their case to Barr, citing the issues of the times, making clear that there was a movement not just at colleges around the country, but rising up in public and private secondary schools as well. Another excerpt from Rojas' book explains this succinctly:

> *The African American community needed its own educational institutions for the cultivation of talent and preservation of culture. Because of a long history of neglect by most colleges and universities, African Americans should take the* initiative to create their own institutions and knowledge base.

Ultimately, the argument made by Eddie and Frank somehow persuaded Donald Barr just enough to save the committee from being disbanded before it was formed, and we were now one of the recognized student committees at the school. But the "brass ring" of creating some sort of Black and Hispanic Studies program was summarily rejected.

I met Kojo Mbogba Odo, an extraordinary Black man who made a powerful impression on me, through Eddie and Frank and the Third World Culture Committee. Kojo was a counselor at the non-profit organization, "Boys Harbor," on Madison Avenue and 104th Street, (now called "Boys and Girls Harbor"), which has been serving underprivileged children and their families from Harlem, East Harlem and the Bronx, for many years. Kojo was one of the first Black men I'd ever met who wore dashikis and Nehru jackets, had his hair braided in various styles, a pierced nose and dozens of silver bracelets from Africa and the Caribbean on both of his arms. Although he appeared eccentric to the average person, his intellect, his eloquence and his purpose in life—to teach young Black and Puerto Rican children about their ancestors' real contributions to history—was quite impressive. The textbooks he used were written and published by African, Caribbean, Hispanic and other "scholars of color;" historians who studied the true wretchedness of the slave trade and the middle passage and its impact on many of the different cultures of the world. My understanding of this country and how Black people were treated would be changed forever.

Those new relationships—from the NTC, to the members of the TWCC (Third World Culture Committee), to Kojo and Boys Harbor—all helped to fill a void in my life at home. My relationship with my father had deteriorated to either shouting matches, or simple avoidance. My mother and he were merely co-existing under the same roof and there were no visible signs of love between them, just an acceptance of their responsibilities as parents. At least that was my mother's outlook on things. My father didn't take the whole parenting part of marriage very seriously. Years later, as an adult, I sat down with my mother and asked her why she stayed with him for so many unfulfilled years. She explained to me in a very matter-of-fact tone that raising five young Black men in Harlem was no easy feat and she felt she needed the physical specter of our father to keep us in line—to discipline us when it was absolutely necessary. I thought about the type of strength and fortitude it must have taken for her to endure those years of neglect, emotional abuse and disrespect by my father, while simultaneously being discriminated against and passed over for promotions at the Metropolitan Museum of Art. All the while scraping the funds together from her job to put three of her six children through private school. She was and is an incredibly strong and principled woman.

CHAPTER 7

ACADEMICS & ATHLETICS

MARK ROBINSON

*"The Negro race, like all races, is going to be saved by its excep-
tional men. The problem of education, then, among Negroes
must first of all deal with the Talented Tenth; it is the problem
of developing the Best of this race that they may guide the Mass
away from the contamination and death of the Worst, in their
own and other races."*

THESE ARE THE FIRST TWO sentences of "The Talented Tenth", an
essay published in 1903 by W.E.B. DuBois as the second chapter of
his book, "The Negro Problem." DuBois makes the argument that the best
and the brightest African Americans—the "talented ten percent"—must
be provided with superior education in order for racial progress to be made.
The ten percent will go on to become leaders through their superior education and will help to bring about positive societal change through their
leadership. The notion of the Talented Tenth, and its role in the uplift of
the Negro race, was DuBois' most significant intellectual and ideological
thesis. It supported the rise and development of historically Black colleges
and universities and anticipated the Harlem Renaissance of the 1920s. The
idea was both elitist and powerfully optimistic, perhaps even inspirational.
Over the past century, literally thousands of social, educational and political

organizations were founded upon this principle. Many are still in existence, reflecting a substantial segment of Black America today who endorse this philosophy.

It is fair to ask and to wonder, was Donald Barr (or any of the trustees) familiar with DuBois' essay on the Talented Tenth when they contemplated their decision to admit a select few gifted Negroes into the elite educational institution of the Dalton School in the mid-1960s? Did they embrace DuBois' thesis that by providing superior education to the best and brightest Negro minds, they were actively supporting and encouraging broadscale social change? Was that—to borrow a phrase—the "Dalton Plan"? After all, isn't that what elite private schools like Dalton are for?

I cannot answer what may have been in Donald Barr's head and heart. I do not know how much of DuBois' thesis of the Talented Tenth he knew or understood or embraced. I do know, however, that Donald Barr's academic credentials suggest that it is quite likely that he had a thorough familiarity with these concepts. As a student at Columbia University, Barr majored in math (mainly statistics) and anthropology. While studying for his Ph.D., Barr taught classes at Columbia in sociology and political science. Issues of socio-economic uplift were part of his curriculum. While he was a graduate student, the School of Engineering at Columbia asked Barr to oversee its efforts to spot promising elementary and secondary school science students, including girls, and enlist them for advanced training at the school to help them rise to the college level. Donald Barr was in charge of recruiting the "talented tenth" in science and engineering for the university. He got the concept. He was fully onboard. His next assignment was as the new headmaster of Dalton.

Among the minority students at Dalton during my time, there was never any explicit discussion—among ourselves or with others—that our presence at Dalton signified some kind of talented tenth. I doubt that most of us were sufficiently conversant in the ideas and essays of W.E.B. DuBois to do that. (At least not until the Third World Culture Committee had begun to take root.) But make no mistake, we knew why we were there. We understood all too well the importance of our place at Dalton. We were there for our families. We were there for our communities. We were there to build shoulders that others could someday stand upon. Even at age 12 or 13, and certainly in our upperclassmen years, we were conscious of the responsibility we carried and the expectation that we would make something of ourselves. For ourselves. For others.

"To whom much is given, of him shall much be required."
Luke 12:48

In Dalton's eighth grade class overall, there were 99 students. Eight were Black and three were Hispanic. Given the very elite—and very expensive—profile of the school, those numbers were not that bad. Under Headmaster Donald Barr's leadership, the trustees and administration of Dalton had made a decision in the mid-1960's to embrace diversity and—at least in terms of recruitment—had done a pretty decent job of it. Dalton had become measurably more diverse than it had been just a few years before. But recruitment was only one small part of successfully transforming the institution. It was still an open question whether Dalton was ready, willing and able to master all of the other challenges. As a school, especially as a school with a distinct pre-eminent educational philosophy and legacy, Dalton had a responsibility to understand, engage, inspire, motivate and educate its students. Dalton was understandably proud of its record of doing this job very well for half a century.

Perhaps, however, it was easy to be successful when your students pretty much all fit into the same mold; when all your students were white, affluent and the beneficiary of quality education virtually from birth. Was Helen Parkhurst's Dalton Plan still a brilliant success if it only succeeded with a certain kind of student and not with others? Did a privileged education only work for the privileged? The question sounds simple enough, but the cultural, social and intellectual implications for national educational policy were enormous. And this simple question gave rise to distinct and sharply conflicting factions within the Dalton solar system.

There were those who were heavily invested in defending and promoting the enduring legitimacy of Helen Parkhurst's educational philosophy and wisdom. For these disciples, there could be no greater validation than the ability to demonstrate how Parkhurst's Dalton Plan could turn even the most under-privileged minority students from the most neglected corners of New York City into bright, polished young scholars who could apply to—and gain admission to—America's elite ivy league colleges and universities. For this faction, Dalton's diversity recruiting was in service to a grand educational experiment that would prove not only that Helen Parkhurst was brilliant, but that they were brilliant too. And by the way, it didn't matter much if these educators did their own liberal tinkering with the original Dalton Plan to adapt to a more contemporary vision of how Dalton should operate. As long as it was still called "Dalton," any alterations that were deemed necessary should simply go unchallenged.

This faction also represented an interesting paradox. They were committed to the success of Dalton's new minority students because they were committed to the successful validation of their educational approach. They wanted—and needed—to be proven right. This was a competition of ideas and they wanted to win. At the same time, however, they were not in any meaningful way committed to the minority students themselves. To them, the young Black boys and girls (but most especially the boys) were little more than man-sized lab rats. We did not have our own destiny, our own identity or our own dignity. We were experimental subjects. What's funny—or perhaps not—is that it did not seem that anyone else at Dalton had any awareness or recognition of this paradox except us lab rats. We knew, even if we were the only ones who did.

In her 1992 book, "The Dalton School: The Transformation of a Progressive School", Susan Semel offered her own interpretation of the school's decision to admit Black boys to the high school.

> "An interesting experiment, too, was attempted by trustee Lawrence Buttenweiser, in accordance with Dalton's traditional commitment to integration. In May 1968, he announced at a board meeting that the school was searching for fifteen Black and Puerto Rican children "whose need is total" from a geographic area around East 104th Street. Furthermore, he stated that entrants would be in grades one through four; contributions of $2,500 per year for twelve years would be sought for each child, and that there were six applicants ready for acceptance. To help children with adjustment problems, a part time psychological social worker would be added to the staff."

Well, for starters, I have to take issue with Ms. Semel's use of the phrase "Dalton's traditional commitment to integration", since those words are not supported by any objective facts or historical record. Dalton's commitment to integration—such as it was—was as new as a bright shiny penny. More important, however, Ms. Semel references entrants to "grades one through four" in Dalton's integration experiment, while completely ignoring the larger and more significant group of minority students being admitted to the middle and high school grades. This is where the school's "transformation" was genuinely taking place. This omission seems hard to explain or justify, since Ms. Semel was teaching history in the high school at the time. I'm pretty sure I had a class with her.

Ms. Semel goes on to observe:

> "Many of the children came from families not committed to the school's particular philosophy, and thus they may not have received appropriate support from the home. Additionally, some of these children were verbally disadvantaged compared to their Dalton counterparts in the use of standard English and middle class communication codes, and quick to use physical actions rather than words when in conflict with their advantaged peers."

It seems very clear from the tone of her account that Ms. Semel, a member of the Dalton faculty at the time, felt very strongly that the "experiment" to admit Black boys into the upper grades was misguided at best and predictably doomed to failure.

I'm sorry, but I believe Susan Semel could not have been more wrong in her observations and conclusions about the minority students who attended Dalton. I cannot speak scientifically or comprehensively about all of the minority students who attended Dalton, but in my five years as a student, and in my many years as an alumnus, I have known a great many of these minority students. I am certain that I know them better than Ms. Semel. She wrote, "Many of the children came from families not committed to the school's particular philosophy..." This is simply wrong. The minority kids who went to Dalton came from families that spanned the socio-economic spectrum, from very poor to very well off. There was no financial common denominator. But every single one of these families embraced the school's philosophy and the value and importance of quality education with far greater zeal and passion than the typical Dalton parent. They understood the transformative power of education—particularly a Dalton education—and invested their children with all of their hopes and prayers for it, usually at great personal sacrifice. Every minority student who attended Dalton was different in his or her own unique way, but this they had in common. This, above all else, they shared.

Even in my own family, tuition and financial circumstance were different for each of the three children that attended Dalton. When my Aunt Milly attended Dalton, she and her parents were unequivocally poor. They were just getting by on my grandfather's income and entirely unable to afford tuition at Dalton. If the school had not offered to cover all of Milly's tuition and expenses, the opportunity simply would not have been possible. When my brother Michael attended Dalton, nearly twenty years later, our parents were "comfortably middle class." But middle-class families do not send their children to elite private schools. Dalton would have been a budget buster. And so—again—if the school had not offered Michael a full scholarship, he would have remained at Stuyvesant, also a good school, but a tuition-free public school. And that is very important.

By the time that I attended Dalton, our parents' income was somewhat better. My dad was working two jobs; in the day at my old elementary school and at night at the Post Office at Kennedy Airport. My mom had received a nice promotion at Time Magazine. But our household income was not substantially better than it was a few years before. But this time Dalton did not rush to offer me a full scholarship like my brother before me. Instead, they sent my parents a thick packet of financial aid application forms and encouraged us to apply for a possible scholarship. My parents took a hard look at the financial aid forms—which seemed to them to be incredibly intrusive—and made the difficult decision that no matter the sacrifice, they were going to send me to Dalton without financial aid from the school. They would pay full tuition, just like Dalton's wealthiest parents, even if it turned our entire household budget upside down. Which, of course, it did.

Three different financial circumstances. Three different family members. One simple shared truth for our parents and grandparents; the unwavering commitment to get us the best possible education that they could. And that was absolutely no different from every other minority family that sent their children to Dalton.

I am sure that it was assumed at Dalton—by both faculty and students—that the Black kids were all attending Dalton on scholarship, that we were all charity cases for Dalton. That was the obvious stereotype. The truth, now that we have interviewed many of our fellow Black students from those early years, is that many of us were not on scholarship. And among those kids who were on scholarship, the story we heard again and again was that our parents made a conscious and principled choice to accept only a partial scholarship while paying a part of the tuition themselves. For these parents, having some financial skin in the game was their way of retaining a degree of dignity and a degree of power over what happened to their children at this expensive private school.

Earlier in her book, Ms. Semel talks about the tenure of Charlotte Durham, Dalton's headmistress from 1942—1960 and heaps praise on Ms. Durham for revitalizing the school during a low point in its history. It was during this time that Dalton admitted its very first Black students, including my aunt Millicent Thomas, with a notable progression of others to follow. And yet Ms. Semel could spare only three words to report on this milestone in Dalton's history.

> "Charlotte Durham served Dalton as headmistress for eighteen years. She reunited a faculty torn by factionalism, revitalized a financially floundering institution, ***introduced racial integration***, continued the Dalton Plan, and routinized and gave the school an air of respectability."

How many words does the topic deserve? I don't know, but I'm pretty sure it is more than three words.

There was another faction that played a critical role in our presence at Dalton. They were all good intentions and not much else; all heart and not much head. These were the folks who believed passionately in two basic truths. First, that minority students had an equal right to the kind of education that Dalton could provide, and that unless these students were able to attend schools like Dalton they were being cheated out of their rightful opportunity for a prosperous, meaningful future. These folks saw themselves as missionaries gathering up as many of us poor Black kids as they could. The other truth that they believed was that our mere inclusion into Dalton automatically made Dalton a better place. They were early believers in the virtue of diversity for its own sake, that Dalton's teachers and students (and perhaps even parents) would become better people as a result of their exposure to and interaction with Black people. They were, of course, absolutely 100% correct. But it would take Dalton decades to recognize and understand this.

That was all well and good. And without the passionate participation of these advocates a lot of us, including myself, might never have attended Dalton and surely would not have graduated. Without these allies, Dalton might never have evolved beyond the quaint progressive private girls' school that it was for the first half of the twentieth century. These parents and trustees were missionaries, social warriors. But they didn't have the first clue what to do with us once we got there. They had absolutely no awareness or understanding of what challenges we might face, nor how to support us with the tools and resources to confront those challenges.

And it was going to take a lot more than smiles and hugs for us to make it through Dalton.

Lastly, there was a sizeable segment of the Dalton community who viewed us incoming Black students as barbarians at Dalton's gate. In their eyes we were an existential threat to their definition of Dalton. Dalton simply could not be what it was if we were there. This was, ironically, a diverse group. There were trustees and administrators who believed that the propagation of minority students at Dalton would trigger financial chaos with the needless expenditure of scholarship money compounded by the anticipated decline in alumni donations. They were certain that Dalton's coffers would quickly dry up, and all for the unworthiest of causes. There were parents who happily paid Dalton's sky-high tuition because the school's reputation bought their child admission to an elite college. These parents were convinced that Dalton's prestige would suffer and that their child's competitive edge would be dulled. Although these parents fully expected Black students to be bringing drugs into the school, this was not something they cared that much about. This was, after all, the late 1960's. These parents—and their pampered children—had far more drugs in their homes than any Black kid could ever afford. In fact, it was the rich white kids who were the school's most active dealers and suppliers. But what these parents did care a great deal about was the dreaded prospect that one of those Black boys at school might decide he wanted to date their daughter. That was taking the whole sixties social experimentation thing a bit too far.

And there were the faculty members—many of them—who had come to Dalton not motivated by a love of teaching, but motivated by a love of teaching *at Dalton*, and knowing that they were teaching the "best" students at the "best" school. Dalton was resume gold. It was your ticket to teach in virtually any prep school you wanted. It was also a huge ego boost. Many of these faculty were themselves the products of privileged upbringings. The Dalton world was their world; where they were comfortable, and where they felt they belonged. They did not feel it was where we belonged. These faculty members were proactive on two fronts. They lobbied aggressively that Dalton must apply the highest possible academic standards to its diversity recruiting. If Dalton was going to admit minority students, those students needed to be only the very best and brightest. Otherwise they would not survive Dalton, did not deserve to be there, and undermined the reputation that Dalton had earned. Of course, these faculty could not imagine that such students actually existed, little Negro unicorns capable of keeping up with whatever Dalton threw at them. These faculty couldn't imagine . . . us. But Dalton's recruiters and admission committee kept faith with the demand for high standards, so they found and returned with some of the most remarkable minority students in the city. Consequently, our presence at the school bred incomprehension, intolerance and indignation. It was a classic case of "Be careful what you ask for, you may get it."

When my brother Michael came to Dalton after attending Stuyvesant for his freshman year, Dalton assigned him to a "remedial" math class, assuming that he would need some extra help to catch up to the other Dalton students. I have heard this story told over and over again by other minority students. Dalton faculty and administrators accepted as fact that minority students were simply not at the same level as the white students and that we would need a special helping hand. Of course, they were happy to offer their hand. They were liberals, after all. It was the least they could do.

After a few weeks of sitting through remedial math, my brother Michael was transferred to advanced math.

I have spoken to several of my Black alumni classmates about their favorite teachers at Dalton and their least favorite teachers. No one disliked a teacher because they were tough. In fact, the toughest teachers were usually the favorites. They were the ones who made higher learning possible for many of us. And, fortunately, they were in the majority. I think that is worth repeating. Most Dalton teachers were terrific teachers. The least favorite teachers were often the ones who just didn't give a crap. And they were the ones whose dislike for minority students was conspicuous and palpable, teachers who made certain we knew how they felt about us.

One of those teachers was Cameron Hendershot. Mr. Hendershot was a social studies teacher at Dalton with a dry, acidic manner. I'm sure that when he was among his friends and peers, he was charming and charismatic. He had an obvious wit. But when he spoke to me it always seemed that he had an unpleasant taste in his mouth, and he couldn't wait to walk away. One year, I took a course with Mr. Hendershot on the History of the City of New York. New York has a great and colorful history and I enjoyed much of the subject matter of the course. But early in the semester Mr. Hendershot offered his own perspective to the class. He said that New York was once a great city, but not anymore. According to him, the unrestrained influx of immigrants from many different countries specifically over the past 20 years had quickly turned New York into a "mongrel city" with no traditional culture and no core identity. He said that the white population of New York was dying out, crushed under the weight of immigrant and ethnic expansion and growth. This perspective would go on to be a theme throughout the course. He might as well have titled the course "The Death of a Once-Great City" because he was convinced that that all of us ethnics had made New York an unlivable dystopia.

The other area where these recalcitrant faculty members were proactive was in the classrooms where they encountered the new minority students.

It is easy to believe that academic performance is a reflection of student meritocracy, that good grades go to those students who invest the most effort to learn and to those students who are most able to learn, who are best equipped to receive learning. If you didn't get a good grade, you either didn't try hard enough or you simply don't have what it takes. But academic meritocracy is only as real as you believe it is. The moment that you begin to question these beliefs, the image in front of you suddenly is not as in focus as it seemed just a moment ago. If you question the objectivity of the teachers who assign the grades, are you still as certain which American History essay deserves an A and which deserves a B? Every teacher has favorites, as well as students they just don't like. But what if all the students that the teacher doesn't like happen to be Black and brown? Is anyone really noticing other than those Black and brown students? And if you were a Black or brown student who wanted to complain about your grade, you don't seriously expect the school administration to take the side of an unhappy teenager over the word and reputation of a teaching professional. Aside from the fact that culturally the administration and the faculty were members of the same tribe, a faculty member accused of racism could sue the school. A student had no such power.

And lest you think that subjects such as math and science left little room for subjective grading by the teacher, there is always the opportunity to evaluate students on the basis of "effort" and "classroom participation" and "shows an understanding of the subject." If the teacher never calls on you, your classroom participation ends up being non-existent, your frustration rises and your interest declines. And if you try to speak up because you have something to say, something to contribute to the discussion, don't be surprised if you are labeled a "disruptive influence" in the classroom. The expectation—by both Dalton faculty and administration—was that incoming minority students would be wholly unaccustomed to the more civilized and genteel manners of a prep school classroom, that there would need to be an acculturation process. This expectation (despite being mostly wrong) was documented in Susan Semel's book on Dalton's history. So, if a teacher suggested that a minority student was struggling to adapt, this assessment surprised no one (except, of course, the minority student).

A few years ago, Dalton hosted its own screening of "An American Promise", a documentary about the experiences of two fiercely bright young Black boys who attended Dalton approximately from 2000 to 2012. Many African American Dalton alumni attended the screening, including several of my classmates. The period covered in the documentary was more than 30 years after the time that we attended Dalton, but the experiences of these two boys were hauntingly familiar. As we watched the film and heard their teachers talk about disruptive behavior in the classroom and how the boys were "struggling to adapt" to Dalton's culture, several of us sat in Dalton's theater and wept as our own memories and emotions overcame us.

Not all of Dalton's faculty were adversaries. Not all wanted to see us fail so that this terrible, terrible idea could finally be abandoned. Some teachers were simply nice people, men and women with good hearts and good intentions. They were welcoming and encouraging. Of course, those nice people assumed that they were doing charity work by welcoming Black and brown kids into Dalton. As happy as they were to have us there, they never actually believed that we possessed the academic and intellectual rigor to keep up with their "regular" students. Upon arrival at Dalton, most of us were assigned to "remedial" classes irrespective of what we might have been doing previously. To be clear—Dalton was a very different educational experience for just about all of us, and that required adjustment and adaptation. None of us simply dove into the pool and swam perfectly right from the start. Dalton was, after all, another planet, another world. But none of us fit their expectations of poor ghetto kids who were tragically and pathetically in over their heads. To Dalton's delight, and very much to their surprise, that was not us. In ways that weren't always apparent to us, and in ways that weren't always beneficial to us, we were genuinely exceptional. And whether they were prepared to do so or not, Dalton had to adjust and adapt to the changes that we brought to the school.

Most importantly, however, there were men and women at Dalton who were truly remarkable teachers and gifted mentors. Dalton was indeed blessed with more than its fair share of inspirational instructors whose impact on the lives of their students was indelible. I have several favorite teachers from my time at Dalton, people from whom I learned a great deal, but there were a few that were genuinely unforgettable. Joe Frank taught me how to write, perhaps the greatest gift anyone has ever given me. Joe frank left Dalton around the time that I graduated. He went on to become a hugely successful writer and radio monologist, frequently performing to packed theaters across the country. Yves Volel taught me the meaning of intellectual curiosity, what it means to love learning. Janet Greene taught me how to look in the mirror and see myself, to understand what I saw in my own reflection. I know that there are others who are genuine Dalton legends, names that get mentioned more often. I don't dispute their rightful place in Dalton's history. But these three were heroes to me.

My academic experience at Dalton—our experience at Dalton—is inextricably intertwined with the school's faculty; a group of men and women who were particular and peculiar to Dalton. I am certain you would not find any of them in a New York City public school classroom and probably not in any of the other private schools either. A French aristocrat taught American and European history. A French count taught French while a Hungarian countess and an aristocratic Yugoslavian, raised in France, taught French and Russian. The high school was headed by a descendent of an aristocratic White Russian family. Apparently, headmaster Donald Barr believed that the natural choice for who should mentor, teach and discipline the children of New York's wealthy elite would be European aristocracy. One might be forgiven for concluding that Dalton's boys and girls were being taught how to become princes and princesses.

When we came to Dalton, Dimitri Sevastopoulo was newly appointed as the head of the high school, a job for which he was wholly unqualified and had no credentials except for his aristocratic pedigree and the fact that he was a protégé of Donald Barr. Barr was meticulously crafting a new image for Dalton as the "hot/elite" school that attracted students—and dollars—from the same cohort. To the degree that image took precedence over substance, Sevastopoulo wasn't so much hired for the job as he was "cast" for it.

Dimitri Sevastopoulo was in his early 30's, tall and one of those people who is all too aware of how good looking he is. He would prowl the school hallways in his three-piece bespoke suits like a lion choosing his next meal. By the time of my senior year Sevastopoulo had left the school, perhaps deciding that he had gotten everything he wanted from Dalton and it was time to move on.

There was another teacher that Headmaster Donald Barr was quite fond of, although for very different reasons. Gambino Roche was a Cuban political refugee who taught Spanish at Dalton, although it is unclear whether he possessed any teaching credentials or experience. "Señor Roche" might well have been some member of the Batista regime before coming to America. It certainly was not hard to imagine him proudly wearing a fascist military uniform. A short, somewhat stocky man, his chest was always puffed up and an American flag always adorned his jacket lapel. He enjoyed intimidating and brow-beating students, both in class or wherever he encountered them. Again, it was not hard to imagine that Roche had experience in the art of interrogation.

Señor Roche had unabashed disdain for Dalton's spoiled, soft, leftist rich kids. And this was, I believe, a big part of his appeal to Donald Barr. Roche could express his distaste and condescension toward the students openly in ways that would have been politically problematic for Barr. In this specific area, Roche was Barr's proxy mouthpiece, his surrogate insult comic. And yet, as much as Roche disliked the rich white kids, his true animosity was reserved for the minority students, the Black and brown kids. Señor Roche felt we were unworthy of attending such an important school. He felt that second class people were supposed to attend second class schools. In his mind, there was no way that any of us belonged or that any of us could possibly succeed there, even if that meant occasionally putting his own thumb on the scale.

I'm not sure how Señor Roche felt about his colleagues in the faculty at Dalton, but I looked recently at my old high school yearbook and saw a photo that might be revealing. There is a page of photos from the Fall Festival, a carnival celebration at the school. Several of the photos show teachers who volunteered to stick their faces through a giant plastic sheet so that students who paid for the privilege could toss giant wet sponges and water balloons at them. Rather than volunteer to make himself a target (which would have been a huge fundraiser), there is a photo of Señor Roche pitching a water balloon at another teacher.

I took Spanish under Señor Roche for eighth and ninth grades. Both years he gave me an F, requiring me to attend summer school to make up the class. This, of course, significantly interfered with my ability to have a summer job, which was essential to having any summer money. And money was essential to having any kind of summer life. My parents were extremely unhappy and troubled by my failing grade. It was, after all, my poor grade in French at IS 59 that brought me to Dalton in the first place. My parents wanted—and needed—to be reassured that the extraordinary effort and expense of getting me into Dalton was not going to turn into an inevitable failure. For me, the pressure and stress were enormous. I could not let my parents down. I could not let myself down. I had something to prove to everyone.

Both summers, under different teachers, I got an A in Spanish. After the first summer, when I returned to school with my A, Señor Roche told me that he was not impressed with my grade. "Women teachers do not grade seriously," he said. When I passed along his comment to Señora Lemme, she muttered something under her breath and shook her head. Completing my high school language requirement was about as needlessly painful and humiliating as it could possibly be. I got through it, but between French at IS 59 and Spanish under Señor Roche, the emotional scar tissue has never fully healed. The wound remains just under the surface, vulnerable to the slightest scratch. To this day I have a profound emotional block against learning a foreign language. My love of words and the English language simply does not—and will not—'translate' into another language.

Yves Volel was another teacher who came to Dalton from the Caribbean. And just like Gambino Roche, Yves Volel was a political exile. But the two men could not have been more opposite; personally, politically and professionally. Perhaps it was precisely this bold and unabashed diversity among the faculty that made my Dalton experience—and the experience of the other minority students—so remarkable and unforgettable. There were misfits, bigots and incompetents who should never have had responsibility over impressionable minds, nor seen the inside of a classroom. And there were giants that you remember with affection and respect for as long as you live. Yves Volel was a personal hero for me. In high school Yves Volel was my geometry teacher. Ten years later, his niece Regine was my secretary at the advertising agency where I worked. Five years after that, I learned of Mr. Volel's tragic death at the hands of corrupt Haitian police. I wept openly over the loss of a personal hero. I don't think there is anyone other than my own family whose death affected me as much as this.

One of my brother Michael's favorite teachers was Mrs. Tuttle. Mrs. Tuttle, by the way, was also remembered fondly by my Aunt Milly, who had her as a teacher nearly 20 years earlier. Lauralee Tuttle dedicated her entire adult career spanning four decades to teaching at Dalton, and she apparently did it masterfully, with grace, wisdom and affection. Michael recalled participating in a history and politics conference hosted by, among others, his Latin teacher, Mrs. Tuttle.

"I talked about American 'Influentialism' throughout the world. Mrs. Tuttle approached me after the meeting and told me I had made an impressive speech, which I assure you was given extemporaneously and without prior thought. She said that I had even coined a new word. I asked her, "what new word had I coined," and she reminded me that it was 'Influentialism.' That really made an impression on me."

In the 1968 Dalton yearbook there are 87 members of the high school faculty and administrative staff shown, not counting group photos of the kitchen staff and maintenance staff. Included in those 87 are three people of color; two faculty members in the Arts Department and one secretary. Unless you were a student who took dance or music classes (not exactly a required subject), you might not have any reason to meet or engage with Mrs. Williamson or with Mr. Moore. Unless you were summoned to Donald Barr's office, you might not have any reason to meet or engage with his assistant, Thelma Blackburn.

Elizabeth Ray Williamson grew up in Raleigh, North Carolina, the granddaughter of Colonel James Hunter Young, one of the most prominent (and politically powerful) Black citizens in the entire state. She graduated from Radcliffe with honors at a time when very, very few Black women attended college (ANY college), and she went on to New York University, where she received her Masters in Dance. Liz studied dance under Martha Graham. As a dance educator, Liz Williamson served on the faculties of Howard University, Tuskegee Institute, and Bennett College of Greensboro, S. C. In 1948 she joined the faculty at Fieldston Ethical Culture School in New York. Throughout the 1950s, she performed on numerous television shows, in film and on the New York City Center stage. In 1958, she performed "Blues Suite" as an original member of the Alvin Ailey Dance Company. In 1959, when Mrs. Williamson joined the faculty at Dalton, she was one of the most prominent and highly regarded African American dancers in the nation. And she was Dalton's very first African American faculty member, 40 years after Dalton first opened its doors.

I never took dance, so I never had a class with Mrs. Williamson, but every Black student at Dalton knew her and was terrifically fond of her—and she of them. She had a smile that could light the way for ships at sea. Her whole body was jazz hands. When she called you "Darling" you knew she meant it. Mrs. Williamson's daughter, Wonza Elizabeth Williamson, was a graduate of the Dalton class of 1964.

Carman Moore was a music teacher at Dalton. Before coming to Dalton, he received his masters degree in music composition from Julliard. Mimi (Mehta) White, a member of my brother Michael's class of 1969, remembers that Mr. Moore produced and directed the high school production of Guys and Dolls. More interesting, and more revealing perhaps, is what the New York Times wrote about Carman Moore in January 1975.

> "Every composer probably has his Walter Mitty fantasy, which goes something like this. Just as he is putting the final touches to a piece that Seiji Ozawa asked him to write for the San Francisco Symphony, Pierre Boulez calls and offers a \$10,000 commission from the New York Philharmonic. As the dream of glory expands, both scores are ready for their world premieres, just a day apart, and composer Mitty must fly the width of the continent overnight so that he may be on hand to accept the intoxicating applause of both great cities.
>
> But wait—all that is no fantasy for Carman Leroy Moore. It's this week's schizoid reality: Moore's "Gospel Fuse" will have its first performance on Wednesday night in San Francisco under Ozawa, and on the next night Boulez will introduce "Wild Fires and Field Songs" to the Philharmonic subscribers. How, in what is laughingly called the real world, does such a golden apple fall into the lap of a Black composer who is 38 years old?"

After he left Dalton in 1969, Mr. Moore went on to become a world-renowned composer, conductor, author, and music critic. Mr. Moore began composing for symphony and chamber ensembles while writing lyrics for pop songs (for Felix Cavalieri and The Young Rascals), gradually adding opera, theatre, dance and film scores to his body of work. A dedicated educator, Mr. Moore continued his teaching at the Yale University School of Music, Queens and Brooklyn Colleges, Carnegie-Mellon University, Manhattanville College, and New School University.

Liz Williamson and Carman Moore's credentials are worth noting simply because of their extraordinary accomplishments, but also—importantly—because of their contrast to the typical Dalton faculty. Dalton certainly had more than its fair share of wonderful teachers. That is undeniable. But the vast majority of teachers hired at Dalton, especially in the 1960s, were young men and women who hadn't yet seen their 30th birthday, and whose resumes could probably fit on half a page. Mrs. Williamson and Mr.

Moore out-classed and out-credentialed them all. It is axiomatic of the Black experience in America that in order for us to get the job, we have to be 2-3 times more qualified than the competition. In more than one respect, Liz Williamson was the Jackie Robinson of Dalton faculty.

There was another Black teacher at Dalton in 1968, although he did not teach in the high school. Chester Davis was a math teacher in the middle school at Dalton. Davis was one of the first African Americans to receive both his bachelor's and master's degrees from the University of Chicago. Following his doctoral work at Syracuse University, Davis joined the Dalton faculty in 1961, and stayed until 1968. Shortly after the assassination of Dr. Martin Luther King, Jr., Chester Davis was recruited to join the Institute of the Black World, a component of the MLK, Jr. Center in Atlanta, GA that was the first and only "Black think tank" to assemble a cadre of scholars to study, write about and advance the Civil Rights movement. Three years later, he left Atlanta to become the first African American Studies professor at the University of Massachusetts at Amherst, MA.

While I was a student at Amherst College in the mid-1970's, I had occasion to meet Professor Davis at UMASS. My girlfriend at the time was a student at UMASS and was an African American Studies major. My girlfriend brought me to some departmental event and introduced me to Professor Davis, who took an instant dislike to me. My girlfriend mentioned that I had attended Dalton and was now at Amherst College. Professor Davis, who decided that I was some over-privileged Black preppy asked me if I was "slumming" by coming over to the UMASS campus. I don't think I accompanied my girlfriend to any more departmental events after that.

One of the Black teachers that was hired at the end of the 1960's was Rolando Reyes. Mr. Reyes was an art teacher at Dalton who joined the school in the 1969—1970 school year and stayed for about a half-dozen years. A tall, young Black man with a big afro and a beard, cool clothes and handmade African and Native American jewelry, he stood out immediately and conspicuously at Dalton. He was a very different kind of presence at the school. Perhaps his "otherness" was a big part of what made him so interesting and appealing to the Black students. Neither Ray nor I had Mr. Reyes as a teacher, but we both knew and liked the man quite a bit. He was a mentor and role model. In fact, a close bond formed between Ray and Mr. Reyes, who offered Ray a job working in the teacher's Greenwich Village store. The job expanded Ray's cultural horizons significantly and put a few extra dollars in Ray's pocket.

Rolando Reyes' "otherness" did not—by definition—fit in well within the Dalton community. He was simply too different. But Dalton was much too civilized and self-assured of its own liberalism to create conflict or confrontation with the new teacher. Instead, it was much easier and much more comfortable to simply ignore him, to pretend he wasn't there at all. In the Prologue to Ralph Ellison's classic 1952 novel, "Invisible Man," he writes, "I am invisible, understand, simply because people refuse to see me." I feel this was the fate of Rolando Reyes at Dalton.

In the 1970 yearbook, he is listed among the Dalton faculty as Orlando Rayes, misspelling both his first and last name, the only teacher to whom this slight occurred. For the next three consecutive years, 1971, 1972 and 1973, Mr. Reyes is overlooked entirely and not included among the faculty yearbook photos in spite of his status as a teacher. In the 1975 yearbook, he is listed as Roland Reyes, and in 1976, he is once again missing completely. Only in 1974, when I was editor of the yearbook, is Rolando Reyes listed properly and accurately.

Was this mistreatment deliberate? Did the school have it in for Mr. Reyes? I don't think so. But I do think that the school made almost no effort to recognize or appreciate him. And I think they simply chose not to see him at all.

In 1968, all we had at Dalton were Williamson, Blackburn and Moore. But when Ray and I graduated in the spring of 1974, our yearbook featured ten people of color among Dalton's faculty and staff. The number had more than tripled in just six years. Dalton had a number of different motives for why it integrated its student body. Each of those motives played a role. So, it is reasonable to assume that there were multiple motives for why Dalton also chose to bring diversity to its professional ranks. The city, the state and the federal government were all beginning to crack down on discriminatory hiring practices and Dalton was always dependent to some degree on government grant money. So regulatory pressure can't be overlooked.

But I also choose to believe that Dalton recruited and hired more Black teachers and staff because we were there, us Black students. I think that Dalton decided that if they were going to have these Black kids attending school, they better have some teachers and staffers who understood these kids, who could liaison, so to speak. But the integration of Dalton's faculty and staff did something else that perhaps was not at all planned for. Dalton's newfound professional diversity had a far greater and more significant impact on our wealthy white classmates because, for many of them, this was perhaps the first time they had any substantive interaction with a person of color who wasn't a domestic servant or a face on the evening news. Encountering us Black kids was possibly the first time that our white classmates ever got to know a Black peer, but this was certainly the first time they had ever encountered a Black person in a position of authority or respect. These were life-altering epiphanies for an awful lot of people. Imagine if these students had never met Yves Volel or known his story.

In what ways did we change Dalton? This is one of the ways.

Image—brand identity—became another one of the important ways that Dalton changed as a result of our presence there. As I have mentioned several times, Dalton's new headmaster Donald Barr was acutely focused on reshaping and refining the image and brand identity of The Dalton School. And he saw this moment in time, the middle of the 1960s, as a nexus of significant change in the cultural landscape. Although Donald Barr was himself a conservative—both politically and in educational philosophy—he believed that he possessed an intuitive understanding of New York liberal elites. He believed that he could reshape and promote Dalton as the school where New York's most important and influential liberals would send their children.

Barr significantly expanded the size of the student body in order to make room for a major influx of new blood. He couldn't (and wouldn't) replace the old family legacy enrollment. They were essential to the financial and operational stability of the school. But he could add to it in a grand way. He also significantly expanded the high school curriculum so much that it rivaled some of the best liberal arts colleges. My brother Michael often remarks—with an undiminished sense of marvel—that Dalton offered more English Department courses than Yale did when he arrived there after graduating from Dalton. The school taught Latin, Greek, Italian and Russian in addition to French and Spanish. Dalton offered courses in philosophy with a bearded, pipe-smoking, ruminating faculty member. Dalton covered the spectrum of technology. We had our own printing press and offered courses in typesetting, but we also had our own IBM 1130 massive computing system and taught classes in Fortran and Basic. And although other schools like Stuyvesant or Collegiate or Horace Mann may have had some of the same bells and whistles as Dalton, we offered all of these wonderful things under the enlightened umbrella of the progressive educational philosophy of the Dalton Plan.

But in order to truly burnish its progressive bona fides, Dalton brought diversity to its student body. Dalton brought Black boys to the high school. Other schools would soon follow, but Dalton took the lead and enjoyed the avant garde limelight. We were exotic, we were mysterious. We were cool. Unlike the caution and trepidation of Dalton's integration of Negro girls into the school in the late 1940s, Dalton had no fear of backlash or white flight this time around. Donald Barr and the Board of Trustees correctly read the moment and watched as parents flocked to enroll their children into Dalton. Artists, entertainers, politicians, authors, activists, philanthropists; the New York elite. And they came because of us. They transformed the school because we transformed the school.

Were the Board of Trustees and Headmaster Barr brilliant visionaries who foresaw a better, more enlightened learning opportunity, building on Dalton's progressive tradition? Were they liberal missionaries who felt an obligation to reach out to the disadvantaged and overlooked students in the surrounding communities, offering a caring and benevolent hand up? Or were they shrewd and cynical businesspeople who understood how to put together a hit show and sell a lot of tickets? I have no idea, but I suppose that the truth is probably a combination of all three.

CODE-SWITCHING AND STRING-CHEWING BASS PLAYERS

English was by far my favorite subject and the remarkable collective of all of my English teachers at Dalton was not merely good, it was great. They were the kind of teachers that you thank in acceptance speeches for awards you receive much later in life. You remember them and what they taught you. Because what you learned did not simply make you smarter. It made you different. These teachers made me different.

I grew up in a household of hyper-articulate, hyper-verbal people. Speaking—in all of its forms—was a skill set each of us learned and mastered at a very early age. Our mother was constantly coaching us in the art of persuasive speaking, how to frame an argument, how to debate, how to enunciate. You could almost envision Professor Henry Higgins drilling Liza Doolittle on "the rain in Spain" in our parents' basement. In the late 1960s newswoman Barbara Walters wrote a magazine article, "**How to Talk to Practically Anyone About Practically Anything**." Our mother was a huge fan of Barbara Walters, a female empowerment role model. Mom used the principles from the Walters article as a syllabus for shaping us into effortless conversationalists. She taught us how to be at ease in virtually any social setting; a skill that would become essential to adapting and succeeding at Dalton. In fact, Mom took great pride and pleasure in inviting us to be part of social events with her office and professional colleagues. She was confident we could hold our own in any social setting and she loved showing us off.

In addition to being told all my life that I "speak so well", I am often asked, "Where are you from? You don't have any accent." All things considered, that was a pretty formidable accomplishment (with all credit to my mother). I am a New Yorker (a Noo Yawka) from Queens, with no trace of a New York accent. I am a descendant of West Indians, with no trace of an island accent. Scrubbing those accents away took a lot of practice. Growing up, we had an amusing little poem in our house that was a mantra for proper articulation; "Not dis, dose, dat, dese, dem or dey. T-H, T-H, dat's de way!" We learned what my mother called the "Network TV news anchor accent", which was in fact no discernable accent at all.

This led to a lifetime of conversations where people felt the need to ask my background, both geographic and ethnic. On the telephone, people who did not know me automatically assumed I was white (based on their own perceptions of what it meant to talk white or talk Black). Many of the same people who made this erroneous assumption also managed to dig a deeper hole for themselves by making some gratuitous racist remark. Eventually these people would meet me in person and be completely embarrassed by the things they had said on the phone. Over the years I have seen more white people with egg on their faces than I can count.

Growing up in the 1960s, my brothers and I had never heard the term "code switching", but we understood the concept all too well. Code switching—the practice of altering one's language or vernacular or speech pattern to suit the context or the audience—was simply something we did, both consciously and unconsciously from moment to moment all day long. It was not simply a matter of talking to kids versus adults, or strangers versus intimates. Black people talk to each other differently from the way they talk to white people. They simply do. The differences can be profound, but far more often the differences are quite subtle and require an attentive ear to notice. This is not about Ebonics or AAVE (look it up). Nor is it necessarily about slipping into (or out of) an accent. It can be about phrases or simple words that have special meaning or relevance. Most Black people in America live in two worlds; the mainstream majority world and the community of Blackness (not just Black people) that exists as a subset of the majority. W.E.B. DuBois wrote extensively and insightfully about co-existing in these two worlds. Language is one of the ways that Black people manage that dual existence. Code switching between two worlds is an essential skill set. It certainly was at Dalton.

And yet, as important as the spoken word has been to my personal success and social mobility, the written word has always been even more important. The written word has been integral to all of the successes in my life; professional, political, personal, even romantic. And whatever facility with the written word I currently possess, I owe to my teachers at Dalton. They taught me the practical mechanics, the interpersonal power and the beauty of words on paper.

I did a freelance consulting project a few years back for a friend and colleague. He needed me to write up my observations about a particular Fortune 100 corporation that would later serve as the basis for a project proposal he would develop. The assignment was no big deal, at least not in my eyes. I wrote my report in less than a week and handed him my bill. He looked at the bill and handed it back to me. He said, "I know you're just trying to be nice because we are friends, but you need to triple this invoice."

I told him that the assignment really wasn't that hard and didn't take me very long to finish. He said to me, "You really have no idea how many people in this world look at a blank piece of paper with absolute fear and dread. You look at a blank piece of paper as an opportunity, as a beginning. That's more than just a gift. That's a super power. Never under-value what you can do with words."

My friend helped me to understand and appreciate what my teachers had given me.

One of my favorite teachers was Jeremiah Evarts, one of the younger, long-haired teachers at the school and the son of Elizabeth Evarts, a Dalton teacher since the 1940's. Mr. Evarts was a Dalton alum himself; class of 1955, although back then boys did not matriculate through the high school, but left after middle school. I suppose since his mom was a teacher and administrator at the school while he was a student, he and I probably had more in common than I realized at the time. Mr. Evarts always seemed to be making an effort to conceal how much he was amused by his students. We were fools—for the most part—but he always seemed to enjoy our foolishness, even to the point of participating and collaborating in some of it. He understood that when we let our guards down some learning crept in. Not only did we accept and retain that learning, we enjoyed it and looked forward to more.

One day in poetry class Mr. Evarts read a poem by Robert Kaufman, an African American beat poet of the 1950's and 60's. The poem was called "Mingus", inspired by the legendary jazz musician.

> String-chewing bass players,
> Plucking rolled balls of sound
> From the jazz scented night
>
> Feeding hungry beat seekers
> Finger shaped heartbeats,
> Driving ivory nails
> Into their greedy eyes.
>
> Smoke crystals, from the nostrils
> Of released jazz demons,
> Crash from foggy yesterday
> To the light
> Of imaginary night....

I was transfixed. I was transported. I was transformed. As I read the words, I could see the musicians and hear their music. I could sense the time of day where it all took place. I could feel it in my bones. A few years earlier I had taken guitar lessons and quickly come to the realization that I possessed absolutely no musical talent. I couldn't even fake it. But I read this poem and I knew that I could make music with words just like Robert Kaufman had done. Well, maybe not as well as Robert Kaufman, but I knew I could be good. I could be very good. That day in that classroom, I don't believe I knew what my own purpose in life would be, but I knew that day what Dalton's purpose would be for me. Dalton would teach me how to use words on paper.

And it was no minor detail that the poem read in class that day was the work of an African American poet writing about an African American jazz musician. Kaufman. Mingus. Mr. Evarts' choice of reading material was brilliantly subversive and powerfully inspirational. I was familiar with several African American authors and had grown up reading some of their work. And I had grown up learning and loving jazz alongside my father in our daily car rides. But this was the first time that any teacher had presented any Black creative work in a formal classroom setting. This was the first time in my life that any teacher (other than my own parents) had recognized and validated that the artistic and intellectual work of Black people should be studied and appreciated. And this was no ordinary classroom. This was Dalton. From the perspective of a little teenage Black kid from Queens, they only taught the best stuff at Dalton. And they had chosen to teach this.

Of course, the beautiful, magnificent irony of the moment was that I was probably the only kid in the entire class who had ever heard of Charles Mingus before or who had the slightest idea what his music sounded like. Maybe because I was Black. Maybe because of my years of car rides with my dad and jazz lessons on the car radio. I was probably the only person in the room besides Mr. Evarts who could experience the poem viscerally. In that moment, I had the advantage over my white classmates. Constantly, they could talk about things where I had no frame of reference. Constantly, I felt as though I was playing an endless game of catch-up, of watching the game from the nosebleed seats or from behind protective glass. But not this day. This day I felt empowered. I felt the physical elevation of an epiphany.

I was ready to begin something entirely new.

In the beginning, I wrote a lot of short stories. Apparently one of the literary forms at which I excelled was romantic literature for men. Put another way, I wrote the high school equivalent of soft-core porn. I wasn't necessarily very good, but I was definitely popular. Most of the students were reading my work. Dalton teachers I had never had a class with were reading my work and coming to me to comment on it. It was the early 1970's version of "going viral." One teacher—the absolutely incredible and inspirational Joe Frank—wrote in my yearbook that he expected to find my work in a Times Square bookstore, but that he would purchase it happily.

One of my own favorite pieces, however, was a simple haiku. We were learning about haikus in Mr. Evarts' class and for homework we were expected to write our own haiku. We had to demonstrate not only our understanding of the form and structure, but also our appreciation for the subtlety of the cultural nature of its expression. Consistent with my own personal style, which Mr. Evarts defined as "adolescent prurience", I wrote my haiku in about two minutes. He gave me an A.

> Sex at the movies.
> I guess it depends on where
> You happen to sit.

Joe Frank had a markedly different pedigree from most other teachers at Dalton. He was not a count or a former military officer. He was not second generation Daltonian, nor the offspring of a prestigious New York family. Mr. Frank's parents were Polish Jews fleeing Nazi Germany in 1938. Joe was born in Strasbourg, France, near the German border as his father and pregnant mother made their escape. They eventually arrived in New York City as refugees the following year. Caroline Love Goodwin, the Democratic Congresswoman from New York, authored a bill specifically to permit the entry of Joe's family into the U.S. and grant them resident visas. President Franklin Roosevelt vetoed the bill, as it had been his practice to oppose the consideration of Jewish refugees. The next day Congresswoman Goodwin resubmitted the bill and Congress overrode the president's veto. Joe and his parents were here to stay.

Joe Frank nurtured his passion for writing from an early age. After graduating from Hofstra—where Francis Ford Coppola was his friend and classmate—he attended the Iowa Writer's Workshop, one of the most prestigious creative writing programs in the country. Their alumni include John Cheever, Philip Roth, Robert Lowell and Robert Penn Warren. Joe turned to teaching as a job, not a career and began teaching at Dalton before he was 30. Although teaching was not the path that Mr. Frank wanted his life to take, he actually enjoyed teaching and was effortlessly good at it. I haven't met anyone who had Joe Frank as a teacher who didn't consider him one of the best teachers they ever had.

Actually, Mr. Frank was more sensei than teacher, guiding students to discover their strengths and skills and how to sharpen them. Joe told my friend and classmate Mickey Rolfe that he didn't need to "try" to write. Mickey should simply write, because he could. That was Mr. Frank. You didn't have to write creatively to understand what good creative writing was. You could understand it, critique it, navigate its layers, even if writing was not necessarily "your thing." Students would workshop their writing with each other, almost like jazz musicians playing off each other in an impromptu session.

Every photo I have seen of Mr. Frank in his life after Dalton shows him clean shaven, looking almost like a Nebraska farm boy. But that was not how he appeared as a teacher at Dalton. Mr. Frank had a full dark beard that brought his chin to a dramatic point and dark unkempt hair that looked like he had just run his hand through it distractedly. Mr. Frank was unfailingly friendly and welcoming, if you knew him. But his dark appearance and baritone voice were closer to sinister. Ironically, later in life, when he was clean shaven and sweet-faced, most people had no idea what he looked like and knew him only as a voice on the radio, where he was unmistakably the "voice in the darkness", a cross between Garrison Keeler and Stephen King.

In addition to being my writing mentor, Joe Frank taught me to embrace whatever it was that made me who I was. He was an advocate for the concept of one's own "personal brand" as a mark of identity; the more unique the greater the value. He encouraged me to see the things that made me different as an act of creativity. It should never be forced or artificial. I should never try to be different, I should simply be who I was; different. Of course, to Mr. Frank I was not different because I was Black. I was different because I was one of the oddest people he had ever met. I was a fearless teenage writer who wrote about experiences I had never had, but still expressed them with an intuitive familiarity. I could make people smile and cringe with the same sentence.

I took my first photography class at Dalton in ninth grade. To describe the experience as life-changing would not be hyperbole. I never owned a camera before that class and there probably isn't a single photo taken before that class where I could say, "I took that picture." Photography had never been a part of my life until that first ninth grade semester. But there it was, this beast hibernating inside me, a leviathan concealing its presence from everyone (especially from me) until it suddenly burst onto the scene and decided it would own me, consume me, redefine me. Photography was my own personal Big Bang creative explosion.

As a young man, just after his service in the Navy during World War II, my father was a professional photographer. Sadly, tragically, I have not seen very many samples of his work. They were lost to time and circumstance and my father never really talked about his days as a photographer. It was something that got left behind. I believe he did mostly fashion photography and social photography. The latter is the kind of photos taken at fancy social events and organization activities, photos where everyone is dressed in their very best. If there were big goings-on in Harlem at the time, my father might have been the photographer capturing the moment. If you were in a Eugene Robinson photo, it probably meant that you had attended something special.

Dad also did fashion photography, capturing beautiful Black women models in stylish dresses and big fancy hats. Back then, you never saw these models in the mainstream fashion magazines, but the newsstands in Harlem and Chicago and other cities around the country were filled with Negro publications that featured and celebrated Black beauty and style. These were the kinds of pictures my father took. And, I'm told, he was very good at it.

Years ago, while rummaging through my parents' basement, I found what is known in the retail marketing business as a riser card. It's a cardboard display piece that's roughly three feet tall and two feet wide and has an advertising image promoting a product for sale in the store. It draws the customer to purchase the product. Beer and soda brands use them all the time. This particular card was for Ballantine Beer and featured five beautiful African American models enjoying the beer. Ballantine, which has been around since 1840, was at its height in the 1940s and 1950s. By then, it was twice the size of Anheuser Busch and was one of the largest privately held corporations in America. The ad, which may have been shot by my dad (I'm not sure) included my mom, Rita Robinson, and another model who was a friend of hers, Audrey Smaltz. That's Ray's Aunt Audrey, who later left modeling to become a fashion runway mogul. The families of Ray Smaltz and Mark Robinson were connected before either if us were born.

So yes, my mom was one of those beautiful Black women models. My father took many beautiful pictures of her. That's how they met. That's how they fell in love. And, oh, how they were in love. If you ever heard either of them talk about their courtship, if you ever heard either of them talk about how they felt about each other, what they saw when they looked at each other, you could not help but become choked up. For me, they were the gold standard of a romantic, loving relationship.

I don't know the details, but the story I've been told is that when my mom and dad went on their honeymoon, they returned to find that all of my father's photography equipment had been stolen, possibly by someone they knew. My dad was young and didn't have much money, so when his equipment was stolen, his photography career was wiped out overnight. He couldn't rebuild or restart. That was it for him. A dream had been snuffed out. When I first began learning photography, I didn't know that my father had been a photographer. He never talked about it. He never said anything to me. Perhaps he didn't realize how passionately I would come to embrace this craft. Perhaps he didn't know if I would be any good at it. But as my learning progressed, I could tell that he was watching. I could tell that he was looking on with interest. And hopefully, he was looking on with pride.

In eighth grade I began writing creatively, I began learning how to flex and build that muscle, make it strong. And by extension, make me strong. By the end of that first year at Dalton I had a handful of friends and people who knew me fairly well. But I had a lot of people who knew me simply as a writer of stories, weird, interesting, sometimes unsettling stories. That was my identity. But now it was ninth grade and all of that was brushed to the side by photography, like sweeping pieces off a chessboard. It would be easy—and very reasonable—to interpret this course change as the ricochet whims and attention span of a typical teenager, jumping from one short-lived passion to another, totally convinced that this "new thing" was the only thing. But for me photography remained a substantial and defining passion and avocation for more than a decade, outliving my teenage years. And once the storm of photography did eventually pass, I returned to writing, which has sustained me and rewarded me for the rest of my life.

In ninth grade I began to learn the technology and technique of photography, learning about cameras and lenses and f-stops and film speeds. I learned how to develop my own film and print my own pictures. After all, Dalton had its own state of the art darkroom, stocked with the best hardware and accessible virtually anytime I wanted. There is a lot to learn in the technical elements of photography; chemistry, math, physics and engineering. And I probably surprised myself (and others) by how easily these skills became integrated in my mind and how quickly I could put them into practice. I realized that if you want something badly enough, you can accomplish almost anything.

Ironically, it was the softer, more artistic skills of photography; composition, lighting that gave me greater difficulty. My teacher, Melissa Shook was a professional photographer hired by Dalton to teach photography. She was a very good teacher for someone who had never studied to be a teacher, but she was often impatient with my inclination to ignore certain fundamentals of the craft. She wanted me to master Photography 101, while I had left that behind the moment I started the class. I knew what the fundamentals were. I just didn't care. I was using my camera to tell stories.

Here again, it would be reasonable to look upon my rebellious, screw the rules approach to photography as typical teenage immaturity. Every teenager thinks they know better than their adult teachers at least some of the time. And I was undeniably immature (or "appropriately adolescent") about many things. I was not "wiser than my years." I'm pretty sure I never was. But from the very first time that I saw photographs that I had taken, from the first time I saw what a camera would do in my hands, it was as though I had just unbottled a genie. When you find yourself in the driver's seat of a Ferrari Testarosa, you don't reach for the glove box and look for the owner's manual. You put on your shades and you floor the accelerator. You just go.

And with my new camera (an extravagance my parents could barely afford), that's precisely what I did.

I was never without my camera, taking pictures constantly during the school day, capturing random candid moments of classmates. Unlike the unrelenting flood of photos that dominate social media today, none of my photographs were posed. I scrupulously avoided taking any photographs that felt intentional, staged or in any way self-aware. My mission was to tell stories by capturing moments as they occurred, not the big moments per se, but the unguarded moments that sometimes go by too fast to be noticed, except that they were captured at 1/1000 of a second.

I was incredibly lucky that people seemed to like the pictures that I took. They saw images of themselves that captured something inside them that they were hoping would shine through, a small piece of personality. My photos weren't glamourous, but they were never unflattering. That wasn't what I was trying to capture. I was always a glass-is-half-full person and that positive bias was reflected in the pictures that I took. I was part photojournalist, part paparazzo, part Boswell. And my camera gave me the confidence to be able to be around anyone, partly because I could hide behind my lens and partly because my camera always seemed to be welcomed. I didn't have to justify my presence. In high school—any high school—this was like having a Kevlar vest against the slings and arrows of teenage social combat.

I didn't much think about it at the time, in fact I didn't really think about it at all, but I spent a lot of my time at Dalton hiding behind my camera lens. Behind the lens I wasn't the Black kid. Behind the lens I wasn't an outsider. The camera always seemed to be welcomed. It always seemed to belong. It just made it so much easier for me to fit in. And people who did not know me well, which was 90-95% of my classmates, knew me as "the camera." My identity at Dalton wasn't me. It was an inanimate object. Looking back, I can't say whether that inanimate object served me or if it prevented me from ever being seen, from ever being known.

The photography darkroom at Dalton was accessible whenever I was available to schedule time, however, it was a shared space used by all of the other photography students. You were rarely alone in the darkroom, but were working alongside another student. Fortunately, of the roughly two dozen photography students at the school, there were probably less than a half dozen who held a serious interest in photography and spent any significant time in the darkroom. I spent most of my darkroom time during ninth grade with two extraordinarily talented upperclassmen, James Cooper and Carl Simmons. James was a senior and, at first, he was completely disgusted with the idea that he had to share darkroom time with a dorky 14 year-old freshman who was just learning photography. James was a tall, lanky hippie with shoulder length uncombed hair and a scraggly beard. His photographic style tended toward late sixties Greenwich Village art house, featuring double exposures and tricks of light, capturing odd unfamiliar images. His work was strange, but it was very good. I liked it.

Much more important, however, James liked my work. He would stand over me (literally) as I selected and printed images. As a print soaked in a tray of chemicals he would look down and say, "I don't think I would ever take that picture, but I like it. You're actually not so bad. Show me something else." Eventually I would seek out scheduling darkroom time when he would be there, so that I could get his feedback and commentary. And he would welcome the exchange.

But James wasn't just a good mentor, he was the head photographer for the yearbook. And one day he said, "Hey, why don't you take some more pictures around school, and if I like them, maybe we'll put them in the yearbook." That became the high school equivalent of a press pass. I could go anywhere and take pictures of anything and simply say, "I'm taking pictures for the yearbook." In particular, this gave me access to the seniors, those people who cared most about the yearbook. And what freshman wouldn't kill for the ability to casually hang around with seniors?

Coincidentally, my friend David Burns (who was a year older than me) also gravitated to the yearbook as an activity that enabled him to integrate into the Dalton social community. He was not a photographer, so I think his role was more on the administrative and organizational side. When Dave was a senior, he was editor of the yearbook and also ran the film society that used as a fundraising vehicle for the yearbook. A couple of fellow seniors were the children of major film studio executives and they were able to procure prints of first run movie releases to be screened at the school for little or no cost. At least that was the case until word got out and a battle over licensing rights and fees ensued.

Unfortunately, David's senior yearbook was also the source of a minor scandal when it came out. The yearbook included a full-page acrostic that featured the names of various Dalton faculty, if you searched for them. Previous yearbooks contained similar name-puzzle devices. But if you searched extra hard you found something more. In the top line of the acrostic, written backward, it read "Mr. Barr eats pussy." Needless to say, David and his fellow yearbook editors got into a great deal of trouble.

From freshman year through my senior year when I became one of the yearbook editors, each year's book had an increasing number of my photographs. In fact, I recently came upon a copy of a book called "Dalton

Memories" published in 1979 to commemorate the school's 60th anniversary. I was quite surprised to find that the book included a couple of my photographs (apparently used without my knowledge) to represent moments in Dalton's history.

The other person with whom I shared time in the Dalton darkroom was Carl Simmons. Carl was a junior when I was a freshman. Carl had an elegant, artistic touch to his work, which emulated and contemporized the photographic style of Henri Cartier Bresson. It was in fact Carl's images that led me to learn and appreciate the styles of the various great photographers; the artists and the journalists. Henri Cartier Bresson was a French photographer of the 1930s and 1940s, considered a master of candid photography, and an early user of 35 mm film and the small hand-held camera. Bresson pioneered the genre of street photography, and viewed photography as capturing a decisive moment. His work, which has influenced entire schools of photography, was very much what I aspired to emulate in my pictures. I hoped to learn—or at least copy—his instincts and his choices.

Carl Simmons was the docent of my photography education. Carl was also the first openly gay Black person I had ever met. Quite possibly he was the first openly gay person of any race that I had ever met, but the fact that he was also one of Dalton's first cohort of young Black men made Carl a rainbow unicorn indeed. I don't know what circumstances or life experiences may have led Carl to choose not to conceal his homosexuality at a time when almost no one except a few notorious celebrities were openly gay. My freshman year was not long after the Stonewall Inn riots and—even in New York—being openly gay could get you arrested, beaten or killed. I doubt that I have ever met another teenage boy—or another person—with as much personal courage as Carl. My admiration for Carl was a significant part of our friendship.

In high school, being "different" was a pathway to alienation, loneliness and social isolation. Life had handed Carl multiple layers of "different." Start with all of the awkwardness and natural insecurities of any teenage boy, take two steps back for not being wealthy, add another two steps back for being Black, and now finish it off with another two steps back for being gay. And although it would be nice to believe that African Americans have learned the hard way through centuries of discrimination and prejudice how important it is to be tolerant and accepting of others who are different, the painfully unfair reality is that the Black community can be even more backward, bigoted and intolerant on the topic of homosexuality than white America. Just to make life that much more cruel.

Virtually none of the other photography kids wanted to share darkroom time with Carl. The mere suggestion of it provoked outbursts of teenage macho bravado and declarations of "He better not try to touch me! I'll beat his ass." I, on the other hand, valued darkroom time far too much to care who I had to share it with. My brother Michael was gay, although it would be another six or seven years before Michael came out. Nevertheless, I knew. I have always loved my brother and never for a moment considered his homosexuality to be anything other than simply who he was. Being around Carl never made me uncomfortable, despite the fact that Carl would constantly test the boundaries of my comfort level in order to test the durability and sincerity of our friendship. An occasional "Knock it off" or—more frequently—a disapproving stare would remind him that I only had a half hour before my next class, and he should stop distracting me from work. I think Carl very much appreciated that he could simply be himself around me and neither of us felt defensive or uncomfortable.

Among the many things I learned at Dalton, things great and small, I also learned to be at ease among all types of people. I learned that I could be around truly brilliant people and not be intimidated by their intelligence, but simply hungry for their knowledge and grateful for their company. I learned that I could be around extraordinarily wealthy people and simply think of them as people that I knew. I learned that I could be around people with whom I had nothing in common and yet discover we had many things in common. I learned that I could go virtually anywhere and be among anyone and not feel out of place or uncomfortable. Dalton gave me this. I am not sure that my white Dalton classmates learned all of these things (perhaps they didn't need to), but I am pretty sure that most of my Black classmates did. Dalton gave this to us.

Every now and then I would show up at a Dalton football game to grab a few photos for the yearbook. I wasn't interested in taking pictures of the action on the field. To me it all looked the same anyway. I was much more interested in capturing the experience of attending the game; the fans and spectators, the cheerleaders, the players who just came off the field bone tired or the ones waiting impatiently to go in. Those were the pictures I took. One of the photos is Ray Smaltz in uniform on the field right after a big play. He is on one knee and the expression of anguish on his face suggests that he will need to marshal every drop of energy just to get back up and get back into the game. It is one of Ray's favorite photos because it captures exactly what he was feeling at that moment.

Of course, not everyone at Dalton liked seeing me with my camera. There was definitely a segment of my classmates that looked at me with a "Who does he think he is?" attitude. For some that might have been borne of racial animus or prejudice. For others it may have been annoyance with my camera's constant presence. And some people just plain didn't like me. I can understand that. I look back on my younger self from time to time and I don't always like the me that I see. But somebody—I never found out who—decided to separate me from my camera. One day at school I opened my locker and my camera was gone. Stolen.

I went home that day and told my parents that I had been "ripped off." My mother was in a panic. She had no idea what "ripped off" meant. She thought that I had been assaulted. I explained that someone had stolen my camera. She was relieved. I was devastated. Good quality 35mm cameras are expensive, and my parents had bought me a Honeywell Pentax Spotmatic SLR with a Super-Takumar 50mm lens that cost a couple hundred dollars. (That was a couple hundred dollars back in 1971!) It was an incredible extravagance and there was simply no way that I could—or would—ask them for another one. Whoever stole my camera from my locker probably figured that I could never afford to get another one, but I was working—because my brothers and I always had jobs—and I had saved some money. At the time, I had no idea how closely my father could relate to my misfortune. I had no idea that many years before, when my father was not much older than me, a thief had stolen his photography career. A thief had stolen perhaps a million unexplored possibilities. My father knew all to well what that meant to me. My father agreed to advance me the necessary money as long as I paid him back, and we set up a repayment schedule. I bought myself a new camera. It was a Nikkormat and it was a badass monster.

About 15 years ago, my brother Michael began taking photography classes after work as a new hobby. Michael began learning the basics, just as I had in my first photography class. And before long, whenever you saw Michael, his camera was either in his hand or somewhere close by, never out of reach to capture a moment. I'm not sure what triggered the interest in photography for Michael. This was not something he had ever mentioned previously. And even though this was 15 years ago, this was pretty "late in life" for Michael, who was already in his 50's. Nevertheless, Michael's commitment to taking up photography was genuine and without compromise, and it wasn't long before he was quite good. After a few years, Michael flew out to California to take a class with a teacher who had been an apprentice to Ansel Adams. I believe that it was through this class that Michael found the place in photography that was his passion and truly his own. Michael has a real gift for photographing nature and architecture, the soft and the hard, the geometry of beauty in the universe. At the encouragement of myself and many of his friends, Michael began producing an annual calendar that features his photographs. If you own one—from any year—you have something quite special. Our father got to enjoy these calendars, and I know that they made him very happy and very proud.

I was always working. As a kid, I never received an allowance. My parents didn't believe in it. You wanted money to buy comic books or candy or barbecue potato chips? (my passion) Go get a job.

And you were never too young to get a job. Before I was fourteen, I had a lawn mowing service and a paper route. Everyone made fun of me because I used to write out invoices for my lawn mowing customers and maintained a detailed accounting system. I made money. I had a paper route for about three years. I inherited it from my older brothers who had the route before me. Delivering the papers on my bicycle was physically hard because 100 newspapers weighed a lot and it was difficult to maintain balance on the bicycle and throw papers with that giant sack slung over one shoulder.

But even harder was the bi-weekly collection work, where I had to go door to door and collect each customer's subscription money. Half the customers would pretend to be not home. You had to be persistent. There was one time, however, when I rang a customer's doorbell and the lady of the house came to the door wearing a lace teddy that was very sheer. She was in her late thirties and very attractive. I was twelve or thirteen; old enough to be extremely turned on, but way too young to have any idea what I would do if she invited me inside. From that point forward, I definitely looked forward to doing my bi-weekly collections.

When I turned fourteen and was now a freshman at Dalton, I took the train to downtown Manhattan and got my working papers. In New York State, if you are under age eighteen you must obtain working papers and show them to any prospective employer in order to get a job. One of my first "official" jobs was working for my Uncle Bill. He and his business partner had their own urban planning firm located in one of the high floors of the Woolworth Building in lower Manhattan. Uncle Bill Lucas (married to my mother's sister Hyacinth) had advanced degrees in urban planning and a bunch of other things, but what excited me most was that he was an entrepreneur. He built his own business from nothing and was quite successful. Uncle Bill was one of my role models. At first, I did general gopher work; making copies, running as a messenger, whatever needed doing. Before long, however, I was promoted to proofreader. The urban planning firm often had to submit proposals and bids for government projects, and the documents would be several hundred pages long. The likelihood of mistakes—and the consequences—were very high, so proofreading was critical. To this day, my proofreading and editing skills have been one of my invaluable strengths.

In my sophomore year I got a job at Dalton, quite possibly the only student to have a job at the school during the school year. (There were lots of camp counselors during the summer.) For the vast majority of Dalton students, the idea of getting a job was simply never a consideration. The fact that I had a job was seen as a novelty and source of amusement by most of my classmates. Dalton kids always had cash in their pockets and never gave a thought to how it got there.

It was also an extremely visible job. In Dalton's lobby there was a giant glassed-in booth where Anne "Goodie" Goodwin, the school receptionist and switchboard operator sat. Goodie was the official welcoming face—and voice—of Dalton. She handled all incoming phone calls and all visitors to the building. Goodie worked from 8:00am to 4:00pm, but life was still very active in the building after 4:00pm, so there was a late shift receptionist from 4:00pm to 6:00pm, when the phone lines shut down for the day. I applied for the job and got the late shift duty.

Even though it was only two hours a day, it was good money. I could sit there and do homework while answering calls. Of course, for the first few weeks, many of my classmates would walk by and stare curiously at me sitting inside the big glass booth. They thought it was a joke and couldn't understand why I would be doing that. But there was another interesting side effect of working there. Dalton's building staff, the maintenance workers, elevator operators, even the kitchen staff, began to see me as someone they could relate to, someone among all of these spoiled rich kids who understood what it meant to work, someone who understood what it meant to cash a pay check. I could see a change almost immediately. They spoke to me differently. They engaged me in small talk. They talked about themselves when they knew that the typical Dalton rich kids had no interest in learning about them. They trusted me not to disrespect them. I also earned a reputation with members of the school administration as someone who was responsible and reliable.

CHAPTER 7

ACADEMICS & ATHLETICS

RAYMOND SMALTZ

M**Y MEMORY OF MY TEACHERS** in 8th grade is pretty shabby; not be-cause they were bad teachers or anything, but because there were other events that shaped my school year and two of them really made an important impression upon me. I got to know Mr. Volel just a little in 7th grade. Now he was my math teacher and geometry was my new challenge. Rulers and protractors became part of the arsenal in my book bag and they caused my head to spin with right, acute and obtuse angles day and night. (I still suffer from occasional geometry nightmares today!) Mr. Volel was there to make sense of it all. We spent extra time during my free periods to make sure I was grasping the lessons. That's when he'd share some more harrowing tales of his time in the Haitian army, where he learned how to shoot and developed the discipline and character he possessed. Geometry was a handful for me that semester, but it would've been far worse if Yves Volel hadn't been my instructor.

My other memorable teacher in eighth grade was Mademoiselle Chaliff, who taught French with one of the cheeriest and most exuberant disposi-tions I'd ever seen in a teacher. Very little ever seemed to bother her, not even the fact that she was cursed with both Jason Ekaireb and myself, the cut-ups of French class. This advanced French—we were there to carry on complete conversations in French without trying to sound like a poor man's Maurice Chevalier. Philippe Bourgois was the star of the class and why not—he had the perfect pedigree, name, accent, and look! Sometimes, it was all I could do to drop the *spanglish accent* from my neighborhood in East Harlem, as I tried to develop my ear for the language that sounded so sexy when she spoke it and so mangled by me. Jason used to nudge me all the time during class pointing out her breasts, as he grew excited each day in anticipation of Mlle. Chaliff's next revealing outfit. I resisted his adolescent urgings as best I could, but he was persistent. I know she caught us staring at her several times, but she was always cool, up until the point when she'd finally had enough of our antics and would then let out a loud shout in English (no French accent, no nothing) as she simultaneously banged a ruler on her desk. Somehow, it made her even sexier, but it must have been our raging hormones clouding our actions at times and we'd then straighten up for the remainder of class.

Eighth grade at Dalton marked the "comin' out party" for me when it came to team sports at the school. Two of the physical education instructors at Dalton—who just happened to be Black—were also the coaches of the middle school football and basketball teams. This was a rarity on any level in the public school system of New York City, never mind at private schools. Booker Quattlebaum and Duerward Middleton came together and groomed me to have confidence in my athletic ability and toughened my spine for the oncoming obstacles at the start of term. Booker and I had a lot in common with both our last names of German origin, and he often joked with me that brothers with names that roughly translated into *fruit tree* and *chicken fat*, "had to stick together!!!"

Mr. Quattlebaum told me in no uncertain terms, that I was going to be his running back on the football team. He also told me that no one was going to stop me on the football field unless I wanted them to, because few teams that we played had opponents my size or speed. So, while my new teammates were the already established members of the middle school team, Booker and Duerward gave me the chance to be the star.

I relished the dream of playing the sport I loved in real pads, with jerseys sporting the school colors, and helmets with a tiger logo on a big grass field (well, maybe not totally grass). Mr. Quattlebaum and Mr. Middleton made the plays fairly simple for our team, Tall, blonde-haired Nicky Blair was quarterback and he led the team. He had a decent arm and decent athletic ability, but he would've been the back-up quarterback to me, if not for the coaches featuring me at running back.

Once practice began in August, the coaches taught us the numbering system we would employ where the gaps between the offensive linemen were given a number. They taught us blocking and tackling techniques which none of us were terribly adept at when we started, but began to improve with time and plenty of practice; especially me, because I *loved* to hit! For me, there was something quite liberating about being able to hit a classmate as hard as I could and look at him and say, "hey, it's only practice," with no repercussions. I never intentionally tried to hurt any of my teammates, but after a while, they began to be on the lookout for whether I was having a "good day," or a "bad day." Carrying the football and running over someone from the opposing team was exhilarating, especially once you got into the open field, because nine times out of ten, the opposing players weren't going to catch me. All that punishment I took from the older guys that challenged me in those neighborhood contests, falling on concrete, getting elbowed in the face, or accidently punched in a scrum, paid off, because I was already hardened for the middle school game.

My father never seemed to make time for my athletic activities. He and I battled constantly over his lack of participation with any of my school endeavors. But the older guys from the high school varsity football team would come out once in a while after their practice to watch our games; guys like Kleon Andreadis, Tony Furnari, Keith Brown, Jose Gomez, Steve Vlamis and a guy I looked up to whenever he was around, Larry Stackhouse. These guys were 4 or 5 years older and part of the first group of males admitted into Dalton when the school went co-ed in 1966, two years before I arrived.

There was one game that fall that I will never forget. As our offense broke the huddle, I noticed the entire high school varsity football team, helmets in hand, cheering on our bunch of misfit 6th, 7th, and 8th graders, as we took our positions on the field. And just a little further down from the varsity players I spotted a woman approaching with a little girl by her hand, watching as we prepared to run our play. It was my Mother. She had walked across the bridge with my little sister Rachel in tow to come support me, even though she was not a big fan of the game. I felt a sudden rush of emotion after noticing her as I set my hand in the grass turf. I almost forgot the snap count as I strained my head to see my Mother at the moment they snapped the ball and pitched it to me. I took off for the sideline where the varsity guys and my Mother were standing. After building up to full stride, all I heard was the sound of the wind as it whistled past the ear hole in my helmet. Opposing players tried their best to cut the angle off and run me down, but I switched to a gear I never knew I had. I was so filled with emotion that I didn't realize I had run through the end zone untouched by anyone from the other team. It was a surreal moment, with tears welling up in my eyes from the joy of knowing my family had come to watch me play. I can't ever recall running as fast as that in my entire life. It was as if I had wings. That day I ran all over the gridiron racking up over one hundred and fifty yards on the ground. That day is indelibly etched in my mind, even though my mom says she doesn't remember it…

Football was a blast. The more I played, the more popular I became at school and the more my classmates wanted me to be a part of their group or clique at school. Mike Nathanson would invite me over to his place to watch the Knicks and the Rangers and even invited me to attend regular season and playoff games. I even (reluctantly) passed on the opportunity to sit in Madison Square Garden and witness the dramatic moment when Willis Reed limped out onto the court for Game number 7 of the NBA Finals of the Knicks against the Lakers, because Jason Ekaireb begged me to come to a party at his parent's apartment that weekend. Boy, was that a mistake! But it was all part of supporting my teammate and sharing in new experiences at Dalton.

My parent's lack of a loving relationship had been established in our household for many years. At one point, because of my father's infidelities, my mother put him out of the house for awhile; believing that if he were deprived of his family, he would straighten up and be the kind of man that she needed him to be. But my father was his own man and he continued his ways. When the Temptations big hit, "Papa Was A Rolling Stone" was released in 1972, they might as well have been singing about our Pop. Pop begged my mom to let him return home (even his mother begged her to take him back). My father, upon his return, was relegated to the living room couch in the evening, while my mother and baby sister shared their bedroom.

By the end of the summer, my mother, thinking that she needed to keep up the discipline that my father failed to provide, matter-of-factly told me that varsity football was "off limits" as I entered the 9th grade. She felt I would need the extra study time to make the adjustment—exactly the same rationale she used when I first entered private school. I guess she figured it worked the first time, why mess with a good thing. As I look back upon her motive, I believe it was imperative for my mother to make me understand that there was only so much rope I was going to be allowed as I went from becoming an adolescent to a teenager and she needed to make an impression on me. That same summer when I screwed up and did something wrong, she made me cut my afro, which I had been proudly grooming for months; ready to intimidate the Dalton community come September. I begged my Mother and tried to explain to her how embarrassing it would be for me have to tell my teammates and coaches that I couldn't play ball because my *mother* wouldn't give me permission. She just looked at me nonplussed and told me that she didn't care what I told anyone—this was her final word. It wasn't a pleasant experience telling Coach Boyers that I couldn't participate in football at the end of the summer and he tried his best to convince me of the opportunity that I squandered away and spots on the team weren't just going to be held for me. Boyers considered talking with my mother about this decision, but she informed me ahead of time that he needn't bother contacting her, because there was nothing to discuss. This insult to Coach Boyers was most likely a "first strike" in our relationship, because normally, within the confines of the Dalton School, he ALWAYS got his way.

THE CAGER TAKES CENTER COURT

Once I'd proven myself academically during the first semester of my freshman year and established whatever additional school activities I was going to be a part of, I carefully approached my mother about joining the basketball team, making sure to point out my first semester grades which were respectable. As with middle school, your parents had to sign a permission form in order for you to become a part of any of the teams. I didn't bother my father because whatever my mother said was the final word whether my father agreed or not. She signed the slip with a warning that my grades can't suffer. I gratefully told her that wouldn't happen and was hopeful that with this freedom I could make the varsity basketball team.

Basketball wasn't my first love as a sport—football was the athletic activity that held all of my "misguided dreams of gridiron glory!" I never believed I was any good on the court, especially over the summers in my neighborhood in East Harlem. If you were a young Black male in the neighborhood, you had dreams of playing professional basketball. If you were a young Hispanic male, pro baseball was the goal. There were many afternoons hanging around the basketball court on the grounds of JHS 45, where I stood for hours waiting to be picked to play in a game where one mistake meant you'd be called out and embarrassed by everyone from blocks around who came to strut their stuff on the blacktop. It was years of sweat and the support of one or two of the better ballers in the neighborhood, along with many one-on-one lessons with my older brother Norman that led to my improvement as a player. If the top guys didn't know you, you weren't picked. So, it was a rite of passage for me to win the confidence of the die-hard players and be picked to play on the court with the serious players "in the hood."

Second semester freshman year at Dalton also began my first full-time exposure to the school's varsity coach and Athletic Director, Allan Boyers. Boyers, otherwise known as "Coach," was a revered fixture at the school. He began his tenure at Dalton in 1957, when Dalton was still an all-girls school and stayed until 1995; an almost 40 year term that saw generations of young men and women influenced by the teachings and coaching of Allan Boyers. A native New Yorker, born and raised in Brooklyn, he brought the grit and toughness of his generation as well as his neighborhood to the re-fined halls of the elite upper east side private school. He was a big man, over six feet tall and barrel-chested with a loud, hoarse voice that penetrated the football sidelines or the basketball court if he wanted to get your attention. If you screwed up a play in football practice, everyone knew to bite their mouthpiece a little tighter because the next sounds you heard were the un-relenting rantings of "Coach." Basketball practice was always worse if you got a play wrong, or weren't hustling enough for his taste, because there was no football helmet to filter his raspy voice.

Boyers' coaching method was simple; do what he told you to do, act the way he felt you should act and don't bring any attention to yourself. These were probably the same principles that were taught to him as a young man and he was convinced that they worked. Boyers was there when Dalton became coed under Donald Barr in 1966. I'm sure the old athlete and competitor in him was excited to have young men attending Dalton. He could fulfill his dream of coaching young men's football and basketball teams, the two sports he loved to coach. As a New York native, Boyers instinctively understood that the school would need to recruit athletes from across the city in order for the teams to be talented and competitive. That meant plucking young men from the tougher working-class neighborhoods of his upbringing and from similar communities across the boroughs. And yes, recruiting some of the very first Black and brown boys to enter this white, extremely affluent school, was an essential part of the plan.

Dalton had been integrated by a few young Black girls back in the 40's, as documented by my co-author, Mark Robinson. Mark's Aunt was one of the first African American female students at the school. But I would've loved to have been a "fly on the wall," when the subject of bringing Black and brown young men to a formerly all-girls school was first discussed. What did Donald Barr think of the idea of an integrated boys' basketball and football team? How would he present that social experiment to the parents and trustees of the school? In my freshman season, the basketball team had a total of eleven players and of those eleven, eight of us were Black or brown.

Coach Boyers was instrumental in integrating young men of color into the Dalton environment and making the school teams competitive with some of the larger private schools across the city. He also made it his business that his athletes were given whatever financial aid or academic assistance they needed to succeed at Dalton (with some serious lobbying of teachers and the administration for those boys struggling academically). This made most of those same young men beholden to "The Coach," for giving them an opportunity of a lifetime at the trendy and prestigious private School. Boyers is still talked about in loving and glowing terms by some of my teammates to this day. That loving and caring relationship was not my history with Boyers. When I entered Dalton in 7th grade, no one had any notion of my athletic abilities; they only knew that I was a bright young man and it wasn't until eighth grade that anyone had a hint of my athletic potential. But Boyers had his eye on me from eighth grade and he thought he could mold me into one of his "star players."

Our varsity basketball team of the 1970-1971 season might have been one of the most talented of all the private schools at that time. But the star player Boyers managed to recruit to Dalton was the late, Wesley Ramseur. As a sophomore, he was a six foot six inch, silky smooth basketball phenom, recruited from the neighborhood playgrounds with curly red hair, an infectious personality and a handsome face that drew the coeds of all colors to him. Wes was a sight to behold and let everyone know what he was at Dalton to do one thing…play basketball. Classes were secondary to Wes and he struggled endlessly to maintain his grades. Tutors were a permanent fixture for him to not flunk out because, despite Boyers' unfailing support for his star athlete, the school maintained its academic standards. Ultimately, Wes flunked out after his sophomore year and went on to become an all-city highly recruited player at Hughes High School and then on to Temple University.

In preparation for each season, Boyers would seek to toughen up the team by having us play a couple of public schools in the pre-season. We would be battle-tested for the year. One of those schools, Harlem Prep, was always on our pre-season schedule. They always brought their entire cheering section to the school, including wives or girlfriends with their kids in tow. Those contests were particularly humiliating if we weren't ready for the highly physical brand of basketball that they played. If we were embarrassed, or played scared, practice the following day would be a brutal affair.

My "identity" as a member of the basketball team cast me in a different light for the white high-schoolers. "Oh, you play for one of the teams. That's how you were admitted to Dalton, right?" This was how it started; the assumption that if you were a Black male in the high school, the only way you could attend was to play a sport. So now high school had its own "caste system", not just based on class or wealth, but also on race and what it implied about you. The white students and teachers never considered that their assumptions toward us were insults. Our feelings were irrelevant to them.

DOUBLE CONSCIOUSNESS

A particular quote from W. E. B. DuBois 1903 landmark book, "The Souls Of Black Folk" accurately described my emotions as I prepared to begin sophomore year at Dalton:

"It is a peculiar sensation, this double-consciousness, this sense of always looking at one's self through the eyes of others, of measuring one's soul by the tape of a world that looks on in amused contempt and pity."

This quote by DuBois always had particular meaning for Black people in America. Unless they were educated in predominantly Black institutions and later worked where they had little to no contact with white people, they had to learn to manage their way through a societal minefield filled with the legacy of slavery, segregation and Jim Crow, a legacy that still persists today. I had thus far spent three years in a school where I was never certain that I was welcome or fully accepted by my teachers and fellow students. The great twelve-story structure on 89th Street between Lexington and Park Avenues was a prodigious monument to the wealth and privilege, but it was never my home.

More than any other time in the past, Dalton had expectations for me academically and athletically that I wasn't certain I could meet, nor if I wanted to. So, I was torn. The Neighborhood Tutorial Center had become such an important part of my life that I wanted to start an after-school Fall program along with several of the other committed students. This would enable us to continue the work we were doing with our children from the summer through the school months. But it would require us to give up the other activities we engaged in at school to begin the program. This was a particularly difficult decision for me because I was finally going to be a member of the varsity football team at Dalton and football practice wouldn't allow me to be available for the start of the transition to the after-school program. However, at the end of the summer fate would cruelly decide my choice for me.

Near the end of summer, I was playing a pick-up game of basketball with a couple of my friends behind our building, when I jumped up for a rebound and came down on the side of ankle. The pain was excruciating—it shot through my whole body and left me in a pile on the hard blacktop. It was no ordinary ankle sprain. I'd had several of those before and always managed to recuperate quickly, but this injury required me being assisted upstairs to our apartment, where my father took me for a visit to the emergency room at Metropolitan Hospital. They took x-rays of the ankle and didn't find anything broken, so they iced it, wrapped my ankle up with a soft cast, gave me a pair of crutches and sent me on my way.

My injury on the neighborhood basketball court was an omen, a sign of things to come for the upcoming semester at school. Coach Boyers was quite annoyed over my ill-timed injury. I wasn't going to be able to join the football team for their twice-daily practices on Randall's Island. Frankly, I didn't mind not sweating my ass off in the hot summer sun gasping for breath as Boyers put us through his version of medieval torture. My only participation with the team was treatment for my ankle under the supervision of our trainer, Joe Webb. He was a slight, red-headed fellow that the school hired as a full-time trainer for all of Dalton's athletic teams.

My accident didn't upset me nearly as much as it did Boyers and the football team. It allowed me to participate in the initial set-up of the NTC After-School Program, as I hobbled on my crutches from Dalton after my treatment sessions and back uptown on the public bus. Mr. Marchal had picked out a storefront near the corner of 125th Street and Third Avenue that needed a lot of work to make it suitable for the children and tutors. With grant money we received, we had new linoleum laid on the floors, painted the walls, bought desks, chairs, pens, pencils; everything we needed to handle the number of kids that would make use of our cozy little space.

It was all exciting, watching the program come to fruition. It gave my comrades and me a tremendous sense of accomplishment even though we weren't getting paid in the fall like we did during the summer. And it eased the pain of my injury aiding young kids from our neighborhood with their studies, because it also allowed me to be nearer my girlfriend Kathy, who was also an after-school tutor.

Coach Boyers grew impatient with my progress in recovering from my sprained ankle. His attitude was it didn't matter whether a limb was hanging off your body, you simply tape it up and get back out on the field. Back then, whether schools had trainers or not, the athletic coaches could easily influence the care of the players, depending on the coaches' needs. Varsity football had begun at the start of the '71 school term and the team had already played several games when I finally practiced regularly, even though I was still experiencing pain in the right ankle. The NTC After School program was established and the kids attended on a regular basis. And although I enjoyed working with the children, my desire to play on the varsity team continued to tug at me and I did whatever I could to be prepared to play; not for Coach Boyers' sake, but for my own desire to become a real part of the team.

It was a beautiful fall day when I got my opportunity to suit up and finally be active to play for the Dalton Varsity Football Team. Because I hadn't been a part of the summer "two-a-days" and wasn't in totally great shape, I was going to be limited in how much I played and was told by the coaching staff of Boyers, Duerward Middleton and Doug French, that I would be available to substitute for one of the defensive ends during the game. The call from the coaching staff came sometime near the end of the second quarter when I was told to go in at the start of the defensive series. Boyers approached me standing on the sideline while the team was prepared to punt the football, looked me in the face with a "let's see what you can do" glare and told me I would be going in when we switched over to defense. I didn't say anything to him—just tightened up my chinstrap and pumped myself up for my chance.

It was exciting to finally be on the same field with my teammates in uniform. We were playing on our home field in Van Cortland Park in the Bronx. The other team ran a running play right at my position. I was able to maneuver my way through the blockers to stop the play for no gain, mostly because I was much quicker than the players who tried to block me. That was why Boyers wanted me out on the field. The second down in that series was an incomplete pass to the opposite side of the field that set up third down for our defense. This time, instead of standing up in a two-point stance at the end of the line of scrimmage, I placed my hand in the dirt to prepare to rush the quarterback. In my mind, I saw all of the great pro football defensive ends I loved to watch as a kid viewing the NFL on television.

This time, the opposing offense didn't line up anyone directly in front of me before the play began. This gave me a direct line to the quarterback, should the blocking break down. I was determined to take the most direct course to the quarterback, come hell or high water. As the football was snapped, I pounced. It was a sprint to the quarterback who moved to his right as I rushed to meet him before he could throw the football. Before he could wind up his arm to release the ball, I jumped in the air on top of his helmet and outstretched arm, causing his throw to wobble toward the right side of the field like a wounded duck, where one of our defensive backs grabbed the football and secured it for an interception. Everyone was elated at our good fortune; the Dalton sideline was going nuts and our defenders were jumping on top of our defensive back. However, back at the spot where the opposing quarterback was lying on the ground, was me, wincing in tremendous pain. I limped off the field toward our sideline and straight to the bench, where our trainer, Joe Webb, came up to me and asked what happened. All I could mutter was, "it's my ankle," as he cut away my sock around the heavily taped ankle. It was almost as tender to the touch as it was when I first injured it during the summer. Joe called the doctor over to examine me.

The Dalton athletic programs were reliant upon the fine orthopedists from the well-known Lenox Hill Hospital on the upper east side of Manhattan to mend the broken bones, dislocations, or ligament tears of the school's athletes, so we were fortunate to have very fine doctors at our disposal. But none of the hospital's doctors had ever examined my ankle before I practiced with the team, nor did Boyers, or Joe Webb ask them to examine me prior to receiving the okay to play in a game. It was a mutual decision by the head coach and the trainer. Let's face it, what did I know? I wanted to play and was willing to endure some pain in order to be a part of the team, but when the doctor examined my ankle after the tape was removed, he looked up at Joe with my ankle in his hand and asked, "why was I even in the game?" Joe gave the doctor a sheepish look and then slightly cocked his head in my direction with an apologetic look. At fifteen years of age, you really don't know any better regarding what's best for your health when you're playing an organized sport. It's up to the professional staff at your school to look out for your well-being and temper your enthusiasm and eagerness to play if you're not physically ready. This doctor concluded after his examination of my ankle that I had not been ready to play.

Moments later, Coach Boyers came over to assess my status and ask when I would be ready to re-enter the game. The doctor told him in no uncertain terms that I was not only done for the day, but probably done for the rest of the season. An unbelievably disgusted look formed on Boyers' face, as I watched him stare incredulously at the doctor, then at trainer Joe Webb, but he never once acknowledged me. He just angrily turned away at the news and left me on the bench, cut-off tape dangling haphazardly off the sides of my right ankle and calf, exposing the neatly shaved leg which had been prepped by me the night before. I was devastated. I was angry at the news, angry at Joe Webb, angry at Boyers who pushed his trainer to have me ready to play before my ankle was properly healed and angry at my sheer lousy luck, as I stared at my throbbing leg in the hopes it would heal itself by my sight. No such relief was coming. I sat there on the bench staring into space, leg exposed, resting on the grass, as several teammates came up to me and patted me on the shoulder pads. I pondered my misfortune on that sunlit afternoon with a new pair of crutches propped up on the bench beside me. "D" tried to console me when there was a free opportunity for him, and he reminded me that it wasn't the end of the world. I would get healthy, come back and kick ass next season. "D's" heartfelt encouragement was only slight consolation for me at that moment, as I sat on the bench wondering who at Dalton was really looking out for my well-being.

The Donald Barr Episode

The incident with my injured ankle left me with an extremely bad taste in my mouth and a total distrust of Boyers and Joe Webb, although I wasn't blind to the fact that Joe only did whatever Boyers asked of him. As an athletic trainer, he should have put the best interests of the injured athlete before the wishes of the head coach, whose main interest was putting his best players on the field. This was the early seventies, and athletes on all levels of sport were expected to play through pain and to play hurt. This was the culture espoused by Coach Boyers. He didn't respect any athlete who didn't sacrifice himself for the good of the team. No player wanted to be labeled "soft" or not tough when it came to the macho sport of football, and players didn't want to disappoint Boyers. Guys played through their injuries and ailments and are paying for those physical sacrifices today, myself included. In my case, the injured right ankle would never be the same.

When I had x-rays taken of the ankle, it revealed a hairline fracture of the tibia that was probably a product of the original injury I suffered playing basketball during the summer, but since a follow-up x-ray of my leg was never prescribed before I was cleared to play football, we never knew the extent of the fracture. I was given a "soft cast" that was wrapped with plenty of gauze and ace bandages around my right leg from the knee down to the foot, as I learned to navigate with the crutches for the next few months around our apartment in the projects, the public buses and subways and the school. From September until at least March my leg was shaved smoother than my girlfriend's, because it needed to be taped for every practice and every game. Otherwise, it would've been susceptible to injury over and over again, since the ligaments were severely stretched, and I'd be screaming bloody murder each time the athletic tape was ripped off my ankle!

As the fall semester ended, my mind wandered to the Neighborhood Tutorial Center and my comrades aiding the children of our area. The prospect of working over the winter months and into the spring gave me and the other tutors a sense of purpose and fulfillment that Dalton couldn't match. Seeing neighborhood children improve their reading comprehension, math and history gave each of us tremendous satisfaction that we had impacted a young life—that they gained enough knowledge to help guide them through the difficult conditions of poverty, inadequate housing, and poor schooling. The percentages weren't great for any of us, much less for these kids, growing up In the projects, hoping to attend better schools with the prospect of one day going to college, choosing a profession and living a better life than our parents before us.

That's what was on my mind as the football season ended and basketball season fast approached. There were barely a few weeks in-between the end of one sport and the beginning of the other, and this never allowed the players that participated in both sports to fully heal from their injuries. It also required them to sacrifice much of their Christmas holiday free-time to practice at the school gymnasium in preparation for the pre-season and the regular season. These sacrifices for the school teams were the context for a critical decision in my Dalton tenure. Was I prepared to put my body through the grind of basketball season when it was still healing from football season? Where would I make the biggest impact on the two communities that I spent most of my time? Who would appreciate and need my commitment to them more?

Sometime in November or December, I made up my mind. I would forgo varsity basketball, where I would play a starting role as a sophomore forward on the team and commit to the after-school program at the NTC. I learned a hard and difficult lesson from football season—my physical well-being wasn't that important to the school if they were willing to have me play on a fractured ankle. The next part of my decision would be much more difficult than making up my mind; how to tell Coach Boyers.

I made my way up to Boyers' office at the top of the gym on the twelfth floor. I could smell the tobacco from his pipe as I walked the narrow hallway of the locker room toward his office to bring him the news. I knocked on the door and he grunted, "come in" as he clenched his pipe through his teeth to yell. I stood in front of him and said that I wanted to know if he had a moment to talk about basketball season. He told me he did, and I sat down in a chair opposite his desk, as he leaned back with an inquisitive look to hear whatever it was I had to say. There was always tension between Coach Boyers and me. He couldn't quite figure me out. He thought he knew all of the boys that played on his teams—understood their motivations, could talk to them about their classes, girls, home life, etc. But he felt he didn't have a handle on me. He was really stumped when I told him that I wasn't going to play basketball that season. I told him it had nothing to do with him or the school, even though deep down inside I still had some resentments. I said I wanted to work at a local community program that I helped to create. His face was twisted with disgust when he removed his pipe from his mouth. He didn't understand my motivations and couldn't understand why I didn't want to commit to the team and support my teammates. I had others I wanted to support that fall and winter and it didn't involve anyone from the school. I made my decision and I thought once I expressed it, that would be it. But Boyers kept pushing, kept prodding, trying to understand me, wanting to know why I was the most militant Black guy on the team (yes, he believed he knew all the other minority athletes on his teams, except me). He thought I was a talented athlete, but that I was never going to reach my potential if I didn't work with him to achieve that end. He couldn't read me and suggested that my teammates couldn't read me either. He said if I went through with this, I'd be letting them down. His attempt to make me feel guilty was kind of humorous, because no one was better at making me feel guilty than my mother and Coach had a long way to go to be in her league.

Our meeting set off a chain-reaction that reverberated through several layers of the school administration. The following week I was summoned to the office of the new Director of Athletics, David Dunkel who, along with Boyers, tried to remind me of the commitment that Dalton had made to me in terms of the scholarship money that I received. Ignorantly, the two of them were under the impression that I was one of their athletic team recruits. Their tactic was to try and make me feel I had an obligation to the school and the teams, but I reminded them that I entered Dalton in seventh grade and NOT high school. Whatever scholarship I received from the school was based on financial need and not on any athletic commitment to perform. This tag-teaming by the two of them over the next couple of days eventually brought us to the office of the Dean of the High School, Dimitri Sevastopoulo. Now the three of them attempted to impress upon me the importance of playing on the school team, the tradition and the honor of representing Dalton in all athletic endeavors. But my mind was made up and no amount of brow-beating from these three members of the school administration was going to change my mind. It was quite silly to watch these men place such a high value on the athletic ability of one young Black boy.

All of these "athletics interventions" finally landed me in the office of the school's Headmaster, Donald Barr. Barr and I had a couple of prior encounters due to some mishaps that befell me earlier in my time at the school, but this was going to be the first time where I would sit down with him surrounded by others; in particular Coach Boyers, Dunkel and Sevastopoulo. The three of them escorted me to the headmaster's office like guards escorting a death row inmate to the electric chair. Barr told me to have a seat in the chair opposite his huge desk in a room with shelves of books from one side of the wall to the other. Then Barr did a very peculiar thing. After I sat down, he told the others that he would see me alone. "WHOA SHIT!" I turned my head around after I heard him say this, to see the stunned looks on the three of their faces and then turned back around toward Barr with a wry smile on my face that they couldn't see. Barr watched the three men slink away and closed his office door behind them. This man, who came from a scientific environment at Columbia University and became headmaster, was a notoriously aloof figure at our school. He had a reputation as a progressive educator, but with zero tolerance for the youth culture of the early seventies and its undisciplined students. Although he occasionally ventured to the gymnasium to watch one of the basketball games, I never considered him a fan of basketball or any other sport.

With his owl-like eyebrows and his buzz-cut hair that formed a neat square on top of his head, and a pair of horn-rimmed glasses, he formed his hands into a triangle in front of his chest, leaned back in his chair, looked me in the eye and asked me why did I think I was summoned to his office. The militant in me wanted to jump up in his face and scream, "I HAVE NO FUCKIN' IDEA!" But I wasn't stupid. I told him I was very committed to an after-school program whose curriculum I helped design for the neighborhood public school children who were far less fortunate than myself. I wanted to share my time and energy and give back some of the benefit of my Dalton education. I also told him that I appreciated that the coaches and administration thought I was an important piece of the team's potential success, but that I needed to see this new project succeed. He sat quietly, listened intently to me, never interrupted or interjected his own personal feelings about the matter, and let me finish my completely unrehearsed presentation.

Everything I told him was from the heart (although I never mentioned my dissatisfaction with the medical treatment afforded me during my injury). When I was done, Barr paused for a second, looked up to the ceiling and then rose from his chair. As he stood up, I figured I'd better stand as well—didn't want him to think that I didn't have any manners at all. He offered an outstretched hand to shake mine and calmly said to me in his most professorial voice, "Young man, your cause is an admirable one and I wish you all the success in the world."

That was it. My ordeal had ended. I was liberated to pursue my involvement with the Neighborhood Tutorial Center, to lend a helping hand to the kids of my building, my projects, my neighborhood. Whether I realized it or not, I became a symbol at the school of someone who "bucked the system," or "beat the man" which was a popular phrase of overcoming white authority figures back in the seventies.

With Donald Barr's backing and blessing, I would no longer be made to feel as if my decision not to play basketball was a betrayal to the school, or that my future at the institution was interwoven with my allegiance to the athletic programs. Boyers, Dunkel and Sevastopoulo believed that I owed the school the benefit of my body and I should have no say in the matter. I think Allan Boyers felt personally betrayed by my actions. I was the student who won a highly contentious battle against the school's administration with the final blessing of the school's headmaster and that did not sit well with him or the others who were unceremoniously dismissed from Barr's chambers. I really didn't give a shit what they believed. I fought for my freedom to make my own decisions. That was worth fighting for.

The backlash and pressure of my decision weighed heavily in everything I did around the school from that point on. Were it not for several supportive teachers at Dalton, I don't know that I would have made it through my remaining years at the school. A quote by poet, singer and actress Maya Angelou seems to fit this part of my story:

"In order to be a mentor, and an effective one, one must care...Know what you know and care about the person, care about what you know and care about the person you're sharing with."

I was blessed to have people who cared for me at Dalton, people who did not just sympathize with my struggles, but empathized as well, people who kept an ear out for any news or rumors that I might need to know in regards to the challenges of the private school. I have mentioned Monsieur Volel, who took me under his wing in seventh grade and was an inspiring figure throughout my entire Dalton experience. Gym teacher, and Assistant Football/Basketball Coach, Mr. Middleton, was one of my first "guardian angels" from the time he started working at Dalton. (As Mr. Middleton and I got to know each other, I learned that it was his younger brother, Delano, who was the high school student murdered on the dormitory steps of the South Carolina State University campus by Highway Patrol Officers during the 1968 "Orangeburg Massacre.") He cultivated my athletic abilities and, as much as anyone, he prepped me for the social challenges at the school. He told me to be wary because not everyone that claimed to be a friend—was.

My sophomore year gave me the chance to get to know and trust the future "Mrs. Middleton." Lucinda Ransom was a dance instructor who worked alongside the beloved Dalton School dance teacher Elizabeth Williamson and who herself performed classical ballet back when dance companies didn't believe Black artists could handle the rigors. She not only danced professionally for more than thirty years, but she also performed on stage with the great Alvin Ailey and his world-renowned dance company and volunteered her time in workshops sponsored by the company to encourage under-privileged children in Harlem to dance. Ms. Ransom was now my house advisor. Ms. Ransom also became the faculty advisor to our Third World Culture Committee. She was very protective of me as we got to know each other through our interactions in the mornings at house meetings, or at various times throughout the school day. I called her my "Dalton Mother."

Rolando Reyes came to Dalton during my freshman year and never seemed to leave the basement area where the art and sculpture rooms were located. That section of the school always seemed remote and separate to me, as if the students curated their own art gallery apart from the school. Dalton had some very talented student artists who exhibited their work around the school, but their craft was nurtured by people like Mr. Reyes. He was Hispanic—not certain if he was of Dominican, or Puerto Rican heritage, but he was a quiet, handsome, gentle man with a full beard that framed his brown skin, a large mole on the side of his face and a medium-sized afro. He almost always wore jeans along with cowboy boots and some sort of authentic western shirt that looked vintage, with Native American jewelry on both of his hands and forearms. He stood out among the Dalton faculty because he looked more like a musician or artist than a member of the school.

I don't recall what brought us together—our relationship just happened. Once I had established myself at Dalton as a student, an athlete, a member of the chorus and determined member of the Third World Culture Committee, I compartmentalized my time at school, interacting with the white students and teachers only when needed. According to many of my white former classmates that I have spoken with at Dalton reunions, this made me an aloof and distant figure; someone to avoid for fear of pissing off. But with teachers like "D", Ms. Ransom and Mr. Reyes, I was able to let my guard down and dispose of the imaginary mask I wore each day to school to cope. Mr. Reyes recruited me that winter to work with him at his store down in Greenwich Village called "The Common Ground." This store was a monument to his love of Native-American culture and artisanship. It featured jewelry crafted by Native-American artists designing pieces with turquoise, malachite, onyx and coral, set inside sterling silver. The Common Ground was an art gallery, a museum and jewelry store all wrapped-in-one. Mr. Reyes gave me a crash course in the history and cost of all the various items in his store and hired me to assist him during the Dalton holiday break in preparation for the Christmas rush that winter. This afforded me the money to purchase the books, supplies and clothing that I needed to put myself through school because it was unbelievably difficult for my mother to afford these items on my family's already stretched household. Not only did my Mother struggle to put me through private school, but she also managed the tuitions of my younger brother Mark, who attended The Walden School and my younger sister Rachel, who attended The Town School and Riverdale Country Day. Yes, we all received scholarships that covered some of the costs to attend these elite schools, but it also meant there wasn't ANY money left for much else in the way of essential school supplies, or entertainment. So if I didn't earn my own money in some way, I was out-of-luck and knew not to bother my parents.

Mr. Reyes' patience with me was admirable during those early days of frantic Christmas shopping by Village residents. There were numerous occasions where he absolutely panicked when I misquoted the price on an item. That was potential cash out the door. And because the shop was always busy on the weekends leading up to Christmas and New Year, he wasn't always available to give me a quote on an item that might not have had a tag on it. It was only when the traffic slowed that he could spend time explaining the origins of many of the pieces he picked out to sell in the store, how different Native-American tribes favored certain stones, or how they favored certain types of silver to create their designs. He taught me about how and why turquoise stones varied greatly depending upon where the stone was mined, and how it could take on the various colors of other heavy metals such as copper, or aluminum. His store also featured incredibly designed hand-made rugs by the Navajo. These were some of my favorite pieces because no two rugs were ever exactly alike. Each one was unique unto itself, so it was always easy to say to a customer that this was a "one-of-a-kind" work. Rolando knew what he was looking at during his numerous trips to the southwest trading posts of New Mexico and Arizona. Through his patient teaching and mentorship, I was given a wonderful gift of the incredible history of the "first true natives" of this land and how they were exploited by the white man.

Of all my relationships with my "guardian angels" at Dalton, my connection with Mr. Reyes lasted the longest. I worked at his shop during every holiday through my graduation at Dalton and into my early college years. He even entrusted me to manage a second store of his that specialized in Navajo weavings when I was just twenty years of age. I sublet a nearby apartment in the Village that summer in order to always be available. Imagine, this man never thought twice about bestowing upon me the awesome responsibility of managing a shop in New York City in a predominantly white neighborhood at a very young age, but the life lessons were invaluable. Especially when confronted with trying to sell to mostly white shoppers who eyed me warily as I expounded upon the origin-stories of the different weavings featured at The Common Ground II. His trust in my abilities gave me tremendous confidence in myself as a young man and the skills to communicate with a world that wasn't always in my corner. His example also showed me the error of my perception of the homosexual community, a lifestyle that was mocked and ridiculed incessantly by most of the athletes on our school teams, including me. Many of the other nearby shopkeepers surrounding The Common Ground were gay and chose the Village because they weren't as threatened as they might have been in other parts of New York.

That sense of safety took a monumental turn, however, during the "Stonewall Riots" of 1969, when The Stonewall Inn on Christopher Street in the West Village became the scene of a violent confrontation between New York City police and the gay patrons of the bar. That moment at Stonewall is considered the "birthplace of the gay pride movement" and as I worked at the Common Ground, I was very aware that I was only a couple of years removed from that dramatic event. Rolando always emphasized to me the importance of service as a shopkeeper—the mantra of "the customer was always right". The whole experience was an awakening for me.

I will never, ever forget the generosity of Mr. Reyes. Not only of his time, but of the many gifts he gave me working with him. If there was a bracelet, or ring, or some other item that I admired but thought I could never afford, by the holiday's end he would present it to me as a gift. I proudly wore my Native-American jewelry at school and later on at college, able to recite chapter and verse the history of that adornment. He also allowed me to purchase gifts for my girlfriend Kathy, my sister and my Mother at tremendously discounted prices, or allowed me the opportunity to work off the remaining balance. These gestures of kindness showed me so much of the person he was, and I will always be indebted to Mr. Reyes and grateful for our friendship. When events around me were sometimes too much to handle, I counted on him to make sense of it all. He was a mentor, a friend, a father when mine was absent, and one of the most special people I've ever known. I am saddened to say that we lost touch over this past decade. Even worse, while writing my story and meeting with other Dalton alumni at a surprise party for one of the contributors to this book, I was heartbroken to learn that Rolando passed away several years ago. I shall forever regret not having the chance to say goodbye and tell him how much I loved him.

Happily, junior year had a calm, positive beginning. Ms. Ransom continued as my house advisor. House now included my closest classmate during my final two years at Dalton. One year behind me, Chris Rose was a brilliant young bi-racial brother who could never quite figure out what to do with his hair, so it sort of fell all over his head with no rhyme or reason. He had a quick wit and a wry sense of humor and an infectious personality that was always entertaining to be around. We hung together in the bass section of the school chorus, which afforded us ample opportunities to scope out some of the young ladies in chorus. If we could be cast as two characters from a "Blaxploitation" movie from the seventies, we would've been "Buck and The Preacher"—me portraying the stoic, no-nonsense "Buck" who was determined to finish whatever his mission, and Chris' engaging and talkative "Preacher." There wasn't a topic that we couldn't discuss together, whether we were in our home room at the start of the day, eating lunch in the cafeteria or in the Dalton chorus. We kept each other entertained. Chris watched my back and kept me abreast of the comings and goings of aspects of the school that I chose to ignore for my own personal, emotional survival.

As students at Dalton, we were told that our junior year courses would count heavily toward the assessment of our eligibility by colleges across the country. And we began to think seriously about which universities and colleges we would apply to. Dalton had a stellar reputation as being a feeder to all of the Ivy League and "little-Ivy" schools, especially on the east coast and New England region. Other schools with wonderful academic reputations like Stanford, Northwestern, Massachusetts Institute of Technology (M.I.T.) naturally gravitated to Dalton for prospective undergrads.

I also tried to focus on the agenda of the Third World Culture Committee. Shelly Anderson, who was a senior, became the new head of the TWCC and relied on my assistance and support for the various projects. It was a constant challenge to convince the various Black and Hispanic Dalton students to commit to the committee's projects. Shelly and I were often disillusioned and wondered why we couldn't better mobilize our brethren. Most of the other student committees had full attendance and devoted participants, but the TWCC suffered from inconsistent participation and a general fear of going against the grain of the school administration or the white student body.

Dalton made it difficult for the Third World Culture Committee to flourish. The Headmaster never wanted the committee to exist in the first place. The school never directly stopped us from suggesting projects, or ideas, but we were never supported. And from my conversations with Ms. Ransom and Mr. Middleton, who were always doing their best to protect me, I knew I was being watched carefully by the school administration. There was no room for any semblance of "Black Power" infiltrating the privileged walls of our hallowed institution.

TELL YOUR STORY WALKIN'!

"Don't tell me how to do my thing
When you can't, can't, can't do your own
Don't tell me how to be a boy
When, when you know I'm grown..."
- James Brown, Talking Loud And Saying Nothing

My old man had a saying he used to bark at people he argued with, "...tell your story walkin'!" This was EXACTLY how I felt about Boyers, Dunkel, Sevastopoulo, after they confronted me the previous semester. The only thing they didn't discuss with me during those interrogation sessions were my "Miranda Rights!" So, after another productive summer of working at the Neighborhood Tutorial Center, I was armed with unbridled confidence in preparation for the start of school and the upcoming football and basketball seasons.

Returning to the school for summer football practices was a surreal experience. Many of my teammates, even the Black ones, were stand-offish towards me. There were also new faces recruited by Boyers over the summer who did their best to impress the coach. The new recruits were part of Boyers "toughening up" his ball club. The new guys were all of Italian descent from some of the "tough-as-nails" neighborhoods around New York City. They were from the same kind of working-class immigrant families that lived in East Harlem and received partial, if not full scholarships to attend the expensive school.

These players were going to be part of a test—a test of my toughness and my will. Assistant Football Coach "D" Middleton quietly let me know that Coach had it in for me, and would start with the practices that summer on Randall's Island. These were brutal practices, where Boyers made us execute a form of the "Oklahoma Drill." This was a drill made famous by the former head coach of the University Of Oklahoma and College Football Hall-Of-Famer Bud Wilkinson. It was glamorized over the decades on all levels of football, but has been pretty much abandoned because of the propensity for players to be injured, some very seriously. Concussions and neck injuries were prevalent from these drills, because we were taught to use the helmet as a weapon when we tackled an opponent. This was the culture of football in the late sixties and early seventies and it was how Boyers evaluated the toughest players on his team.

When my turn came, Coach barked out the players he wanted lined up against one another, and I took the defensive player position opposite Tom Fedele, who stood around five feet eight or nine inches tall and was the blocker for the ballcarrier. I wish I could tell you who the player was running the football, but it didn't matter, because I was too quick for Tom and maneuvered my way around him and made the tackle. The Coach was so annoyed that he yelled at Fedele to move out of the way and ordered Larry Schau to take his place and for me to stay where I was. I glanced over to "D", who gave me the look to watch out for this new kid who was supposedly "a little crazy, high strung" character. Larry was a slightly bigger version of Tom and was determined to take a piece of my ass with him when he challenged me, but after we came together with a loud "clap" from shoulder pads and helmets smashing together, he looked up amazed because even after his ferocious contact, I still brought down the ballcarrier. This angered Boyers even more, and he fumed on the sidelines for a couple of other players to complete their drill.

When it was my turn again, standing on the other side opposite me as the blocker was Fred Baldino. Freddie was right around six foot four and upwards of two hundred and fifty pounds, so he was a little taller than me, but outweighed me by close to sixty pounds (back then I weighed around one hundred and ninety pounds, and that was only after a big meal). It was time for me to tighten up my chinstrap and bite down a little harder on my mouthpiece, because this confrontation the coach thrust upon me was about my manhood. I decided that the ballcarrier didn't matter this time—it was the time to make a statement to my upcoming challenger, to the Coach and the rest of my teammates; you're NOT going to intimidate me and you're NOT going to get the best of me. So, when the whistle was blown, and Freddie charged at me, the only thing that was on my mind was at least a stalemate. I got just a little lower than him as we attacked each other and brought the crown of my helmet right across his face mask, which nine times out of ten always forces your helmet to impact against the bridge of your nose, causing a moment when you can see stars from the contact. As the ballcarrier scurried past us as if we were two bighorn sheep challenging for dominance in the herd, we looked at each other with a mutual respect after our violent contact and walked back to our respective lines. As I walked away, I glanced in the direction of Boyers, who was now preoccupied with yelling at someone else after our exhibition was over and I knew that I got my point across… Coach could throw whoever he wanted at me, and I would give as good as I got.

If Coach Boyers was hoping to break me in front of the team with this drill, his plan backfired. Instead of creating a wedge between my teammates and me, he succeeded in making me a "de facto" team captain. Fedele, Schau and Baldino looked up to me after we completed our summer pre-season practices and I happily offered whatever assistance I could helping them make that transition to Dalton. I went out of my way to befriend them just to piss off Coach, because I knew these guys. I knew where they came from, how they ticked. They were from the same kind of neighborhood that I lived in.

THE HEADHUNTER EMERGES

As varsity football season began, my excitement was palpable. There's no way to describe the feeling I had when I pulled on my pants with the thigh pads in the pockets, taped my knee-high football socks around my calves, tied the shoelaces on my football cleats, tightened the straps on my shoulder pads and donned my brand new Riddell air compression helmet. One of the advantages of going to a well-funded private school was that all of the athletic teams' equipment was top-of-the-line. The school spared no expense. We could put on as many elbow pads, forearms pads, sweatbands, and never felt we had to worry that the equipment had to last us till the end of the season.

From the first game junior year, I was determined to make an impact. But it wasn't going to be on our team's offense, because Coach Boyers admired the type of offense the Oklahoma Sooners ran back in the sixties and seventies: "The Wishbone." It was geared toward a quarterback that could run the football. Roy Samuelson, who has been involved with and worked for the school since he first stepped through its walls, was a talented, three-sport athlete in football, wrestling and baseball, and was our quarterback. He was given the direction to run the wishbone until ours, or the other team's tongues were hanging out. For Coach Boyers, it was about force-feeding the football down the throat of the opposing defense and may the toughest team win. All of my ambitions of being a tight end that caught the football downfield, like some of my NFL idols from the seventies, were dashed because of Boyers' choice of offense. My job was to block my ass off for our quarterback and running backs Jason Ekaireb and Kenny Collins.

Fred Baldino and I manned the right side of the offensive line as the team's right tackle and tight end. We got a thrill whenever Roy recognized a blitz coming from the other team and signaled an audible. An "audible" is a verbal signal that the quarterback shouts out before the snap of the football. It lets his team know they're changing from the original play called in the huddle, to another different play, because of how the opposing team has lined up. When it worked, it was a thing of beauty. In one game, the other team's linebacker jumped into the gap between Fred and me. Since I was quicker than Fred, it was up to me to get to the right spot first. Fred would follow behind. When the snap count came, I sprang to my left and plowed my helmet directly into the chest of that linebacker, and forced him into his own defensive lineman. Fred slid to his right, securing the other lineman at the end of formation. This created a huge hole for Jason to scurry through untouched for fifty-plus yards and a touchdown. Fred and I slapped each other five as we watched Ekaireb sprint to the end zone. When Jason joined the huddle for the extra-point, he excitedly mumbled something through his mouthpiece about how big the hole was for him, and we were both like, "No Shit!"

Every once in a while, one of our audibles was a quick pass to the tight end…meaning me. I always got a real burst of energy when Roy called this particular audible. It was all I could do to not give away the fact that the football was finally coming to me. I made many a big play downfield with this call, and enjoyed dragging defenders who were draped all over me once I caught the football. Sometimes, I was a sitting duck for the defensive backs to line me up and take a running shot at my head. During one game against Fieldston, I jumped into the air to catch a football and was rudely low-bridged and landed on the back of my neck and shoulders. My helmet to flew off and rolled along the field like a soccer ball. Fortunately, my head wasn't in it, as it scooted along the grass. When I ran to grab it and place it back on my head, I couldn't put it on. I turned my helmet around to look at the face mask. It was bent from the top bar, down to the bottom part of the cage, which caused the sides of my helmet to compress so much that I couldn't put my head into it.

Obviously, I couldn't stay on the field without my gear, so I was forced to run off for a play to find another helmet. I now had to canvas my teammates to see if someone had a comparable-sized one for me to finish the game. Finally, I came to another junior teammate named Billy Rudin. His family was very wealthy and was involved in expensive commercial real estate in New York City. They were major donors and always took out expensive full page ads in the school yearbook to support the students. Billy wasn't much of an athlete and only entered the games whenever it was a blow out, either in our favor, or the opponent's. But since he was the only teammate whose helmet I hadn't tried, I implored for him to let me borrow his equipment. He vehemently objected, until the Coach intervened and yelled at him to give up his helmet. Needless to say, he was none too pleased about being embarrassed in this way, but since I was a "two-way" player and Billy was a "no-way" player, he begrudgingly surrendered his helmet.

As I mentioned at the outset of this chapter, Dalton's football offense was offered only a very limited opportunity for me to show my abilities, so because of that, I took out my frustrations against the opposing team on the defensive side of the ball, much in the same way that I harassed my teammates during practice when I was in a foul mood. It was during a game against the New York Military Academy at their home field in Long Island, NY where my varsity football nickname was born.

I was having a particularly rambunctious defensive game against the NYMA when, on a third down play, they brought into the game a little "wingback" who lined up on the opposite side of the field from me. I noticed this kid because it was the first time he had entered the contest and we were already well into the second half, so I assumed he was placed on the field for a reason. I was in a three point stance with my hand in the grass, because I knew it was going to be a passing down. When the ball was snapped, the quarterback dropped a few steps back before he slowed down. I told myself that I had this guy dead to rights; only, instead of him raising his arm to throw the football downfield, he handed it off to the oncoming wingback from the opposite side of the field. My eyes grew wide as I rushed full speed toward the intersection of the quarterback and the wingback's exchange of the football, stuck my right arm outward from my body and whipped it underneath the helmet of the ballcarrier. This maneuver was commonly called a "clothesline"—not a gentle way to bring down any ballcarrier. My arm completely wrapped itself around his neck and slammed him headfirst to the ground, while his legs jutted out in front of him and the football shot out of his hands like a pumpkin seed. My team recovered the fumble and the other team's trainers carried the little wingback off the field.

Our school newspaper, "The Daltonian," recounted the big moments from our victory against NYMA, and they highlighted my "clothesline tackle," whereby they dubbed me "The Headhunter." It was never my intention to harm anyone—it was just a reflexive action during a football game that has many violent moments. But I have to confess, I kinda' dug the new nickname. It elevated me to a new level of notoriety within the football team and at school; a level I didn't shy away from.

The toughest team we ever faced was the Eastern Military Academy. These were a bunch of big, tough white boys from Long Island, who prided themselves on punishing their opponents; especially if the opposing team had any Black athletes on their squad. I never heard the word "nigger" used as much as I heard spew from the mouths of the players from EMA, who consistently taunted me with the racial epithet.

"We're gonna' kick your nigger-ass, 89!"

"Hope you're ready for an ass-whipping today, nigger', cause we got your number, 89!"

"Better not turn your head nigger—cause we're taking it off!"

By halftime, I thought I was playing a football team from the deep south, like Birmingham, Alabama, or Jackson, Mississippi. I became unbelievably frustrated and angry throughout the game from all the late hits, the unnecessary piling-on after a play was over, the pulling of my hair (a tuft of my afro always stuck out the back of my helmet, making it an easy target to grab, or pull) and the constant nuisance of having your foot, leg, hand or other body part stepped on by their cleats. If their intention was to take me out of the football game mentally and emotionally, they succeeded.

By the second half, we were being shut-out and completely out-classed and I had had enough of the double-team blocks, the post-play thuggery and the racial slurs. So, on a passing down late in the game I was finally able to break through their blocking and lined up their quarterback for a hit. By the time I was almost in position to deliver a satisfying blow, their quarterback had released the football downfield. Even though he was now officially off-limits, I never stopped my momentum and hit him after the whistle was blown, square in his chest with my shoulder pads and all of the fury I could muster. A melee broke out on the field, the referees stepped in between me and several of the EMA monster offensive linemen and I was tossed from the game. It was the angriest I had ever been during any athletic event in my life and I trudged off the field and threw my helmet on the bench, as Boyers glared at me from the sideline. "D" tried to calm me down, but he knew what I had gone through, because he watched it all day long. I stood there and fumed over the almost sixty minutes of degradation and humiliation from those military white boys. Boyers never came over to me, never said a word before, during or after the game. What would he have told me; that I needed to develop thicker skin? I shouldn't have let them goad me into a stupid play? I let the team down by getting ejected? Shit, at that point, our team was so demoralized, we had basically rolled over on our bellies and given up halfway through the game, so my getting tossed had no bearing on the final score.

It was a difficult lesson. I learned what my limitations would be on the gridiron. And I learned how much support I'd receive from my teammates—practically none. Not one of them stepped in to protect me from the racist chants and taunts throughout the ballgame. But if any of the EMA players took too long to get off the pile on one of my teammates, I was in the fray peeling punks off of my guys. I'll never forget the feeling of being alone in a jungle of belligerent white boys who thoroughly enjoyed verbally and physically battering me. "The Headhunter" was turned into the prey on that day.

CHAPTER 8

BLACK GIRLS AT DALTON

HERE'S AN OLD SAYING; "GINGER Rogers did all the same dance steps as Fred Astaire, but she did them backwards and in heels."

The intention of this book has been to focus on the influence and experience of being a young Black man at Dalton in the late 1960s and early 1970s. It was during this window when boys, including Black boys, were first introduced to the high school at Dalton. It was a unique time for Dalton, for us and for the country. We also conceived this book from that perspective because, well... because Ray and I are guys.

But we have interviewed many of our classmates, including female classmates, in preparation for this book, and it has become unavoidably clear that their stories have a place in this book as well. Their stories are inextricably bound with ours, yet their stories are unique and their own. Our story would be incomplete without their voices.

When I started at Dalton in eighth grade, there were two Black girls in the class of 1974; Carol Chaderton and Kendall West. Kendall left Dalton after eighth grade and Carol left after ninth grade. For almost all of high school, there were no Black girls—or any girls of color—in our class. And as we began to conduct a census of the Black students from the surrounding years, we began to see a trend emerge. When the Black boys began populating the high school, the Black girls at Dalton started to disappear.

In 1969, the first graduating class of boys, the ratio of Black girls to Black boys was 3/2. The next year, in the class of 1970, the ratio had flipped to 2/4, now favoring boys. The class of 1971 had an even balance of three each, however, the following year in 1972 there were six boys and no girls at all. The class of 1973 started high school with five girls and seven boys, however, three of the girls left after freshman year and the ratio became 2/7. The class of 1975 had only one Black girl (who didn't arrive until senior year) and four Black boys.

For a school that had been all-girls up until the class of 1969, Dalton seemed to have abandoned Black girls, or they abandoned Dalton.

There were many reasons why Dalton decided to make the high school coeducational. The move was essential to the growth and expansion of the school. The parents wanted it. They were tired of having to transfer their boys to other schools when they reached high school age. This was a critical political salve to Dalton's relationships with parents. It meant that Dalton did not need to give away valuable parent and alumni loyalty to another school. And that translated directly into fundraising dollars and cents.

Once the school made the decision to have boys, that meant that Dalton would have boys' varsity athletic teams in the high school. That opened a whole new, important door for Dalton. Varsity athletic teams meant an entirely new kind of publicity and exposure for the school; the reporting of sporting events, school rivalries and the achievement of championships. It also meant the opportunity for passionate boosterism—and fundraising— among parents and alumni. Nothing raises money like team spirit.

But team spirit requires a winning team. So, Dalton athletic director Alan Boyers set out to recruit a winning team. This meant reaching beyond the preppy Upper East Side boys who were now coming up from Dalton's middle school. This meant scouring the city to find boys who were natural athletes, boys who played on winning junior high school teams. And—most fortunately for Mr. Boyers—Dalton was now interested in recruiting Black boys to the high school.

There's an old story about the University of Alabama's legendary football coach Bear Bryant. Bryant's all-white University of Alabama football team went up against the University of Southern California's all-Black backfield (the first of its kind in NCAA history) in a larger-than-life confrontation that showed Alabama to be woefully out-matched; an embarrassment watched by 60,000 home team fans in Alabama's Denny Stadium. After suffering a humiliating loss to USC at the hands of USC's star fullback Sam "Bam" Cunningham, Bryant walked off the field muttering "We gotta get us some of them." The sentiment seems to have contributed to the long overdue integration of southern college football.

Coach Boyers undoubtedly felt that he needed to get him "some of them" too, as he worked to build his varsity teams.

The first two Black boys at Dalton, members of the class of 1969, were my brother Michael and Travis McDougald. Neither one was much of a "natural athlete." Neither one was destined for varsity basketball or football. But the next year included four Black boys, including Larry Stackhouse who played varsity basketball and football, and David Garrison who played varsity football. Things were just getting started, but Dalton's competitive team sports were on their way.

The 1968 varsity basketball team was the first year that I have found any photographs or records. The team photo shows eleven players standing with Alan Boyers, two of them are Black; Larry Stackhouse '70 and Keith Brown '71. The 1969 team photo adds Jose Gomez '72, along with Larry and Keith. The 1970 team photo shows that five of the ten team members are now either Black or Latino. And by 1971, the team photo reflects seven Black or Latino players. We had taken over the neighborhood. Indeed, if you were a minority student at Dalton and you didn't play a sport, you were something of an anomaly. And if you were a female minority student at Dalton, you weren't just an anomaly, you were an endangered species.

People grow up at different rates and at different times. But it is fair to say that most of us, both Black students and white students, grew up during our high school years at Dalton. It is also generally accepted wisdom (and my own experience as a parent) that girls grow up faster than boys. I think that the Black girls at Dalton were quicker to recognize distinctions based on race and gender. They were aware of—and perhaps more sensitive to—the daily micro-aggressions inflicted because we were not all the same at Dalton and those differences were creating gaps that could not be skipped over. Teenage boys can possess an almost boundless capacity for cluelessness, for not noticing or sensing things that might be right in front of us. There are so many chaotic things going on inside of us, that we sometimes seem to have zero external perception. Teenage girls, on the other hand, notice and feel everything. Consequently, I think that it is possible that for some of the

Black girls at Dalton, the "time to move on" simply came sooner for them than it did for us boys. Perhaps this contributed to the attrition of Black girls in the high school at Dalton.

Among the Black girls at Dalton, those who graduated tended to be among those that arrived during their high school years. And so for them, Dalton was a relatively new experience. More often than not, Dalton's "new experience" was better than whatever school experience they had before.

CHAPTER 9

COMPLETING THE DALTON EXPERIENCE
AND MOVING ON TO COLLEGE

MARK ROBINSON

I WROTE CODE

ONE OF THE REQUIREMENTS FOR students who had reached their senior year was the creation and completion of a "senior project"; something each senior would do in their spring semester (as a possible antidote for senior-itis) based on independent study under the supervision of a faculty advisor. Projects were as varied as the students who undertook them and ranged from the truly scholarly to efforts that were community service focused, to schemes to avoid doing anything that required effort.

The project that I chose was a bit out in left field and was certainly the first time that any student (perhaps even the first time that anyone) had attempted something like this. But my proposal represented a good deal of work, a lot of thought and the generous application of math, so my project would not be dismissed or rejected as frivolous. As I mentioned previously, Dalton had acquired—at considerable expense—an IBM 1130 computer and used it to teach students the brand-new discipline of computer science. The IBM 1130 computer was extremely advanced for its day, as advanced as the computers that took Apollo 11 to the moon and back. It took up an entire 10 x 20 room, not to mention the elaborate cooling system that it required. In a separate room down the hall was a keypunch terminal where operators used a special keyboard to write programming instructions that were punched onto 3x7 cards and fed into the computer mainframe. It was extraordinarily tedious and time-consuming. But it was also thrilling. Back then, no one could have imagined the almost limitless computing power or ease of use that we take for granted inside our smartphones today. Back then, these giant machines were the edge of science fiction. I took the class and loved spending time on the computer. I was in serious danger of becoming a math geek.

For my senior project, I chose to write a computer program that was capable of reading Tarot cards and telling your fortune. A few months earlier, the James Bond movie "Live And Let Die" had been released. (I'm a huge James Bond fan. Our son was named after Sean Connery, who—according to my wife—is the only man she would ever leave me for.) Jane Seymour played a Bond heroine who read fortunes on Tarot cards. I actually own a set of Tarot cards that were created for the movie. How cool. I wondered; what if I could program a computer to do that?

And I did. I actually wrote code!

In order to simulate dealing hands of cards that were individualized and personalized, I created a random number generator, so that every hand dealt was different. Then I had to input the meaning of each individual card from the deck. But the most important step was to input the meanings or interpretations when cards were in combination with each other. In other words, not just what the six of hearts means, but what does it mean when it is combined with the four of clubs. And so on.

The program actually worked, assuming of course that you believed in Tarot cards. But if you did, then it was not a giant leap of faith to also believe that somehow the computer knew you were you and was magically reading your fortune. Mr. Rice, the head of the computer sciences department, gave me an A for my project, but the real reward was that lots of my very pretty female classmates wanted their Tarot cards read, and of course I obliged.

I can't imagine that anywhere but Dalton it would have been possible for a middle-class teenage Black kid to be trained how to use—and program—a state of the art computing system in 1974. And I can't imagine that anywhere but Dalton would a student have been given the freedom to explore his own intellectual curiosity and come up with his own offbeat, personal use for the computer, to make the computer a tool of my imagination. The experience has forever shaped my interactions with technology.

In the early 1980s, Chemical Bank became one of the pioneers of electronic banking when it launched Pronto, its own proprietary home banking system. At a time when only 21,000 customers nationwide were willing to sign up for this revolutionary new service, I was doing my bank transactions on my Commodore 64 home computer. When Chemical abandoned Pronto because there weren't enough early adopters, I moved to Citibank and did my electronic banking there.

In 1998, I left the advertising industry for a few years and launched my own company, Heritage Apparel. We manufactured and sold clothing and collectibles that celebrated African American history and heroes like the Tuskegee Airmen and the Buffalo Soldiers. The company started around the time that many companies were creating websites to establish a presence on the internet, so of course Heritage Apparel had its own website. But what was still fairly uncommon at the time were businesses conducting retail transactions online, enabling customers to purchase goods directly from the website. That's called "ecommerce." As a result, Heritage Apparel earned the distinction in 1998 and 1999 of being recognized as one of the "top 10 minority owned companies doing ecommerce." It was a bit staggering that my little company had earned this status, but it wasn't because we were so big or so successful. We weren't. We were just way ahead of our time.

Shortly thereafter, I was advising the political campaign of a candidate for mayor of our town in Connecticut. We built a website for him and created an entire digital platform at a time when such things were relatively unheard of in local politics. And we created a mechanism for collecting campaign contributions online. It probably magnified his fundraising capabilities three-fold. And that paid for image-building advertising. On election night our guy trounced his opponent 63% vs. 37% and became the first Democratic challenger to defeat a Republican incumbent since before World War II. The headline in the local newspaper, in giant letters, simply read, "WOW!"

I can never overlook the role that Dalton has played in the events, choices, and possibilities in my life, long after graduating from the building on East 89th Street.

It is both inevitable and unfortunate that this book will be compared to "American Promise", the documentary film about two young Black boys who entered Dalton in the Lower School and continued there through High School. Inevitable because these are both chronicles of the experiences of two Black boys at Dalton. Unfortunate because—in a lot of ways that matter—our stories have very important differences.

Let's first look at the ways in which our stories are similar. Even in first grade, the two young boys, Idris and Seun, immediately recognize that the environment at school—culturally, socially, and of course demographically—is fundamentally different from the environment of the neighborhood where they live. Those differences force these two boys to straddle two worlds, to create dualities and dichotomies in their own day-to-day lives. This is extremely difficult for a 15 or 16 year-old dealing with teenage identity issues, and virtually impossible for a 5 or 6 year old. The psychic burden and emotional stress is almost unbearable. Being entirely unsure how to act—in either setting—becomes a daily dilemma.

In the documentary, we saw Dalton teachers and administrators who seemed much too quick to surrender to the challenges faced by their minority students. They were much too quick to throw up their hands and tell parents, "Dalton might not be the right school for your son." That is what was so sad for us older alums who watched the film. We saw a school that invited us in and then was ready to right us off at the first sign of trouble, a school that didn't fight for us when we needed them to. We saw the conspicuous unfairness of this because we knew all too well that no one was "more trouble" than the typical wealthy, spoiled white students who were our classmates, and Dalton never gave up on them. Never.

In the documentary, a Dalton administrator talks about the problems these two boys are having and concedes that while Black males statistically do worse at Dalton, she can't say exactly why. To me and to my Black alumni classmates, this moment is infuriating.

Goddamn.

This administrator has not looked closely enough or clearly enough to realize that her statement is completely untrue. It is not true that Black males statistically do worse at Dalton. Why doesn't she know this? Why doesn't Dalton know this? Why do they think it is true? This negative assessment flies in the face of readily available empirical data.

In the seven year window from 1969 to 1975, those first years when Dalton admitted Black boys into the high school, there are 45 Black alumni. These are the alums who paved the way. These are the alums who went through Dalton with the least amount of safety net from the school or from any outside organizations. There was no Prep-For-Prep back then, no Early Steps. None of these alums came from Jack 'N Jill. There was absolutely no institutional or organized support system to help prepare those boys for the radical dislocation and bombardment of Dalton.

We had no net. If we fell, there was nothing beneath our feet except cold hard pavement. We. Were. On. Our. Own.

Those first 45 Black alums are the alums who made sure that the whole "minority student experiment" did not fail. In the writing and preparation of this book, Ray Smaltz and I have been in touch with 28 of those alums, talking with them about their Dalton experiences and their lives after Dalton. 23 of those 28 alums are professionals, that's 82%. In that cohort there are 3 attorneys (including 1 judge), 2 doctors, 3 in banking, finance or business, 5 professional writers. There are TV producers, teachers and retired military officers. Those Black alumni who had the odds most stacked against them, still managed to defy those odds and were extraordinarily successful.

Black males did not do worse at Dalton. They did great. They probably did better than the average Dalton student, and that is extraordinary. I'm proud of that. I'm just pissed that Dalton doesn't seem to know that. I'm frustrated that Dalton has not looked at us closely enough or clearly enough to see that. Why is it that our alma mater treats us like invisible men?

Earlier, I recalled how Dalton treated one of our Black teachers, Rolando Reyes, by alluding to Ralph Ellison's classic 1952 novel, "Invisible Man." In his Prologue, Ellison writes, "I am invisible, understand, simply because people refuse to see me." Of all the things good and bad that Dalton did to us Black boys, this was the worst. They refused to see us. We were simply invisible.

Important elements of the American Promise story, however, are specific to these two boys and are not projectable to Dalton Black alumni more broadly. American Promise, and the parent/filmmakers who produced it, want to suggest that race was the source of the problems for Idris and Seun at Dalton. These two young boys struggled at Dalton for a number of reasons. Although they were both fiercely bright, even gifted young men, Idris was diagnosed (far too late) with ADHD and Seun was dyslexic. Those are very specific, individual challenges. Idris' parents seemed far more invested in filmmaking than in parenting. Dalton was not a perfect partner in their education, but neither was it—in my opinion—to blame for the walls that these two boys sometimes could not climb. I cannot look at the successful experiences of my Black alumni peers and not acknowledge the positive influence that Dalton had in our lives. That would simply be dishonest.

American Promise is a compelling, emotional film. It should be seen. There are moments in this film that resonate hauntingly for me and many of my classmates, moments that are painfully familiar. But it is not a film that tells my story. And if the message of the film is that young Black men cannot succeed at Dalton, then this is a message that I do not share. I just wish that Dalton cared enough about me and all of the other Black male alums to recognize and appreciate our success. Even now, in Dalton's eyes, I feel like we are "invisible men."

Recently, I attended a focus group discussion among Dalton alumni of color. We talked about our experiences and our perceptions and attitudes toward Dalton. One alum felt strongly that we should not look to Dalton or to any other external party for validation of who we are or for recognition of our accomplishments. This alum felt that we should look only to ourselves for validation. Anything else was dependency.

Although I can understand this sentiment, I do not share it. I think this attitude misses the point—or at least it misses my point. I believe that any relationship—any healthy relationship—requires mutuality. I must see you, respect you and appreciate you. And you must do the same for me. If Dalton wants a relationship with its Black alumni, if we want a relationship with Dalton, there must be reciprocity. Reciprocity—even after 50 years—is the ingredient that is still missing from our relationship with Dalton.

THE "RACE" FOR COLLEGE

Throughout its history, Dalton has had two core missions; to ignite and inspire the imagination and intellect of its students, and to train them in the art of self-discovery, so that they may "Go forth unafraid" according to the school motto. All of the specifics of educational theory that are packed inside the Dalton Plan are in service of these simple yet significant goals. I have read many critiques and analyses of whether Dalton has lived up to its promise in delivering on these objectives. Most agree that Dalton has. Most agree that in spite of (or because of) tinkering with the formula from time to time, Dalton has been faithful both to its roots and to its long-term mission. Dalton was—and is—a noble success. I consider my time as a Dalton student and my life since Dalton to be a demonstration of its positive impact. I can see that. I'm not entirely certain that Dalton can.

Somewhere along the way, however, a third mission was added. Somewhere along the way, Dalton added a razor's edge to its profile. In the 1960's Dalton became a prep school that could virtually guarantee that your child would be admitted to a prestigious college or university, probably on one of the Ivy League campuses. Everything changed.

After World War II, the Servicemen's Readjustment Act (the GI Bill) made it possible for millions of American veterans to go to college. This was a wonderful thing, except for the fact that now a college degree was no longer reserved for the elite. The majority of Americans were going to college. And that changed things. That meant that if you wanted to *have* more and *do* more in life, make more money, achieve more status, be the best, then you had to do more than simply go to a good college, you had to go to one of the *best* colleges.

The best colleges and universities, the Ivy League schools and such, always had their standards. These schools were always difficult to get into. The difference now was that many, many more students were knocking on their doors and applying for admission. So many more applicants for just the same limited number of openings. And this ferocious competition only added to the prestige of these respected institutions.

Again, Susan Semel, in her book "The Dalton School" provides some perspective on the far-reaching effects of this expansion of the educational market.

"Ultimately, the expansion of post-secondary education resulted in a credential expansion making not only a college education necessary, but more importantly, where one went to college. For schools like Dalton, this post-World War

II credential inflation resulted in a far greater emphasis on college admissions than ever before. Concurrently, as very selective colleges placed more emphasis on grades and SAT scores as the basis for admission, Dalton responded in kind."

Meanwhile, parents were becoming desperate for some competitive edge that could help assure their children a seat at the best colleges. Parents, especially parents of means, would do just about anything to gain an advantage for their child. And that's right where schools like Dalton came in; providing a valuable and necessary service to New York's wealthy elite moms and dads. An article from the July 29, 2014 New York Times describes the desperation of these parents.

> "The frenzy over getting children into elite New York pre-schools is well documented. Parents sweat, barter and bribe to get their 4-year-olds into prestigious early education programs. Toddlers take achievement tests and participate in observed playgroups to prove their potential.
>
> Other things contribute to the prekindergarten mania... Mostly, there's the implicit belief that a premier prekindergarten program guarantees an early leg up in a nearly 14-year battle to gain admission to the country's most competitive colleges.
>
> If getting into college requires a high school degree, getting into an elite college (or so we have come to believe) is made easier by an elite high school degree."

Dalton fit perfectly into this new marketplace equation. Dalton's board of trustees understood that parents would pay a handsome premium for the cachet of a Dalton diploma. And Donald Barr understood that changes like coeducation and integration and a fresh roster of bright young teachers were more than necessary tweaks to a grand old school on its way to its 50th anniversary. It was smart marketing. Donald Barr understood that at this moment it wasn't enough for Dalton to be a great school, which it was. The time was right for Dalton to become an "it" school.

I say all this to establish context for my senior year. It was time for my classmates and me to apply to college and see if all that Dalton time and money was worth it. We were leaning up against one of Dalton's primary load-bearing walls. An awful lot of hopes and aspirations were tightly packed into an anxiety-laden few months, from late fall to early spring senior year. Dalton was always a competitive place; fashion, social stature, vacations, boyfriends, girlfriends, even grades. Dalton students could compete for just about anything. But the middle months of senior year went way beyond mere competition. We were in full bore Hunger Games territory.

It was all a matter of simple—yet high stakes—math. The senior class was roughly 100 students. The Ivy League and top tier colleges were likely to accept 3-4 students each, with some overlap factored in. That meant that at least half of the senior class would not get in to a first-choice school, maybe not even a second-choice school. The great students in the senior class would have an easy time of it. They would have multiple choices and they would all be happy choices. But that didn't mean that the not-so-great students felt any less entitled. It did not mean that the average students had lowered their expectations in any way. This was Dalton, after all.

What it did mean, however, was that the average students suddenly began looking at their minority classmates—at us—in a whole new, cold unfriendly light. Not only did they begin to see us as trying to eat from the same plate as them, they began to look at our Black and brown skin as an unfair and undeserved competitive advantage in the college application contest. In the 1960s, the policy of "Affirmative Action" introduced by President Kennedy was used mostly to address inequities in employment, especially public sector employment. But by the late 1960s and early 1970s, the practice of Affirmative Action was being embraced by college admissions. It did not take very long at all for privileged society to feel completely under assault.

As the adage goes, "when you are accustomed to privilege, equality feels like oppression."

Based on my own observations and experiences, Affirmative Action was a concept that was almost universally loathed by Dalton's various constituencies. The white students saw this as grabbing the magic carpet they had been riding and pulling it out from under them. No one had ever taken privilege away from them before and they didn't like it. Not one bit. Never mind, of course, the fact that Affirmative Action didn't take anything away from anyone. That simply was not how it worked. But that's how it felt to them and that is all that mattered.

Several of my classmates would ask me how I felt about Affirmative Action. Didn't I think that it was fundamentally unfair? Wouldn't I rather succeed or fail on my own merits? Wasn't I concerned about the stigma of being associated with Affirmative Action? I explained that I didn't know if the principles of Affirmative Action would be used when colleges evaluated my application. That would be their choice, not mine. I didn't make the rules, they did. And if a college accepted me, I wasn't going to lose any sleep over why they decided to say yes. My focus would be on succeeding once I got there. My focus would be on taking the opportunity and making the most of it. I doubt that I changed many minds. The response I received most often was, "Well, I wish I could use Affirmative Action."

When I spoke with Wendy Jones, a graduate of the class of 1971, she shared this story of her own experience with Dalton classmates during the college application process.

> "One of my classmates thought that I shouldn't have received the National Merit scholarship. Another was upset that the University of Chicago sent me round trip airplane tickets to visit the campus to decide if I wanted to go there. I had visited all the east coast colleges on my list. When I told her I couldn't afford it otherwise, she said there was another (white) student who couldn't afford it but wasn't sent tickets.
>
> I pointed out that she had the benefit of a two-parent family that I was sure made more money than my single-parent family. My mother worked three jobs to pay her half of the tuition at Dalton. She was offered a full scholarship for me, but refused it because she wanted to have a say in my education. If Dalton had paid for all of it, she felt she wouldn't be able to complain if problems arose. And complain she did when she felt I wasn't being treated right!"

It speaks volumes about both the presumptive privilege that some Dalton students felt, as well as how much they believed their privilege was being threatened, that Wendy's classmate felt confident that it was her place to judge, critique and challenge anything positive that Wendy received.

My brother Michael was the recipient of a National Merit Achievement Scholarship. Michael, our brother David, and I all grew up in a house where our mother often admonished us, "Don't let other people know your business." However, this did not stop people at Dalton from knowing Michael's business or, apparently, from talking about it. One day, completely out of the blue, a Dalton teacher approached Michael in the school hallway (not one of the teachers that had Michael in any class) and said that she had heard that he had received a National Merit Scholarship and wanted to know if that was true. Michael did not know the teacher, but there was something about her question that did not seem entirely friendly or benign. She seemed to be challenging what she had heard.

"I received a National Merit Achievement Scholarship." Michael explained. "It is awarded by the National Merit Scholarship Foundation, but it is a scholarship specifically for minority students."

"Well that hardly seems fair. Don't you think?" The teacher was not at all pleased. "That's reverse racism."

Michael does not recall his response to the teacher, only the awkward feeling that she had left with him.

It seemed to me that the faculty didn't like the idea of Affirmative Action because they saw it as taking away their proprietary power to choose who the best students were. They felt that this was rightfully their exclusive province. It was as though someone else held veto power over the grades that they handed out. An important part of the college application process was obtaining good letters of recommendation from your teachers. And teachers loved being asked to write them because it enabled them to select and support their favorite students. Receiving requests from multiple students was a bit like a faculty popularity contest. The whole thing was a monumental ego boost for teachers. But the teachers also knew that they had to "manage their brand" and not simply hand out recommendation letters willy-nilly. To be valuable they had to be scarce.

And the school administration felt that Affirmative Action college admissions potentially compromised their ability to deliver against that important 3rd mission; getting rich kids into elite colleges. That was, quite literally, an existential threat to Dalton's stature in the private school universe.

In the late 1960s and early 1970s, many of the Black kids at Dalton were probably the first ones in their families to go to college. That is a very big deal, a powerful transformation of a family's history and future trajectory. It changes not just the individual, but the whole family. It is not so hard to understand the sentiment of others that perhaps we minority students should step back from the golden trough and be grateful for whatever college we ultimately attended. Dalton had invited us in. They brought us to this special party and educated us right alongside the rich white kids. Now we were graduating, and we were expecting to have post-Dalton lives just like the rich white kids. Was that reasonable? Was it naive? Was a Dalton education a guarantee of anything? Should it be?

Honestly, I don't think I have any of those answers.

For me, the process of applying to college resulted in a few very different Dalton experiences, good and bad.

Early in my junior year, I accompanied my cousin Diane, who was a year older than me, as she and her mom (my Aunt Thelma, the one who was also my third grade teacher) drove back and forth through New England visiting and touring colleges for a week. Half of the colleges we visited were all-girls schools; places like Smith, Mount Holyoke and Wellesley, perhaps because Diane attended a Catholic high school, or perhaps Aunt Thelma chose them. But we also visited Yale and Williams and Wesleyan and a few others. And so, the trip was quite worthwhile for me as well. I was able to tour several of the campuses that made it to my own short list. We didn't visit Amherst because at the time Amherst was all boys and of no interest to Diane, but I visited Amherst later when my friend David Burns was a freshman. I had also visited Yale before, because my brother Michael was enrolled there.

And so, after sending away for dozens (yes, dozens) of college brochures and application packets, I had a pretty good feel for the colleges where I wanted to apply. I had chosen seven. They were all in the northeast. That was partly regional chauvinism on my part, but also a formula that I had developed. I wanted the school to be close enough to home that I could get home easily when I wanted to, but not so close that my parents could drop in on me on a whim. No less than a three-hour drive, no more than six hours. I wanted a liberal arts college with a strong humanities curriculum, preferably a small college, although Yale and Princeton were included in my list.

Amherst College, Brown University, Bucknell University, Hampshire College, Princeton University, Williams College, Yale University. That was my list of seven. Amherst was my first choice.

Back then, applying to college was an arduous and elaborate task. For starters, there were no personal home computers or laptops. You used a typewriter, or you wrote by hand, filling out questionnaires and typing essays. And there was no internet, no filling out applications online. And, unlike today, there was no "Common Application" that you could fill out once and have it sent to all the schools on your list. Nope. Each one was separate, each with its own small mountain of paper. Even the minor task of making copies (like all of the financial aid documents, etc.) was a big deal. Copy machines were not commonplace. Or cheap. You had to go to the library with a roll of quarters. And—believe it or not—credit cards were pretty uncommon as well in the early 1970s, so you had to pay each college's application fee by personal check. Applying to college was more complex than filing your taxes.

After finishing and mailing away all of the applications, the next step was requesting letters of recommendation from your best teachers. And I am tremendously grateful that there were Dalton teachers that believed in me and supported me and who were willing to write letters of recommendation on my behalf to some of the colleges where I applied. After all, the best teachers were in high demand, receiving requests from lots of other students. They couldn't say yes to everyone. In order for their letters to be valuable, they had to be rare. If a college received ten letters from the same teacher, that meant that he or she would write nice things about just about anyone. That defeated the purpose. The two teachers that I asked were Mr. Frank and Dr. Greene, two people who knew me well and who could say more than standard platitudes. Teachers never let you see the letters they wrote, so I have no idea what they said. But I trust they did a pretty good job.

Some colleges ask for a letter of recommendation from a peer, a fellow student. Interestingly, I was asked by two of my classmates to write letters for them. I was flattered by the request. I decided that I would ask Mickey Rolfe to write a letter for me. Mickey and I weren't particularly close, but we were friends who always regarded each other well. In fact, one summer I got a job working in the mailroom for Mickey's dad at his real estate management firm. Sulzberger-Rolfe managed about a third of all the residential apartment buildings in Manhattan, or so it seemed. Donald Trump was an insignificant pip-squeak by comparison.

Mickey, who was the president of the student government at Dalton, handed me a sealed envelope and said, "Here's the letter I wrote for you. I mailed it off to the colleges you wanted. Your copy is sealed, because I didn't know if you wanted to read it or not. Thank you, Mark."

"Thank you...?" I asked, since I was just about to thank him.

"Yes, thank you," Mickey said. "I'm honored that you asked me to write a letter for you. It made me feel like somebody really cared what I thought. And writing about you was easy. I had lots of nice things to say."

"Wow. Thank you, Mickey. I'm really grateful for this."

Mickey laughed and waved his hand dismissively. "Please. Just be grateful you didn't have to come up with nice things to say about me."

I actually waited about three or four years before opening that envelope with Mickey's letter. After reading it, I cried. I could never have written a letter as kind and generous and wonderful as the letter that Mickey wrote for me. It was both humbling and a tremendous ego boost that someone else saw that much in me. I didn't see or have contact with Mickey until many years later when we connected at a Dalton class reunion. The first thing I said to him was thank you for the letter. I don't know if he even remembered it, but I did, and I probably always will.

Of course, the opposite of Mickey was Dennis Phillips. Mr. Phillips was a history teacher at Dalton who somehow got the job of replacing Mrs. Cameron as Director of Admission, although he clearly lacked any relevant qualifications whatsoever. While Mrs. Cameron had a genuine warmth and a demeanor that put you immediately at ease, Mr. Phillips came across as the guy who was ready right now to put you in the car of your dreams for a price you won't believe. He had a smarmy smile that looked like he had practiced in the mirror, and he always seemed to be wearing his prep school blazer, even when he wasn't. I don't have any idea what was in his head or in his heart, only how he came across to me and to my fellow minority classmates. None of us liked him. We suspect the feeling was mutual.

In addition to being the Director of Admission, Mr. Phillips was also the college advisor for the senior class. It was his job to help Dalton students successfully apply to college. He would counsel students on how to come up with the right list of schools, how to navigate the difficult and unfamiliar application process and how to emphasize the elements needed for a strong application. Dalton faculty were responsible for getting you all the way down the field to the one-yard line. Mr. Phillips was responsible for getting you across the goal line.

When the time came for me to meet with Mr. Phillips to talk about colleges, I had no real expectations. Despite the fact that we had both been at Dalton for the past five years (since he arrived when I was in eighth grade), we had no relationship with each other. We had no history of interaction with each other—good or bad—which is unusual, given Dalton's small size. But I did have my perception of him, and he apparently had one of me as well.

He began the conversation by asking me if I had given any thought to college, which seemed like an odd question, since 98% of Dalton graduates go to college. Of course, I had thought about college. I guess he assumed that we were going to start from a blank sheet of paper and cover the basics. I wanted to discuss which colleges had a stronger humanities program. I handed him the sheet of paper I had typed with the list of seven colleges I had selected.

Mr. Phillips looked at the piece of paper as though I had just taken a dump on his desk. "Where did you get this?" He asked.

I explained the investigation I had undertaken and the process I had used to narrow my selections.

He looked again at the list and laughed somewhat nervously. Then his expression changed to one of irritation. "I want to help you, but you are making that very hard. I don't know what would make you think that this is a realistic list for you, but it's not. None of these schools are realistic options for you."

"Excuse me?" Like I said, I had no real expectations for my meeting with Mr. Phillips, but I definitely wasn't expecting this.

"Mr. Robinson," he said to me sternly. "You are wasting your parents' money and my time with this list. If you want, we can sit and try to come up with a more realistic list, or you can come back when you have discussed this with your parents."

"Thank you, Mr. Phillips." I got up from my chair. "I'm glad that we talked, but I won't be coming back. I won't be asking for your help with my applications." I would like to say that I stormed out of his office, but mostly he shooed me out of the room. In any case, that was the last time we spoke to each other. A few months later, before the school year ended, Mr. Phillips announced his resignation and left Dalton to work for a small-time law firm in upstate New York, a setting that probably suited him better.

As we were working on this book, I told Ray Smaltz my "Mr. Phillips story" and he shook his head in disgust. Ray said he never got along with him either.

From Ray

Dennis Phillips, Dalton's college advisor, played a critical role in one of my most exasperating experiences at the school. He single-handedly motivated me to apply to nothing but Ivy League schools, which was the exact opposite of his intention.

When we sat down for our initial discussion about where was I interested in applying, he scoffed at my mentioning an Ivy League school like Princeton. It was an important choice for me, because one of my best friends from my neighborhood, Keith Small, had already begun his university experience at the school. I was also fortunate enough to have a close friend of my mother's who was the Head Track and Field Coach at the university; Lawrence Ellis. He was the very first African American coach of any kind hired by an Ivy League school in 1970, a milestone at the time. His wife, Shirley Ellis (maiden name Beard) and my mother were lifelong girlfriends from Harlem. Our families were close for many, many years; so close that we always referred to Lawrence Ellis as "Uncle Larry" and my mom's girlfriend was affectionately known as "Aunt Shirley." Their children, Leslie Smalls, Robin Williams, Joanne Glenn and Larry, Jr., for all intents and purposes were our cousins. We were terribly saddened when the Ellis family moved from Queens to Skillman, New Jersey, just outside of the campus of Princeton University, but we were proud of the opportunity my "Uncle Larry" had earned. Keith and "Uncle Larry" gave me hope that attending Princeton would become a reality for me as well.

Mr. Phillips, however, repeatedly urged me to consider playing either football, or basketball when I was applying to college, because based on my PSAT and SAT scores, he did not consider me a "legitimate candidate." None of my other school activities or grades were ever factored into his equation. He simply determined that based on my athletic talents, that was my only path to attend a college of that kind. I was taken aback by his matter-of-factness, but I wasn't dismayed by his advice. I was angered! I cut short our meeting and abruptly left him in the classroom that we had commandeered for our meeting and I vowed to show him that sports would not be the reason I would go to an Ivy League school.

I applied to Princeton (my first choice) and was accepted. I was also accepted to Columbia, Brown, Amherst, and it gave me untold, great pleasure to let the smug SOB know I'd be attending Princeton in the fall of '74.

Like Ray, I applied to my list of seven schools. My list. I was offered admission to six of the seven schools, including Amherst, my first choice. The one school that rejected me was Princeton (*where Ray went to school*). I don't know why Princeton rejected me. They never tell you such things. But I have my own crazy theory. I met with one of the admission deans from Princeton who was conducting interviews at the Princeton Club on West 43rd Street in Manhattan, just off Fifth Avenue. For the most part, the interview went fairly well. However, there was one question that I obviously answered very poorly. He asked me if Princeton was my first choice.

I told him that I would be incredibly fortunate if I were accepted to Princeton. It was one of the finest schools in the country, if not in the whole world. I told him that it would be a life altering experience and that I would have to work extremely hard to prove myself worthy of the opportunity. But I did not say that Princeton was my first choice. I dodged the question and he knew it. I have always believed that the admission dean decided that if some other college was my first choice, I should go there.

CHAPTER 9

COMPLETING THE DALTON EXPERIENCE AND MOVING ON TO COLLEGE

RAYMOND SMALTZ

THIS IS A TEST...

WITH THE NEWFOUND NOTORIETY AT school that came with my participation on the varsity football team, a strange new question crept into the everyday queries of the white students and teachers at Dalton; "…Are you on scholarship?"

In the minds of the majority of the white students and faculty, if Black students like me stood out on the football field, or on the basketball team, I must've been on an athletic scholarship. It didn't matter that I had matriculated at Dalton in middle school, four years prior to any athletic activity. The assumption was automatically made that I was a "dumb jock," because that's exactly how the most of the white Dalton community viewed the Black AND white male recruits to the school by Boyers… Dumb jocks who needed extra care and attention. Otherwise, the recruits would never make it past the demanding curriculum at the prestigious institution. It didn't matter that I was a "B/B+" student at Dalton, with an occasional "A" if I was energized by the teacher and the subject. Once you donned a uniform, you were stigmatized and put into a "special box."

The constant slights and condescending comments carried on through-out the rest of my time at Dalton. And while I did my best to not let these stereotypes affect my academic and athletic performance, I wasn't always successful. If I wasn't taking my frustrations out on the football field, I was arguing with teachers in the classroom; especially those who taught American history covering the period of the Civil War.

On many occasions during my junior year, I'd do battle with Fredrik Hufnagel. He was one of the history teachers at Dalton. We had crossed paths previously during seventh and eighth grade. He had been very tough on most of my tests and my papers. However, studying the history of the Renaissance Period in middle school was one thing. Now in my junior year in high school, my newfound understanding of "America's Sin" and the effects of slavery on our society and the barbaric treatment of the Native American people by white settlers became a problem for me in the class-room. I was no longer intimidated by the other students, or the teacher's prejudices anymore. I had no issues standing up for what I believed was right and now I was ready to challenge the history of America that was taught in the textbooks we used. It was a never-ending struggle; many times with just he and I as the only participants debating in class, while the other students rolled their eyes, seemingly weary of the constant conflict. There was one class where we were arguing over the slave trade through the Caribbean and Mr. Hufnagel became frustrated over my insistence that the indigenous Taino Indians of the island known as Borinquen (now Puerto Rico), were summarily murdered like the Native American tribes in the United States. I tried to introduce some of the historical materials that were shared with me by Kojo Mbogba Odo from Boys Harbor, but Mr. Hufnagel had no patience to see these books placed alongside his recommended textbooks. For me, it was a fight worth having simply to enlighten him that there were other resources out there regarding world and American history, if he only took the time to explore. I don't know if it would've changed his thought process, but I wasn't prepared to accept the history of this country unconditionally.

My grades suffered with Mr. Hufnagel. Although he didn't fail me, he didn't exactly grade me on a curve. He cited my disruption of his class on several occasions when it came time for meetings to discuss my report card with my house advisor and my mother. Was I a disruptive student? Was I argumentative with him in class? I would say that those observations are in the eyes of the beholder, but if standing up for my own beliefs was an annoyance for this history teacher, or any other teacher at the school, then I probably was "annoying as hell."

Another constant test for us Black Dalton students, was where we would apply to college once we began our senior year. There was a significant amount of status attributed to the choice of schools for your college experience and whether or not you were going to meet the academic requirements. This time-honored questioning by every student was meant either to fulfill someone's curiosity and compare their choices to yours, or simply to embarrass you, because so much importance was placed on each student's wish list. The students from middle-class and working-class families had little or no vision of an "Ivy League" education dancing in their heads. The academic and financial burden would be extremely challenging. Not to mention, every school application had a considerable fee attached, and in my family's case, I shared that burden with my mother by saving as much of my summer earnings as possible. That was the only way those application costs were going to be met. There was a definite "turning up" of noses when Dalton students asked one another where they were applying. And there was a healthy amount of snickering if you dared name a school where they didn't think you'd ever be accepted.

On this almost exact same track, I was being pestered by Coach Boyers to schedule meetings with college recruiters who were interested in me playing football for their school. During my junior and senior seasons on the football team, I made "Honorable Mention" in New York City for the "Little Ivy League" schools, as a select group of private schools were referred to back then. The coach would be able to burnish his credentials if he were able to send his athletes to big-name, or prestigious ivy league schools. The coach was getting a lot of requests to have recruiters come and visit the school to speak with me, but because of my animosity toward Boyers and the many instances where he tried his best to make an example of me, I told him don't bother, I'm not interested. One of those examples was not declaring me one of the captains for the football team my senior year. It was his choice to name the players he felt were deserving and he chose Jason Ekaireb and Doug Frank to be his team leaders, even though assistant coaches Duerward Middleton and Doug French both told me in private that everyone knew I was the best player. But Boyers was never going to make me a captain. Granted, I was participating for only my third season on the team and one of those seasons I played in only one game before my injured leg sidelined me for the rest of the season—the other two guys were on the squad for all four seasons (at least this was the rationale given to me for their elevation).

This slight didn't sit well with me all season-long and it probably fueled a confrontation between Doug Frank and me that occurred during a game. After a particular play against New York Military Academy at their home field, our defense was gashed on a running play through the middle of our defense. Players were getting frustrated and tempers were flaring. In the aftermath of one of these plays, captain Doug Frank, who played an inside linebacker position, kicked sophomore Larry Schau in the ass right after a play and yelled and screamed at him in front of everyone on the field and observers on the sidelines. This upset and angered me so much that I ran toward him, spat out my mouthpiece attached to my helmet, grabbed him by the facemask and yanked his head as hard as I could and screamed:

"Who the fuck do you think you are—Dick Butkus?" I angrily shouted at him.

"But he screwed up the play and they're killing us," he excitedly mumbled, because he still had his mouthpiece in his mouth.

I violently yanked his facemask once again and bellowed, "He's your teammate and you don't EVER show up your teammate. You do it again and I'll kick your fucking ass all over this goddamn field!"

He was still trying to plead his case as I disgustedly turned away to ready for the next down and noticed the thankful look on Larry's face as he tried to show me his gratitude for coming to his aid. Looking back on the incident, I guess it was my not-so-subtle way of showing the coach that he made a mistake by not naming me as captain, but I was too angry to be conscious of how Boyers would interpret my attempt at "team discipline." All I do remember is that we settled down and eventually won the game and my "de-facto" captaincy senior year was firmly established.

So, this was the backdrop when coach Boyers told Jason and me that a recruiter from Columbia was coming to talk with the two of us about playing for his university and all that the school had to offer. My protestations to coach about not scheduling any of these recruiting sessions had gone in one of his ears and out the other, so I was forced to sit with Jason in a darkened classroom with a film projector playing back scenes from a particularly big game I had against some forgotten opponent. I tried my best to be cordial to the recruiter during the entire process when I was asked questions about the performance unfolding on the wall of the classroom, but inside I was seething. When the session was over and the recruiter took his leave, I went up to the coach one last time and told him, "don't bother setting any more of these up, because I won't be around if you do."

Call it arrogance, call it lack of foresight, call it whatever you want, but as my time came to an end at Dalton, I was motivated to prove to men like Dennis Phillips (the college advisor), and Boyers, that my worth wasn't only displayed on the athletic field—I had many other redeeming qualities that weren't going to be quantified by them. My self-worth was going to be determined by me and on my own terms.

After the basketball season ended, and by the time spring arrived during my senior year, many, if not most of the other seniors had already heard from the colleges of their choice and they were already mentally packing their bags as they dreamed of life after Dalton. For me, it was a long, drawn-out process waiting to hear back from the schools where I had applied for the following fall semester. I was nervously waiting for any acknowledgment from any school. It wasn't until after the passing of my grandmother Smaltz (my father's mother) in the month of May, that I finally heard from any college. I remember it distinctly, because I was never able to let her know that I was accepted by Princeton University and would be attending the prestigious institution the following fall. I wasn't terribly close to my dad's mom, but she always doted on her grandchildren and I knew she'd be pleased to hear of the accomplishment.

As for Mr. Phillips and Coach Boyers, it gave me untold pleasure to walk confidently into a classroom that Phillips occupied by himself one sunny afternoon and smugly told him,

"Oh, by the way, Princeton accepted me, and I'll be attending the school in the fall."

His mouth dropped open and he turned red as a beet when he heard my news and he quizzically asked, "You're playing football, right?"

"Nope," I remarked as I turned toward the door with a smirk on my face, and left him to ponder how in the world he could've been so wrong. Shortly after that delicious affair with Phillips, I found out that I was accepted into all of the other schools I applied to such as Williams, Brown, Tufts, and Columbia; none of them with the commitment to playing football, or basketball. It was an accomplishment at that time in my young life that made me truly proud, because it was the culmination of six years of constant mental, emotional and physical testing. And until that point, I questioned whether or not I would pass.

But that proud feeling didn't translate to my graduation ceremony. That was a surreal moment for me. I remember looking out into the audience and feeling like I was an attraction at a carnival show—not really feeling satisfied, happy, or thrilled at what I had managed to achieve. I do remember seeing my family in the audience: my father, my mother's mother, my flamboyant Aunt Audrey and smiling back at them; especially my mother, who was beaming with pride from the "experiment" and personal sacrifice to furnish me with an educational opportunity that was denied to her and to our ancestors. My mother believed that by my matriculating through—and surviving—this incredibly challenging experience, I opened the door and made it possible for my younger siblings to circumnavigate the same kind of educational and social opportunity that was afforded to me. My Mother had no idea whether I would succeed or fail—all she knew was that it was important for me to be exposed to the world of the privileged. It was the only way to open my eyes and toughen my hide inside and out, if I was ever going to be given a chance to make a mark on this world.

CHAPTER 10

AND IN THE END . . .

I N AUGUST 1969, THAT SUMMER after my brother Michael graduated and before I came to Dalton, the Beatles recorded "The End", the penultimate track on their Abbey Road album. It is the last song ever recorded by all four Beatles together. It concludes with a simple couplet written by Paul McCartney.

"And in the end, the love you take is equal to the love you make."

The through-line and over-arching theme of this book has been the question, "How were our lives changed by having attended Dalton, and how was Dalton changed by our presence there?" I think that Ray and I are comfortable answering the first part of that question by saying that we came to Dalton as good, strong people and we left Dalton as better, stronger people. Dalton did not transform us or alter our essential nature. There were many very good qualities and strengths that put us on the path to arrive at Dalton in the first place. We got there because of who we were, which was something quite special. We also got there because of where we came from; the families that raised us, surrounded us with love and care and nurturing, that invested us with purpose and ambition. Our families understood that education meant everything, literally everything and they inspired us with an insatiable appetite for it.

Undeniably, however, we were stronger, better, most definitely smarter and more focused and resolute in purpose when we graduated from Dalton.

Dalton took what we had, what we brought, and fortified it. Dalton put muscles on our muscles. Dalton did this by continually challenging us and by occasionally assaulting us. Dalton taught us that the metric we used to measure our achievements was inadequate, that the upper range of our scale should always be open-ended and infinite in its possibility. Dalton taught us that learning and growing were bigger than the classroom and were part of a larger, more holistic experience. Dalton gave us room to grow and room to fail. And when we failed, Dalton helped us grow from it, becoming more resilient, more resourceful. And like a referee's advice to boxers, Dalton taught us to "defend ourselves at all times"—including, occasionally, defend ourselves from Dalton, which wasn't always the most caring alma mater. Some lessons were learned in spite of Dalton. More than anything else, Dalton lived up to its core mission because it taught us to "Go forth unafraid."

And what of Dalton? What did Dalton receive from this transaction?

It seems pretty clear, from our perspective, that Dalton did not bring Black kids to the school as any grand act of nobility. There were, we believe, multiple motives and predicates for the integration and diversity of Dalton, but benevolence and beneficence were probably not high on anyone's list of priorities. Dalton did the right thing, the wonderful thing, and it worked out great for us and for Dalton. But some element of self-interest was almost always an "active ingredient" in the formula.

Donald Barr came to Dalton in the early 1960's with very ambitious plans and intentions. He wanted to grow Dalton's treasury, grow its capital footprint and resources, grow the curriculum and grow the school's enrollment. Barr wanted to transform Dalton from a modestly successful, reliable niche institution of the independent school community, into New York's "It" school, the hot school, the place that all of New York's wealthy liberals wanted to send their kids. Opening the high school to boys, and including Black boys, was critical to making that happen. We helped make Dalton cool. We helped make Dalton "sexy."

Did this formula succeed for Dalton? As Ms. Tuttle might say, "res ipsa loquitur."

Boys in the high school made it possible for Dalton to build a regime of varsity athletics. **Black** boys in the high school—not surprisingly—filled out those varsity team rosters and turned Dalton's new athletic enterprise into a succession of winning seasons that inspired parent and alumni loyalty and largesse, opening quite a few purses and wallets. Win-win.

Because Dalton began to have diverse students, the school began to hire diverse faculty, first in the arts and athletics, then finally in traditional academics. For a great many of Dalton's student body, this became the first time that these students interacted with Black adults who weren't there to serve them food, open their doors or babysit them. This was the first time that these students experienced a Black adult who was a mentor, a teacher and an authority figure, as well as—simply—someone to be admired and respected. And to Dalton's credit, it showed exceptional wisdom and good fortune in the Black teachers it chose. Those men and women were giants. And for more than a few of Dalton's faculty, this was the first time that they had ever had a Black professional peer, an intellectual equal. And you can bet that this truly rocked some deeply held belief systems. It re-ordered their universe.

Because we were there, friendships were formed across the picket fences of various ethnic communities. Friendships that broadened everyone's horizons and shattered well-meaning stereotypes. White kids discovered that just because you were Black did not mean that you were—or knew—a drug user. White kids discovered that not all Black kids are good at sports. Rich kids discovered that their Black friends were sometimes more likely to be the product of a stable, traditional, two-parent nuclear household than they were. And we learned that money could be pretty damn cool, (and fun) but it didn't make you a better person, or a happier one.

In the beginning, diversity at Dalton was a means to an end, a way to accomplish certain other objectives. The objectives were honorable and reasonable, but back then we were not the objective. We were simply the tools by which those objectives were achieved. And without a doubt, those objectives were achieved in spades (forgive the pun). Dalton achieved a level of status and prestige that was unprecedented in its history, and it has successfully held onto that status ever since. Today Dalton is not just bigger, it is greater—in so many ways that truly matter—than ever before.

But because we were there . . . something more happened. Because we were there, Dalton's diversity became its own sentient presence. The first generation of diversity at Dalton was one thing, but subsequent generations were something else, something adaptive, something progressive. Over time, in the years beyond our graduation, Dalton's diversity evolved and became self-aware. Over time, in steps that were imperceptible at first, gradual at first, Dalton's diversity evolved from being a means to an end and became an end unto itself. As Dalton entered the new millennium, diversity became a core value of the Dalton community. In 2007, diversity was formally written into Dalton's official Mission Statement.

In 1996, Elisabeth "Babby" Krents became Dalton's new Dean of Admission, nearly 30 years after she graduated in 1968. This was a role of such extreme importance to New York City parents that Bill Keller of the New York Times dubbed her "the most powerful person in New York" and meant it with a straight face. Another New York Times reporter wrote, "... in certain living rooms, in coffee shops and on Web sites, Ms. Krents, 61, incites the kind of fear and fascination usually reserved for a head of state or an over-covered celebrity."

Having met and spent time with Babby, I have found her to be warm, charming and genuine, a thoughtful and reflective person with a quick wit and an easy smile. In ways that might be impossible to pin down precisely, she reminds me of Teddy Cameron, the Admission Director who interviewed me nearly fifty years ago. Babby seems well-suited to the task of populating Dalton's classrooms.

Babby was part of the very last all-girls class to graduate from Dalton, the year before my brother Michael's graduation. Babby was part of closing the door on a certain phase in Dalton's history. She saw the conclusion of one era and the birth of another following behind her. But in 1996, when Babby returned to Dalton as its new Admission Dean, and with some encouragement from the headmaster, she began to move the school— to transform the school yet again—toward significantly greater diversity and inclusivity. 1996 also brought the arrival of Dr. Lisa Yvette Waller to Dalton as Assistant to the Head of School for Academic Affairs and Associate Director of Admissions. Lisa, who holds a Ph.D. in history, had done her dissertation on the integration of New York City schools from the 1940's—1960's. Dr. Waller's scholarly work was instrumental in pivoting the study of the Civil Rights Movement from the American South to the urban North. She brought an ideal expert background and credentials, along with her own personal perspective as an African American woman, on how Dalton should advance into the new millennium and she became an invaluable partner to Babby Krents.

When Babby and Lisa arrived at Dalton in 1996, the incoming kinder-garten class included 6% minority students. Babby and Lisa, supported by a core team of a half dozen parent volunteers, set about almost immediately to change that, pushing the percentage of minority students up each year. Together, Babby and Lisa have been Dalton's diversity change agents, each year increasing the percentage of kindergarten entries who are children of color. Currently, and for nearly a decade, children of color represent about 45-50% of the kindergarten class. That means those numbers are now wash-ing across Dalton's middle school grades and will soon cross into the high school. It won't be long before that ratio is school-wide.

Over the course of 23 years at Dalton, Lisa Waller held a number of positions, including Head of the High School and Assistant Head of School for Progressive and Inclusive Practice (*a job title that would have been un-imaginable during my years at Dalton*). Through these roles she was able to complement Babby's admission work with transformative influence inside the school. Dr. Waller promoted the expansion of Dalton's curriculum to become more globally oriented and developed and implemented diversity, equity, and inclusion curricula for all faculty and staff members.

Sadly, however, there will always be people who believe that any positive step forward for people of color must automatically represent a sacrifice and unfair step backward for everyone else. Affluent New York City parents who are desperate to get their child into Dalton believe that the school's diversity progress comes at their own child's expense. They are convinced that the only reason their child did not get accepted was because some Black or brown child took their place. It was perfectly okay when Dalton had just a small handful of minority students. That made it a cool school, a liberal school. They were not a threat nor an obstacle. But now quite of few of these parents feel Dalton has taken this whole diversity thing too far, and it is crowding out the students who are supposed to be there.

Not surprisingly, alumni were originally resistant to Dalton's diversity initiatives, perhaps because their strongest connection to the school was based upon a frozen moment in time, a memory that is unchanging. That seems to have eased a bit, although not entirely. I am told that one of the complaints voiced by parents was that the increase in student diversity re-sulted in a noticeable decrease in playdates, especially weekend playdates in the Hamptons. (No. I'm not making that up.) And more recently, Dalton's diversity has given rise to a new problem. As we experience a moment of national racial and social justice reckoning, Dalton's students and alumni of color are seeking redress of grievances that date back years, or even decades.

For now, Dalton seems determined to weather this storm and persevere in the face of some angry parental and alumni resistance to its present diversity posture. And we applaud that. Dalton is still very much a work in progress, and we hope to see that progress continue. But pendulums swing both ways. Diversity comes at a cost, especially when there are pockets of parental and alumni resentment. If Dalton's ideals become financially painful, we could see a readjustment in Dalton's diversity statistics.

We hope not.

At a recent lunch with Babby, I asked her if she thought that Dalton's current forward momentum on diversity could be reversed. I expected her answer to be a quick and confident "No." But it wasn't. The smile disappeared from her face as she looked at me, then paused to give her words weight, and said, "People come and go. Change is unpredictable. New administrations can make different choices. There are no guarantees." Babby's response is a useful cautionary note.

Shortly before her retirement, Ray and I sat down with Ellen Stein, Dalton's recently retired Head of School, for a conversation about this book. The book was not yet finished, and we had not yet shared any of its contents. Ellen asked if she was going to like the book. We told her that our relationship to Dalton was like that of an old married couple (us and Dalton). We are well aware of each other's faults and foibles, and not the least bit bashful about talking about them. But we love each other and wouldn't have it any other way.

AFTERWORD

In the past several months, Ray and I have spent a good deal of time communicating with several of Dalton's recent graduates of color; Black men and women. And by "recent" we mean graduating after 2000, young enough to be our own children. We have gotten to know some of them, and they have shared their stories of their own Dalton experiences. The process of learning and understanding their stories has been enormously valuable and instructive. It has made it possible for us to re-examine our own experiences from an objective distance and ask questions of ourselves that we had not previously asked. It has also enabled us to draw a continuous line from fifty years ago to the present and find the connections.

And the broken connections.

America is a different place from what it was fifty years ago. Is Dalton a different place? And if so, how different? In what ways different? When Ray and I attended Dalton fifty years ago, the school was changing radically and had a full head of steam for reinventing itself. What did Dalton do with that momentum, with that potential? How has Dalton changed and how has it failed to change?

Some of the answers, in fact a number of the answers, surprised us.

The first thing we learned was that no one was reluctant to talk or to share. This was not an eagerness to boast about personal success stories or to reminisce about nostalgic memories. For the most part, these were stories that unearthed painful memories, even trauma, and that includes people who described their time at Dalton as "happy." But the issues and experiences that they wanted to talk about, needed to talk about, were therapeutic, sometimes cathartic.

Several of these alums were the children of immigrants. Others were simply the first in their families to have the privileged educational opportunities that Dalton afforded them, the first in their families to go to college. All of them told us that their parents saw education as an essential ingredient in their children's future success. Their parents had struggled all their lives and they fully expected that their children would struggle too through their Dalton experience, but that didn't matter. Struggle builds character. And struggling through Dalton would get them to a better life. "You're not going to Dalton to be happy" was a familiar refrain these alums had heard at home.

Most of the alums we spoke with told us that they had "stayed away" from Dalton and avoided contact since their graduation. Even those alums who told us that their Dalton experience was a happy one, admitted that they were not motivated to return to the school. The consensus of their attitudes was that they put in their time at Dalton, it was a necessary and important stage in their lives, but when it was done there was no compelling reason to look back and there was no longing for those memories. Once the connection had been broken, there was no driving force or motivation for reconnection.

This had been true for Ray as well. From 1974, when we both graduated, until roughly 2010, after he and I reconnected, Ray had no communication or interaction at all with Dalton, nor did he have any desire for it. Unlike the robust loyalty and affinity that Dalton's white alumni demonstrate year after year, there is no strong bond between the school and its Black alumni. In many cases, no bond whatsoever. As any alumni director or development director will tell you, that is a very bad thing. It is bad for the financial health of the institution as well as the cultural vitality of the school community. And yet, year after year, Dalton has never made any focused outreach to its Black alumni. Dalton has never tried to woo back or re-engage its Black alums. Until the summer of 2020, the school had never sent a mailing (or email) specifically to its Black alumni.

Ray is an alum of Princeton. Amherst College is my alma mater. Both schools have left no stone unturned in establishing and maintaining an active and robust relationship with their Black alumni. There is a regular schedule of targeted mailings (email), promotion of relevant events and activities on campus, a Black alumni listserv and a tradition of biannual Black alumni reunions. Of course, the schools want our money. And they'll hold you upside down and shake you if they have to. But they also recognize that they get a lot more from the relationship than just cash.

Since Dalton's apparent 'alienation of affection' is contrary to the self-interest of the school, it begs the question, "Why not?" Why hasn't Dalton ever made the effort? Does Dalton have a philosophical or policy reason against targeting an outreach in this manner? Has Dalton never thought of the idea before? Or are Dalton's Black alumni simply invisible to the school? Do they simply not see us? Only the school's administrators can answer these questions.

I know that on several prior occasions Ray and I have asked the school to create a Black Alumni Directory, simply to help Black alumni to find each other and also to help current students find us. Others have made this request as well. Their response has been that they don't have one and don't have the ability to create one. If they are being sincere, then they are also being incompetent. Creating the directory would be very easy to do. But the more likely scenario is that they simply have never bothered to try. That would be consistent with the school's pattern of behavior toward Black students for the past fifty years.

Among the recent alums that we spoke with, there were two exceptions to the pattern of "staying away." One of these two alums actually returned to work at Dalton for a couple of years, while the other has been actively participating in the school's annual diversity conference (something I have been doing as well). For them, there was a palpable sense of unfinished business between the student and the school, unresolved feelings and emotions that subconsciously called out for a way to seek closure. Both alums acknowledged that—in returning—they found the closure and resolution they had been seeking.

Everyone spoke of dealing with—and living with—the micro-aggressions of daily life at Dalton, the remarks, the looks, the exclusions and the occasional overt bullying. These micro-aggressions succeeded in eroding their self-confidence and their self-esteem. But in almost every case, the alums agreed that the petty assaults from other students were not the hardest things to deal with. What was much harder for them was the feeling that there was no one they could go to about their problems. No one who was a sympathetic ear. No one who would take up their cause.

As we said before, many of the families of these students were working class or immigrants. They did not necessarily have the frame of reference or the perspective to understand and support what their children were experiencing at school. And, too often, they simply did not have the time. These parents told their kids just to tough it out and keep going. Sad, but perhaps also understandable. It was, however, the responsibility and the duty of the school to be proactive and empathetic advocates for their students, **all** of their students. And story after story suggests that Dalton did not do that.

One student tells of being bullied multiple times. When she stood up to the bully, the school threatened to penalize her for standing her ground. This only emboldened the bully, who came after her again, publicly calling her a "nigger cunt" to his friends and other onlookers. When she defended herself, the school reacted by suspending only the student of color. The bully publicly gloated about the outcome.

Another student of color tells how, during his very first week at Dalton, he was followed to the bus stop after school by four white students who encircled him and flicked lit matches at him and told him he did not belong at Dalton. He was terrified. The next day he went to the administration and was told there was nothing they could do unless they caught someone in the act.

Here is the story of a recent alum who always dreamed of a career in the STEM fields, but saw those dreams wither on the vine at Dalton.

> *I have always loved Math. I was fortunate and skilled enough to be in advanced math classes for most of my Dalton career and had the most engaging and patient teachers (Ms. Aziz, Dr. Mason). They were constantly checking in, engaged in my overall learning and class fit. I had some of my first conversations about personal goal settings in these classes.*
>
> *As I progressed through Dalton, however, I found that there was little attention paid to the experiences of students of color and specifically Black girls in STEM fields. When I was in my sophomore year of math I asked about resources for tutoring and instead I was told that I would be a "better fit" and "more comfortable" if I moved down a math level. I lost confidence in my abilities. I found myself drifting away from math and other STEM fields.*

Again and again, the stories we heard were about the absence of support, the absence of encouragement and practical guidance. Ray and I are not quite sure just how to describe it. We are still processing what we heard and what we learned from these younger alums. But the picture they painted was something a bit worse than just benign neglect. What surprised the two of us more than anything else were the repeated confessions of self-doubt, of uncertainty that they really belonged at Dalton. Dalton left them questioning their goals and dreams.

"When you and I graduated in '74, self confidence was not a problem for us." Ray said, as we discussed our notes from our conversations with the other alums. "We were definitely going to go forth unafraid and we believed we could do anything. What these guys are telling us is that was not true for them at all."

I agreed with Ray.

It was remarkable to hear and to take note of the consistency of certain stories told by all of the alums. Perhaps the most common theme of all was college application guidance and the monumental failures of the school in helping its minority juniors and seniors. Literally everyone said they received "no useful guidance" from their college advisor. There were three areas in particular where the college counselors were notably unhelpful:

- **Explaining and navigating financial aid applications.** This is especially important information for students of color for two reasons. First, their families are much more likely to have a greater financial need of college tuition assistance. Second, their families are far more likely to be unfamiliar and inexperienced handling the complex and somewhat arcane financial aid process. And of course, minority students are substantially more reliant upon support from college scholarships, but Dalton did not provide its minority students with information or resources to find and apply for scholarships. Of course, at an elite place of privilege such as Dalton, the typical Dalton student probably has little use for or interest in scholarships.

- **Providing support and encouragement in applying to "reach" schools.** For Ray and for me, Dalton taught us that we were being prepared to do anything, that there should never be an upper ceiling on our dreams or ambitions. And so when our college counselor scoffed at the Ivy League schools on our application lists, Ray and I both told Dennis Phillips to go screw himself and we applied (successfully) anyway. But for some reason, Dalton never gave these recent alums the same self confidence to remain steadfast in their goals and ambitions. That is a grave disservice.

- **Becoming familiar with and giving consideration to HBCUs.** Half of the alums we spoke with said that when speaking to their college counselors they inquired about applying to HBCUs, but got nothing in response. The other half said that they never really inquired because they didn't know enough about them and were never offered information. Some alums expressed regret at a missed opportunity. Some of the alums mentioned that their white classmates were not shy about discussing HBCUs with them. Some thought that was where all Black students went to college, or ought to. Others mocked HBCUs as not truly rigorous or legitimate academic institutions.

Here is one story from an alum from the class of 2007:

> *Mr. Koppert, the then college counselor, explicitly told me that I had very little going for myself and that he hoped I could get into a SUNY University. I had to fight to add other schools to my list. He told me that I had a chance if I made my application's personal statement as ethnic-centralized as possible, as affirmative action was a trend. There was very little advocacy—I took everything on myself with little help from Dalton. During one of my few meetings with Mr. Koppert, I arrived a bit early and overheard him tell his assistant that he would not be "pushing to any admissions officers" for any of the schools on my list.*

Another student from the class of 2013 told us:

> ***NOT HELPFUL AT ALL.*** *They did not provide information on financial aid or college selection and fit.*

Another alum from the class of 2001 explained that it was the support system from the organization Prep For Prep that came to her rescue with college application guidance. Prep For Prep is a leadership development and gifted education program that offers promising students of color access to a private school education. It is targeted toward high achieving New York City minority students. Some of the minority students at Dalton come through the Prep For Prep program, and even after matriculation at Dalton, the program continues to offer support to its students.

> *My college counselor was not very encouraging. She told me that my top choice was a serious reach (she drew an arrow off the page to signify how much of a reach) and told me that I shouldn't really apply. Luckily, I also had a college counselor through Prep For Prep, who encouraged me to apply. I did manage to get some fee waivers to help offset the cost of the application process. There were schools that my Dalton counselor encouraged that I either did not visit, or had no interest in applying to, but because I also had my Prep For Prep counselor, I had another advocate to help me create a final list.*

The importance of programs and organizations like Prep For Prep cannot be overstated. PFP, A Better Chance, Jack & Jill, the Hord Foundation and a number of others; their mere existence is a gift and a minor miracle. They make a world of difference in the lives of minority students. Not only do these organizations help make it possible for academically talented minority students to attend schools like Dalton, they consistently and persistently remain present in the lives of these students as a support network and as a safety net. They are the proactive and empathetic advocates that we hope and expect the school to be.

They are the proactive and empathetic advocates that the school _ought to be_.

These organizations and programs weren't around fifty years ago when Ray and I attended Dalton. They didn't exist yet. It would have been great to have them, but we survived—and thrived—even in their absence. But our experience was different from these recent graduates. And here is why we think that is.

Ray Smaltz and I were among the very first young Black men to attend the high school at Dalton. Other young Black men just like us were among the very first to attend the other elite private schools, the places of privilege. We were pathfinders. There was no roadmap for us to follow, no prior experience or point of reference. But that was 100% equally true for the school administrators, guidance counselors and faculty. They had never done this before either. They had no handbook for this.

They were as intimidated by us as we were by them.

Neither Dalton nor any of the other elite private schools had yet mastered the game of "How to manage your minority students." All the new rules were being written as we lived them. And so in many respects, we had a freedom that no longer exists today. We didn't know that we weren't supposed to be self confident. So we were. We didn't know that our place at the school was not "probationary." So, we stood our ground. We didn't know we weren't supposed to fight the school. So, we did. And sometimes we won. It was all quite unpredictable. By the time that we graduated, we were battered and bruised. Some of us were bitter, but all of us were better. And we knew it. We were cocky SOBs and we felt that we earned it.

One of the questions we asked in our interviews with alums was, "If we say that Dalton's mission is to create future leaders, future members of America's elite, would you say that Dalton lived up to its mission for you?" The answers we got were equivocal. Every one of them. That is definitely not the Dalton that Ray and I used to know.

So, what happened?

Time is what happened. And time was not on the side of students of color. Every year, students of color would graduate and move on. Every year, new students of color would come in. New kids on the block, exposed to the elite private school experience for the first time. Fresh teenagers, afraid of failing, afraid of not fitting in, afraid of disappointing their families. Meanwhile, as each year went by, the school acquired and accumulated experience. They got smarter and savvier. They learned how to serve the needs of the students, but also how to "manage" the students, how to protect the interests of the institution.

The result, we believe, is that Dalton and other elite private schools, the places of privilege, were able to master the diversity numbers game, increasing their enrollment while carefully controlling what impact this increased diversity would have on the institution. The public relations benefit is obvious and substantial. The cultural, institutional and financial risk is minimal.

You could call it "diversity on a leash."

A natural by-product of diversity is creativity. This principle has been studied exhaustively in both business and science. When new and different elements are introduced to the ecosystem, new and unanticipated outcomes emerge. Creativity and innovation are sparked. Genetic innovation is Darwinism at work, making species better, stronger. The opposite is inbreeding. It is possible, we believe, that what elite private schools like Dalton have been doing is trying to have the appearance of diversity—the statistics—without the unpredictable outcomes of diversity; creativity and innovation. Diversity on a leash.

Clearly, this is not working.

This is hard for me. Writing this Afterword is very hard for me. My story of Dalton is not a perfect one, and certainly not always a happy one. But, by and large, I left Dalton pretty happy with what they had given me. I left better than I went in. And over the years I have maintained a connection and a relationship with the school. I attend reunions and I volunteer for other activities and programs. So, it is difficult—and painful—for me to hear that the school that I have always known to be imperfect and occasionally disappointing has actually been quite careless and uncaring toward other students of color. It is hard for me—and for us—to make this how our story of Dalton ends. On this, Ray and I agree.

In recent weeks, Dalton has literally made history by reaching out specifically to its Black alumni for the first time ever to initiate a dialogue about positive change. In an email letter from the Head of School, he states that Dalton has begun to recognize the magnitude of its shortcomings with regard to matters of diversity, equity and inclusion, and asks for help in making the school and the school community better. That letter has set in motion a virtual tsunami of conversations—both with the school and about the school. And it has set in motion a sincere and heartfelt desire among Black alumni to step up, step forward and help.

To be clear, there are many mixed and conflicted emotions among the Dalton Black alumni community. There are many still left hurt or damaged by Dalton. There are many who are angry or distrustful of Dalton. But common throughout is a sincere desire to see Dalton be better, perhaps mostly for the students of color who are there now and will be there in the years ahead.

In our conversations with the recent alums, Ray and I asked if they thought that the letter from Jim Best, expressing Dalton's commitment to becoming a better, more anti-racist community, was genuine. The responses were mixed; from yes to probably to maybe to a few no's. But when we asked if they thought that Dalton was capable of making the necessary positive changes, there was an optimistic chorus of yes. At the end of the day, that probably matters more.

Ray and I want Dalton to be better. And we want to help get it there. We are prepared to put in the time to do what we can. Over the past several years, Ray has been actively involved with the Dalton Mentorship Program and serving as a mentor to minority students. I have been involved with Dalton's annual Diversity Conference, serving as a facilitator. Immodestly perhaps, we believe that this book can be a part of helping Dalton to do some needed introspection. And perhaps this book can help the students who are there now and will be there in the years ahead to understand what it is like to go to school in a place of privilege.

ACKNOWLEDGEMENTS AND APPRECIATION

In the research and preparation for this book, the authors consulted and conducted interviews with more than 100 people, including Dalton alums, administrators, faculty and students, as well as numerous others in the solar system of elite (and ultra-elite) independent schools. The authors wish to express their sincere thanks and appreciation to them all.

In particular, the authors wish to thank the following people for their substantive contributions to the completion of this book: Desiree Pilgrim Hunter, Robert Hunter, Duerward Middleton, Michael Robinson, Christopher Rose and Lisa Ann Waller.

ABOUT THE AUTHORS

Mark Robinson has spent the past 40+ years in advertising at some of the industry's most prestigious agencies. Mark has been featured in <u>Fortune</u> magazine, <u>The New York Times</u>, <u>The Wall Street Journal</u> and <u>Advertising Age</u>.

Mark is a past member of the American Advertising Federation's Multicultural Marketing Leadership Council, a national touring lecturer for the American Educational Foundation, and an ongoing mentor for MAIP (Minority Advertising Internship Program) for the American Association of Advertising Agencies.

Mark was chosen by filmmaker Spike Lee to co-found and manage his new agency, Spike/DDB. In 1998, Mark launched Heritage Apparel, an internet-based clothing company that celebrated African American history and heroes. In 2001, he was recognized as the Entrepreneur of the Year for the successful launch of his next company, S/R Communications Alliance; the first 100% minority-owned network of 10 multicultural advertising companies, with combined business of $225 million.

Mark was nominated for the 1994 Connecticut Human Rights Award for his community service and work in multicultural education. In 2000, Mark was appointed by the Governor to serve on the State's Martin Luther King Commission. And in 2009, he was chosen by the State of Connecticut to receive the Martin Luther King Leadership Award.

Mark lives in Connecticut and is a highly sought after strategist and advisor to various political campaigns and community organizations.

Raymond B. Smaltz, III has traveled the globe producing, directing & replay directing major sporting events for most of the various broadcast and cable networks. Ray's production company, RaySun Productions, has worked with every major professional sports producer and broadcaster, including the NFL on FOX; the National Football League of Europe (*highlighted by three nationally televised World Bowls*); ESPN Championship Week College Basketball; the Foot Locker Track & Field Series on CBS; amateur events such as the Pan American Games on Telemundo; a total of twelve Winter and Summer Olympic Games; combat sports such as EliteXC, Metamoris 5 and Strikeforce MMA; and professional boxing for EpixHD Boxing, ESPN Boxing, HBO Boxing and Showtime Championship Boxing, featuring the highest grossing pay-per-view boxing event in history—Mayweather vs. Pacquaio.

During his thirty-plus years in sports television, Ray has garnered four Emmy Awards; 1988, 1992, 2002 & 2004 for "Best Live & Edited" Olympic coverage, three Telly Awards in 1993 and 1996 for "Best Music Video" & "Best Production & Graphics for the Foot Locker In-Store Video," the prestigious Olympic Golden Rings Award (Silver Rings) in 1996 from the International Olympic Committee for "Atlanta Olympic Broadcasting - Weightlifting," and a NATAS Award in 2005 for his production of Seattle Seahawks Pre-Season Football.

Ray currently resides in Orange County, New York with his wife, Teri Williams Smaltz.